The Piety of JOHN CALVIN

An Anthology Illustrative of the Spirituality of the Reformer

Translated and edited by

Ford Lewis Battles

Music edited by

Stanley Tagg

BAKER BOOK HOUSE
Grand Rapids, Michigan

Copyright 1978 by
Baker Book House Company

Harmonizations
copyright 1977 by
Stanley E. Tagg

"A Communion Hymn"
copyright 1976 by
United Church Press
and used by permission

ISBN: 0-8010-0701-1

Library of Congress
Catalog Card Number: 77-88698

Printed in the
United States of America

To
John Leith
instrument of God's gracious providence
but for whose timely pastoral intervention
both this book and the life of its author
would not be

Contents

List of Abbreviations

Benoît   Calvin, John. *Institution de la religion chrestienne.* 5 vols. Edited by Jean-Daniel Benoît. Paris: Vrin, 1957–1963.

CSEL   *Corpus scriptorum ecclesiasticorum latinorum.*

Herminjard   Herminjard, Aimé-Louis, ed. *Correspondance des Réformateurs dans les pays de langue française.* 9 vols. Geneva: Georg, 1866–1897.

LCC   Library of Christian Classics.

LW   Luther, Martin. *Luther's Works.* 54 vols. to date. Edited by Jaroslav Pelikan and Helmut T. Lehman. St. Louis: Concordia; and Philadelphia: Fortress; 1955–   .

McNeill-Battles   Calvin, John. *Institutes of the Christian Religion.* Edited by John T. McNeill. Translated by Ford Lewis Battles. LCC, vols. 20–21. Philadelphia: Westminster, 1960.

OC   Calvin, John. *Opera Quae Supersunt Omnia.* 59 vols. Edited by Guilielmus Baum, Eduardus Cunitz, and Eduardus Reuss. *Corpus Reformatorum,* vols. 29–87. Brunsvigae: Schwetschke, 1863–1900.

OS   Calvin, John. *Opera Selecta.* 5 vols. Edited by Petrus Barth and Guilielmus Niesel. Monachii: Kaiser, 1926–1952.

Pannier   Calvin, John. *Institution de la religion chrestienne.* 4 vols. Edited by Jacques Pannier. Paris: Société les belles-lettres, 1936–1939.

PG   *Patrologia graeca.*

PL   *Patrologia latina.*

SC   Calvin, John. *Supplementa Calviniana: Sermons inedits, iussu corporis presbyterianorum universalis.* Neukirchen Kreis Moers: Neukirchener, 1936–   .

Schipper   Calvin, John. *Ioannis Calvini Noviodvnensis Opera Omnia: In novem tomos digesta.* 9 vols. Amstelodami: Schipperi, 1667–1671.

WA   Luther, Martin. *Werke. Kritische Gesammtausgabe. Weimarer Ausgabe.* Weimar: Nachfolger, 1883–   .

Preface

The present collection of texts was originally made primarily to acquaint Roman Catholic students with the spiritual teaching of John Calvin (1509–1564), the Reformer of the Swiss city of Geneva and the chief architect of the Reformed tradition of Protestantism. In its several printings, however, it has found a wider audience. To Allan Fisher and Baker Book House I am indebted for their willingness to publish it for an even wider circle of readers—laity, clergy, students. For those who wish to pursue the subject beyond the confines of this book, we commend the endnotes, key to a larger literature.

Calvin was a far more systematic writer than was Martin Luther; but this very fact, while it makes easier a superficial effort to attain a rudimentary notion of his teaching, actually works against a warm, personal grasp of the man himself. It is for this reason that something other than the totality of the *Institutes of the Christian Religion,* masterpiece of theology that it is, is here placed before the reader.

By way of introduction to Calvin's spirituality, there has been included an essay on "True Piety According to

Calvin." This is primarily an extended word-study of *pietas,* exhibiting its classical and Christian roots in Calvin's thought and examining how it was exemplified in his life.

The first aim of this anthology is to know the man as he saw his own life. The second is to see the Christian life as he understood it. The third is to examine both his theoretical exposition of prayer and his own prayers, in the liturgy and for other occasions. Related to this is the effort to get at his own poetic expression of the faith. Here, in fact, is the order of the present book, divided as it is into seven chapters. Let us look briefly at each of these in turn.

The spiritual pilgrimage of Calvin. Unlike Luther, Calvin was a most reticent man. While we know the outlines of his life and have the lineaments of his character from his letters, tracts, and other writings, we do not have from the Geneva Reformer the treasure-trove we possess in the Table Talk of Luther. Calvin has given us one brief tantalizing sketch of his spiritual pilgrimage, found in the preface to his *Commentary on the Psalms* (1557). We have chosen to translate this mainly from the French, because of its more familiar quality, but not without some glances at the Latin original.

It was no accident that Calvin chose the preface to the Psalms commentary for his spiritual autobiographical sketch. As it was for Luther, the Book of Psalms was for Calvin, next to Paul's Epistle to the Romans, the most important book of the Bible, if frequency of citation is a reliable criterion. For both Reformers, each in his own distinctive way, the "constellation" of these two Biblical books is the foundation of the Christian faith. There is in fact much intimate detail concerning Calvin's inner life of faith to be found both in the *Commentary on the Psalms* and in the distinctive use of Davidic materials in his other writings, especially the *Institutes.* Calvin himself speaks

of his life as a kind of *imitatio Davidis.*[1] The preface, therefore, is a fundamental piece for understanding John Calvin and the nature of his faith.

The kernel of Calvin's faith. Our second selection affords a bridge between the life of Calvin and Calvin's view of the Christian life. His great work, *Institutes of the Christian Religion,* was first published in Basel in 1536. Concentrated in the first few pages of chapter 1 ("On the Law") is the kernel of Calvin's faith. In later editions of the *Institutes,* this compressed statement was vastly elaborated and at the same time dispersed to various contexts. Here it is adapted from my own translation of the 1536 edition[2] and put in strophic form.

This short passage presents the familiar insights from Paul's Epistle to the Romans with Calvin's own distinctive working out of the relation of law, gospel, and conscience. Here is the foundation of Calvin's understanding of faith-righteousness and of his later elaborate critique of works-righteousness.

Calvin on the Christian life. Our third selection addresses Calvin's understanding of the life of the Christian. It was in the second Latin edition of the *Institutes of the Christian Religion,* published at Strasbourg in 1539, that Calvin included a concise treatise on the Christian life. Slightly expanded and edited, this little tract ultimately became chapters 6–10 of book 3 of the *Institutes* of 1559. Here we have chosen to translate "On the Christian Life" from the French version of 1541, using the text established by Jacques Pannier (1939). Calvin, resting his teaching on Scriptural foundations, pictures the Christian life as a process of spiritual growth never completed in this life. He finds the essence of the Christian life in self-denial, particularly as it is expressed in our bearing a cross after the pattern of our Lord. The goal is of course the life to come, but while Calvin seems at times to speak like a "medieval" *contemptor mundi,* he holds a lively and healthy view of the present life which is, with due restraint, to be enjoyed by the devout Christian. The tension between the two lives is characteristic of the often noted Calvinian trait of *complexio oppositorum,* the yoking together of opposites. Or, for our purpose here, we might describe his style as the juxtaposition of antithetical views in the effort to find a middle way between extremes.[3]

This little treatise on the Christian life was the first substantial work of Calvin's to be translated into English; it appeared in 1549 as *The Life and Conversation of a Christen Man,* translated by Thomas Broke.[4] Thus it was with this aspect of Calvin's thought that Englishmen who knew no Latin first became familiar. One may be so bold as to suggest that the seeds of later Puritanism are, in part at least, to be found in this, which was chapter 17 of the *Institutes* of 1539 (Latin) and 1541 (French). The French version was used for the present translation because of its less formal, less technical, less compressed character.[5]

Calvin on prayer. With our fourth document we turn to the third aim of this anthology, to examine Calvin's understanding and practice of prayer. The second longest chapter of the *Institutes* in its final Latin edition of 1559 is chapter 20 of book 3, "On Prayer." In it is contained a full but concise commentary on the Lord's Prayer. But the ancestor of this longer treatise is to be found in chapter 3 of the original 1536 edition. This has been adapted from my translation of 1968, mentioned above. The familiar three "moments" of prayer, drawn from the apostle Paul, are here spelled out: (1) our realization of our own inability, unaided; (2) our discovery of Christ's power; (3) our appropriation of Christ's power through God's grace.

Prayers of Calvin. Essentially the same lesson is taught by *The Form of Prayers and Songs of the Church* (1542), Calvin's second blueprint for Protestant worship, stemming from his Strasbourg experience. We may be overwhelmed by the sheer weight of assertions about human sin and inability voiced in the prayers of his liturgy. But this was the way the Reformer chose to drive home to his flock the lessons of *sola gratia.* Only the shock of exaggeration and constant reiteration could bring to the common Christians the force, the insights of the new Augustinianism or, more precisely, the renewed evangel of the Protestant Reformation.

Yet with all the unkind things Calvin had to say of the Roman Catholic Mass, his own liturgy derives, as do Luther's and Cranmer's, from the Latin rite of the Western church. Calvin's first effort, made while he was exiled at Strasbourg from Geneva (1538–1541), was related to Bucer's German Strasbourg liturgy, coming from the earlier German translation and adaptation of the Roman liturgy by Diebold Schwarz. Alert students of the Western liturgy may detect some of these family connections.[6]

Our next selection provides examples of prayers used in the weekday services and of those prayers introducing and concluding Calvin's exegetical lectures, or *praelectiones.*

No comprehensive collection of Calvin's prayers as such exists in English translation, although the 524 prayers which he used to end his lectures on Jeremiah through Malachi are all translated in the Calvin Translation Society series of these commentaries.[7] The prayers which conclude the *Praelectiones* follow a set form (a modification of the Latin *collect* form?), but they carefully articulate the essence of Calvin's faith. In fact each prayer encapsulates the whole of theology; the whole of the Christian life; earth, hell, and heaven.

While we have included a portion of the liturgy for the Lord's Supper, apart from a hymnic summary (in chapter 7) we have not supplied here any theological statement on that sacrament. To include everything is not possible! The centrality of the Lord's Supper for Calvin and the realism with which he viewed the presence of Christ in the eucharist have stimulated in our generation great interest and study.[8]

For Calvin the mystical union of the believer with Christ, felt in the eucharist, is sensed as a drawing of the worshiper to heaven, in the spirit. Luther had conceived it more as the coming down to the worshiper of the glorified body of Christ, everywhere extending. Both of these views are found in late-medieval thought and practice.

Metrical Psalms translated by Calvin. An important place in Protestant worship was taken by the vernacular Psalm and hymn. However, Lutheran and Calvinist church music took quite different directions, from the contrasting personalities and views of the two Reformers themselves. Calvin's was the more circumscribed and the less rich. While he was at Strasbourg, Calvin produced in 1539 his first Psalter.[9] From it we have made fairly literal but unrhymed translations of the six metrical psalms held to be from Calvin's pen. An effort has been made to approximate the metrical form of the French, so the English translations may be sung to the original tunes. They have been arranged for congregational and choir use by Stanley E. Tagg, minister of music, Eastminster United Presbyterian Church, Pittsburgh. A separate introduction has been provided for this section of the anthology.

Prose-poems adapted from Calvin. These six "hymns" are derived from strongly lyrical passages in some of Calvin's writings, spanning the years 1534–1539.

On Christ and the church. Here the two chief loves of Calvin's life, Christ and His church, draw testimony from two of the most passionate passages in Calvin's writings.

In all the pieces included in this anthology, the reader will note the powerful impress of the Psalms. One of the mysteries of the Hebrew-Christian tradition is that so many pieties, so many ways of worship, can derive from the same book. Perhaps Calvin is right in seeing the Psalter as the mirror of all the spiritual states of the human soul.[10] Certainly his own Christian faith was articulated through a soundly historical exegesis of the book, but one that dared see the moral and spiritual parallels between David's Jerusalem and Calvin's Geneva, yet through no veil of distorting allegories. In this last respect Calvin ceases to be a child of the medieval world. Can we, in our advanced stage of secularity and technology, still find a pattern in this hymnbook of the ancient Jews?

It is to be noted that the "prose-poetic" form of the translations has been adopted to give the reader some taste of Calvin's style. The prose of the sixteenth century was not the flat, limping prose we so easily fall into in twentieth-century America.

If readers desire a short biography of John Calvin, John T. McNeill's *History and Character of Calvinism,* T. H. L. Parker's *Portrait of Calvin,* or Parker's fuller *John Calvin: A Biography* is recommended. The edition of the *Institutes of the Christian Religion* edited by John T. McNeill and translated by Ford Lewis Battles will afford an introduction to his thought. The much shorter first edition has been translated by F. L. Battles; *An Analysis of the "Institutes of the Christian Religion" of John Calvin* is a summary of the great Protestant summa.[11]

The author of this present anthology wishes to extend his grateful thanks to all who have made this little book possible: his wife Marion; his daughters Nancy and Emily; his colleagues and students, first at the Hartford Seminary Foundation and since 1967 at Pittsburgh Theological Seminary; to Peter De Klerk of Calvin Theological Seminary, for bibliographic assistance; and to the scholars, living and dead, whose names are recorded in the pages that follow. Without their labors this would have been a poorer book. Lastly, to Stanley E. Tagg for his labors as musical editor goes warm appreciation.

FORD LEWIS BATTLES

Notes

1. The Davidic parallels to Calvin's life and thought are explored in John R. Walchenbach, "The Influence of David and the Psalms on the Life and Thought of John Calvin" (Th.M. thesis, Pittsburgh Theological Seminary, 1969). See chap. 1, line 773 (note) below.

2. *Institution of the Christian Religion . . . 1536: Now Englished Completely for the First Time by Ford Lewis Battles. . . .* (Pittsburgh: Pittsburgh Theological Seminary, 1972). This is a facsimile edition with English translation in parallel columns and textual notes relating to subsequent editions. The translation alone, augmented by an introduction and critical notes, was subsequently published as *Institution of the Christian Religion . . . 1536,* trans. and an. Ford Lewis Battles (Atlanta: John Knox, 1975).

3. See Ford Lewis Battles, "The Antithetical Structure of the *Institutes,"* in Battles, *An Analysis of the "Institutes of the Christian Religion" of John Calvin,* 2nd rev. ed. (Pittsburgh: Battles, 1972), pp. 28*–31*.

4. See initial note in chap. 3.

5. Readers who would like to pursue the study of Calvin's doctrine of the Christian life more fully may find an excellent guide in Ronald S. Wallace, *Calvin's Doctrine of the Christian Life* (Grand Rapids: Eerdmans, 1959). The social and economic aspects of his ethic are admirably set forth in André Biéler, *La pensée économique et sociale de Calvin* (Geneva: University of Geneva, 1959). In English on the latter topic is W. Fred Graham, *The Constructive Revolutionary: John Calvin and His Socio-Economic Impact* (Richmond: John Knox, 1971).

6. The most recent book-length study in English on the Reformed liturgical tradition is Hughes Oliphant Old, *The Patristic Roots of Reformed Worship* (Zurich: Theologischer Verlag, 1975), which at some points corrects the pioneer work of William D. Maxwell, *John Knox's Genevan Service Book, 1556: The Liturgical Portions of the Genevan Service Book Used by John Knox . . . , 1556–1559* (Edinburgh: Oliver and Boyd, 1931). For the main liturgies with helpful notes, see Bard Thompson, ed., *Liturgies of the Western Church* (Cleveland: World, 1967).

7. For a survey of Calvin's prayers, see my essay "The Future of Calviniana," in Peter De Klerk, ed., *Renaissance, Reformation, Resurgence* (Grand Rapids: Calvin Theological Seminary, 1976), pp. 150–53.

8. Among contemporary Roman Catholic theologians who might be mentioned are Eduard Schillebeeckx and Luchesius Smits. The latter has studied Calvin's use of Augustine in detail in the first two volumes of his *Saint Augustin dans l'oeuvre de Jean Calvin* (Assen: Van Gorcum, 1957–1958); a third volume will assess Calvin's faithfulness to Augustine in the chief theological doctrines that concerned both, the eucharist in particular (1:275). Jill Raitt considered Schillebeeckx's transignification in the light of Beza's eucharistic teaching in "Roman Catholic New Wine in Reformed Old Bottles," *Journal of Ecumenical Studies* 8 (1971): 581–604. Kilian McDonnell, an American Benedictine, has written *John Calvin, the Church and the Eucharist* (Princeton: Princeton University, 1967) and various articles on this subject. Joseph Tylenda, an American Jesuit, has written "Calvin on Christ's True Presence in the Lord's Supper," *American Ecclesiastical Review* 155 (1966): 321–33; and "Calvin and Christ's Presence in the Supper–True or Real?" *Scottish Journal of Theology* 27 (1974): 65–75. The bibliographies that appear annually in the *Calvin Theological Journal* (and that cover the period 1960 to the present) report a number of essays in this field.

9. We have worked from the facsimiles of this rare work that appear in Richard R. Terry, *Calvin's First Psalter* (London, 1932; reprint–Ann Arbor: University Microfilms, 1965).

10. See chap. 1, lines 13–19 below.

11. New York: Oxford University, 1967; London: SCM, 1954; Philadelphia: Westminster, 1975; LCC, vols. 20–21 (Philadelphia: Westminster, 1960); *Institution of the Christian Religion . . . 1536* (see note 2 above); 2nd rev. ed. (Pittsburgh: Battles, 1972); respectively.

Introduction

True Piety According to Calvin

Piety Defined in Word and Act

Piety defined by Calvin. In his first *Catechism* (published in French in 1537 and in Latin in 1538), John Calvin defined the untranslatable word *pietas,* which for him was the shorthand symbol for his whole understanding and practice of Christian faith and life:

> True piety does not consist in a fear which willingly indeed flees God's judgment, but since it cannot escape is terrified. True piety consists rather in a sincere feeling which loves God as Father as much as it fears and reverences Him as Lord, embraces His righteousness, and dreads offending Him worse than death. And whoever have been endowed with this piety dare not fashion out of their own rashness any God for themselves. Rather, they seek from Him the knowledge of the true God, and conceive Him just as He shows and declares Himself to be.[1]

Calvin more succinctly defined *pietas* in the *Institutes* as "that reverence joined with love of God which the knowledge of his benefits induces."[2] Beside *pietas* he set *religio:* "... faith so joined with an earnest fear of

God that this fear also embraces willing reverence, and carries with it such legitimate worship as is prescribed in the law."[3] Note that in these definitions of *pietas* and *religio*, a number of other basic terms are interlaced: *faith, fear, reverence, love, knowledge.* One might diagram their interrelationship thus:

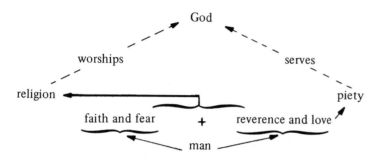

To grasp the full amplitude of *pietas*, let us examine a few of the many references to the word scattered through his commentaries and other writings. In the *Commentary on the Psalms* (119:78f.) he taught that the true nature of *pietas* is seen in the two marks of believers: (1) honor, the obedience rendered to Him as Father; (2) fear, the service done Him as Lord.[4] Distinct from this is the unbeliever's fear which rests not upon faith (*fides*) but upon unfaith (*diffidentia*).[5] Knowledge also enters largely into the concept of *pietas*. In the *Commentary on Jeremiah* (10:25) Calvin spoke of knowledge of God (*cognitio Dei*) as the beginning of *pietas*. Calling upon God's name (*invocatio*) is the fruit of the knowledge of God and is evidence of *pietas*.[6] In the *Institutes* Calvin spoke of the first step toward *pietas* as "to know that God is a father to us."[7] Elsewhere he asserted that there is no *pietas* without true instruction, as the name *disciples* indicates.[8] "True religion and worship of God," he said, "arise out of faith, so that no one duly serves God save him who has been educated in His school."[9]

Calvin also related piety and love (*caritas*). In *Praelectiones in Ezekiel* (18:5) he spoke of *pietas* as the root of *caritas*.[10] *Pietas* means the fear or reverence of God; but we also fear God when we live justly among our brethren.[11] This relationship between our reverential attitude toward God and our attitude toward neighbor is further developed in a sermon on Deuteronomy 5:16:

> And this is why the heathen have applied this word *pietas* to the honor we render to father, mother, and all those in authority over us. *Pietas*, properly speaking, is the reverence we owe to God: but the pagans, although they were poor blind folk, recognized that God not only wills to be served in His majesty, but when we obey the persons who rule over us, in sum, He wills to prove our obedience at this point. And thus, inasmuch as fathers and mothers, magistrates, and all those who have authority, are lieutenants of God and represent His person, it is certain that if one show them contempt and reject them, that it is like declaring that one does not want to obey God at all.[12]

Yet Calvin places *pietas* higher than *caritas*, for God towers over man; still, "believers seriously testify, by honoring mutual righteousness among themselves, that they honor God."[13]

The connection between the pagan and Christian notions of *pietas* is pursued further in the *Commentary on John*. Here Calvin admitted "that some grains of *pietas* were ever scattered throughout the world" but "that by God, through the hand of philosophers and profane writers, were sowed the excellent sentiments to be found in their writings."[14] Aratus's couplet quoted by Paul (who spoke to infidels and men ignorant of true *pietas*) is "the testimony of a poet who confessed a knowledge engraved by nature upon men's minds."[15]

That Calvin's youthful classical studies had laid the groundwork for this classical as well as Christian understanding of the word *pietas* is clear from his *Commentary on Seneca's "De Clementia,"* published in

1532 when Calvin was twenty-two years of age. In explaining the Senecan phrase "nor the piety of his children," Calvin drew together what we may assume were the chief classical texts that were mingled, after his conversion, with Scriptural and patristic uses to shape the word in his thought. Note that among the pagan classical writers is to be found a quotation from Augustine's *City of God*. Here are Calvin's words:

Cicero, *Pro Plancio* (33.80): *What is piety, if not a benevolent gratitude to one's parents?* Quintilian (5.10.12): *Just as those things that are admitted by the general consent of mankind, such as that there are gods, and that piety is to be shown to parents.* Yet in order that my readers may understand what piety really is, I shall append Cicero's words from the *Topics* (23.90): *Equity is also said to have three parts: one pertains to the gods in heaven, the second to the spirits of the departed, the third to men. The first is called "piety," the second "sanctity," the third "justice" or "equity."* Thus far Cicero. But since parents are for us so to speak in the place of the gods, to them is diverted what Augustine hints at (*DCD*, 10.1.3): *Piety, properly speaking, is commonly understood as worship of God, which the Greeks call eusebeia. Yet this eusebeia is said to be exercised by way of obligation toward parents also.* But we also use the term when we wish to express a particularly forceful love. Cicero (*Ep. Fam.*, 1.9.1): *I was very much pleased with your letter, which made me realize that you fully appreciate my piety toward you; for why should I say "my good will" whenever the term "piety" itself, most solemn and sacred as it is, does not seem to me impressive enough to describe my obligation to you?*[16]

As this collection of classical passages indicates, the words *pius* and *pietas* in classical Latin referred first to the relationship of children to their parents.[17] In the Roman family of the *paterfamilias* and the *materfamilias*, children were expected to fear, honor, obey, and love their parents. *Pietas* bespoke the mutual love and care between parents and their offspring.

The state was, after all (as Aristotle described it in his *Politics*),[18] but the extension of the family. The king or emperor was the *pater patriae*, the father of his country.[19] Parricide, in Roman eyes the most horrendous crime of which man is capable, and subject to the cruelest and most unusual punishment of all, was extended to assassination of the ruler, as the parent of all.[20] *Pietas*, then, in the larger sense summarized all the feelings of loyalty, love of country, and self-sacrifice for the common good which marked Roman citizenship.

The early Christians, whose supreme Ruler and Father was God, without divesting the word *pietas* of its familial and national meaning, carried the word to a higher use. For them the whole complex of relationships between God the Father and His earthly children was summed up in this one word. For Calvin, then, there is in the word the classical overshine of filial obedience. *Pietas* bespeaks the walk of us adopted children of God the Father, adopted brothers and sisters of Christ the Son.

So far we have dealt mainly with the "inner" meaning of *pietas*. It also had an external meaning for Calvin. In *On the Harmony of the Gospels* (Matt. 12:7 and parallels) he argued, with our Lord, that certain types of manual labor were permitted on the Sabbath—those connected with the worship of God—and spoke of the *officia pietatis*, which we might render "religious duties." In the same passage Calvin suggested the modern hypocritical connotation of *piety*, speaking of the "hypocrites who pretend *pietas* by outward signs and grievously pervert it by sticking in carnal worship alone."[21]

Calvin's meaning will emerge more clearly as we seek out the Scriptural basis of his concept of *pietas*. The New Testament word uniformly rendered by the Latin *pietas* is εὐσέβεια. It is found almost exclusively in the Pastoral and General Epistles, appearing elsewhere in the New Testament only at Acts 3:12. Of the fifteen refer-

15

ences in the former, the RSV translates all but three as "godliness." The word is used in the Septuagint to denote "the duty which man owes to God—piety, godliness, religion."[22] In the Septuagint the word is chiefly found in the Apocrypha.

Piety mirrored in Calvin's life. If this then is what piety meant for Calvin, we will certainly find in the accounts of his conversion, however meager, help in understanding how this concept was shaped in his own life.

Much ink has been spilled in discussion and speculation on the date, circumstances, and character of Calvin's decision to accept the Reformation faith. I have dealt with the shape of his conversion in my translation of the *Institution* of 1536.[23] Classic accounts of conversion usually cite some verse of Scripture as triggering the change. Augustine's experience of *"Tolle, Lege!"* ("Take up and read!") in the garden near Milan led him through Romans 13:13f. to Bishop Ambrose and Christian baptism. Luther was captivated by Romans 1:17. We have no such definite information on the specific scripture that brought Calvin's change of heart. A close study of the evidence has, however, led me to suggest that it very probably was Romans 1:18–25. More specifically the text may well have been Romans 1:21 (". . . for although they knew God they did not honor him as God or give thanks to him, but they became futile in their thinking and their senseless minds were darkened"—RSV).[24]

The central themes of Calvin's piety are the honoring of God and being thankful to Him; they are interwoven in the recital of his conversion in the preface to the *Commentary on the Psalms*[25] and in the account of the Reformed Christian's confession before God's judgment seat in Calvin's *Reply to Cardinal Sadolet.*[26]

Calvin's new-found faith is early expressed in his preface to the French translation of the New Testament made by his cousin Pierre Robert (Olivétan).[27] Almost contemporaneous with this are the early pages of chapter 1, "On the Law," of the 1536 *Institution.* I call this in chapter 2 "The Kernel of Calvin's Faith."

It is the intolerable contrast between God's absolute perfection and man's fallenness that initiated Calvin's religious quest. Like Augustine, he saw no instant perfection succeeding the event of conversion however *"subita"*[28] it seemed; there is rather a growth into the Christian life to a perfection beyond death—all the gracious gift of God in Christ. So he begins this "kernel" account of faith with the two knowledges: of God's glory, justice, mercy, and gentleness; and of fallen man's ignorance, iniquity, impotence, death, judgment. In the third place, we are shown the law, the written law of the Old Testament and the inwardly written law of conscience, as God's first effort to bridge the gulf between Creator and created. The law is for us a mirror in which to discern and contemplate our sin and curse. It leads us to the impasse of being called to glorify, honor, and love our Lord and Father, but unable to perform these duties. Therefore we deserve the curse, judgment—eternal death. This was indeed the sequence of Calvin's experience, or more accurately, it was the shape which in retrospect he gave his experience in the light of the Pauline-Augustinian tradition and which he generalized in his teaching.

But the impasse, through God's mercy, is breached; another way is opened to us. It is forgiveness of sins through Christ. Calvin's "kernel," in its fourth and final section, comes back once more to the knowledge of ourselves, of our poverty and ruin. The lesson of this knowledge is that we learn to humble ourselves, cast ourselves before God, seek His mercy. Thus will Christ, our leader, the only Way to reach the Father, bring us into eternal blessedness. Our piety then is our pathway, in grace, from estrangement to reunion with our Creator. It is the way of suffering, but also of joy.

Thus Calvin's conversion took a lifetime to be worked out. We cannot here summarize that brief but crowded life. But we can look at several episodes in it that will explain why he believed in the third use of the law—its pedagogical use as tutor to converted Christians—and denominated it the law's chief use.[29] His life will also exemplify his teaching on calling, that the Christian must, like a sentry, stand guard at his post while he lives.[30]

First, look at how Calvin was called to his initial ministry in Geneva. His initial vision of the Christian life (like Augustine's) was that of a retired, contemplative, intellectual study of the faith. William Farel, that hot-headed pioneer of the French-language Reformation who was spurned in his invitation to Calvin to work with him in Geneva, a city that had just chosen the Reformed faith, had recourse to imprecation and threat: "You are following," he thundered at Calvin, "your own wishes and I declare, in the name of God Almighty, that if you do not assist us in this work of the Lord, the Lord will punish you for seeking your own interest rather than his."[31]

And so, against his will, Calvin took up the task at Geneva as at the invitation of God Himself. After Calvin's banishment in 1538 from Geneva, Bucer used the same threat to persuade him to assume pastoral and teaching duties at Strasbourg.[32]

Calvin was subsequently importuned from his happy pastoral relationship with a tiny French congregation in Strasbourg to return to Geneva.[33] It must be said that the Strasbourg sojourn was crucial in working out pastorally and practically and liturgically the full meaning of *pietas*. In his study of the sufferings of the patriarchs, Calvin mirrored his own *tolerantia crucis:* Abraham, Isaac, Jacob, and the rest, David included, withstood terrible hardships, pain, suffering, because they were on pilgrimage. The hope that was to come fed them on their journey.[34] This too was the secret of

Calvin's triumphant struggle against the overwhelming odds that faced him and his world. This too kept alive his feeble body, taxed as it constantly was beyond its strength. This too enabled him to maintain a ceaseless literary output of the highest order and one so decisive for posterity.

Piety in Calvin's view of the Christian life. We have endeavored to define *pietas* in Calvin's own words and his own acts. Let us now turn to the principles of *pietas* as he worked them out in his *Institutes of the Christian Religion.* In doing this, it will be necessary to examine more fully the transition years 1538–1541 of the Strasbourg exile, which we have just now lightly sketched.

The portion of Calvin's *Institutes* on which we would like to concentrate our attention at this time comprises, in the final Latin edition of that book printed in the author's lifetime (1559), chapters 6–10 of book 3.[35] One may search in vain the pages of the first edition of that work (1536) for any section corresponding to this one on the Christian life.[36] Actually (with some subsequent additions) it dates from 1539, the year of the second Latin edition, and remained in all editions from 1539 to 1554 the final chapter of the *Institutes.* Why was such an important subject so belatedly treated by Calvin?

The clue to the answer lies, I believe, in a comparison of what Calvin wrote before he went to Strasbourg in 1538 and what he wrote after that date. On the one hand, examine the *Institution* of 1536, the *Articles Concerning the Organization of the Church and Worship* of January 1537,[37] and the *Confession and Catechism of the Church of Geneva* of 1537–1538.[38] On the other hand, examine the *Institutes* of 1539 (in which he placed the treatise "On the Christian Life"); his *Several Psalms and Songs Set for Singing,* also of 1539;[39] and his 1540 *Commentary on Romans.* Add to these the literary output immediately following his return to

Geneva from Strasbourg in 1541—that is, the *Draft Ecclesiastical Ordinances* of 1541, *The Form of Prayers* of 1542, and the third Latin edition of the *Institutes* (1543). What does a comparison show?[40] We see a real growth in Calvin the churchman, in his grasp of the practical problems both of individual Christians and of the church as the society of Christians. All of these works are directed to the perfecting either of the Christian life or of the liturgical and disciplinary functioning of the church. Together they mark the significant changes that were later to be incorporated into books 3 and 4 of the 1559 *Institutes*. Both the *Institution* of 1536 and the *Catechism* of 1537–1538 were cast in the traditional catechetical mold: Decalogue, Apostles' Creed, Lord's Prayer, sacraments. In Geneva the efforts to enforce acceptance of the *Confession and Catechism* of 1537–1538, household by household, and oversight of morals, district by district, ended in failure and banishment from the city for both Farel and Calvin, as we have seen, in April 1538. What had gone wrong? Let us quickly review the facts.

On Sunday, 21 May 1536, the General Council of Geneva had unanimously voted by a show of hands to abolish the Mass and other papal ceremonies and abuses, images and idols, and had sworn with God's help to live in the holy gospel law and Word of God. The duly appointed Reforming pastors, William Farel and John Calvin, had taken their city fathers at their word and had planned literally to transform the city into a gospel community which had its true center in the Lord's table. This was not to be, however. The public documents of 1536–1537, as a consequence, underwent (after Calvin's Strasbourg sojourn) a clarification of disciplinary procedures and a development of church polity in those of 1541–1543. The *Institutes* of 1539 shows a greater maturity and fullness in its understanding of the formation of the individual Christian than does the *Institution* of 1536. Similarly, the next

edition, that of 1543, quite surpasses both the first and the second editions in its grasp of ecclesiology. Calvin indeed learned from experience, both in the first two years in Geneva and in the three-year interim in Strasbourg under Martin Bucer's tutelage.

We may infer that the short treatise "On the Christian Life"[41] is in a sense the first fruits of Calvin's reflection on his 1536–1538 failure. He realized, it would seem, that catechetical statements on such topics as faith, repentance, justification, regeneration, election, and related heads of doctrine—however clearly stated—would not suffice to transform men's hearts, even though their minds might give intellectual assent to the new faith. A deeper reflection on the Christological foundations of the Christian life, particularly as they had been set forth by the apostle Paul, was called for. This short treatise supplied the lack we have noted in the 1536 *Institution* and the *Catechism* of 1537–1538.

We must, however, slightly qualify this judgment. The 1536 *Institution* contains certain short blank spaces in the text as printed, called *alinea*, at which points—in later editions—expansions of materials were made. This fact seems to bear out what Calvin himself says of his progress through the various editions of the *Institutes*, as he speaks to the reader in 1559: "I was never satisfied until the work had been arranged in the order now set forth."[42] Also, the *Catechism* of 1537–1538, while largely an epitome of the prior edition of the *Institution*, does presage important changes to come in the *Institutes* of 1539.[43]

What then does the short treatise "On the Christian Life" tell us about Calvin's continuing pilgrimage of faith?

First, we see further reflection on the contrast between the philosophers and Scripture.[44] He had, in his conversion, already rejected the Greek and Latin authors as moral guides. Here the contrast between them becomes sharper and more detailed. But some vestiges of their influence still remain. This can be illustrated by his attitude here expressed toward Stoicism. Rejected are Stoic notions of fate and of the passionless wise man and Stoic strictures against pity. We might here note in passing that even before his conversion Calvin had begun to show such an attitude, as his *Commentary on "De Clementia,"* which we previously quoted, reveals. But the Stoics' call to follow God, their insistence that we are born to help one another, and their preaching of moderation and frugality[45] are sufficiently close to Calvin's Christian piety to remain a part of his moral teaching.

Second, since penning his first great theological essay of 1536, Calvin had come to know the early church fathers, both Greek and Latin, far better. The homilies of a Basil or of a Chrysostom or the writings of a Cyprian or an Ambrose filled in gaps in his pastoral knowledge. Most important of all, Augustine brought him to a deeper understanding of Paul.[46] He was therefore in a position in the spring of 1539, after five months as pastor of the French congregation in Strasbourg and a brief visit with Bucer to Frankfurt, to write this portion of his forthcoming second Latin edition of the *Institutes.* On 12 May Calvin began to lecture on the Epistles of Paul to the Corinthians.[47] On 16 October he dedicated his shortly-to-be-published *Commentary on Romans* to the Basel savant Simon Grynaeus. This concentration on Pauline studies is reflected in the treatise "On the Christian Life." Not only is it steeped in Paul's thought; Calvin's very purpose smacks of Paul's way of working in the churches: ". . . to show some order whereby the Christian man may be led and directed to order his life aright." This is Calvin's announced intention.

The treatise "On the Christian Life" is a marvel of brevity. After a call to the holiness that God demands of His children, a holiness deep within the heart, Calvin began to describe the lifelong process of growth into Christian perfection in and through Christ.[48] Here Calvin was consciously standing on a middle ground between the two-tiered Roman Catholic notion of the Christian life[49] and the instant perfection he rightly or wrongly inferred from the teaching of the Anabaptists.[50]

He then moved on to describe the Christological pattern as it unfolds inwardly in the heart—"Denial of Self."[51] The same following of Christ is then traced in the outward life as the "Bearing of the Cross."[52]

He next turned to an examination first of the present,[53] then of the future life.[54] I have sometimes asked my students reading book 3 in the *Institutes* to stop after reading chapter 9 and write down their impressions, then go on to chapter 10 and do the same once more. At the end of chapter 9 Calvin sounds like a medieval monk, reflecting on the vanities of the world; at the end of chapter 10, he is clearly free of medievalism! The secret? *It is the hope of the life to come that gives meaning and purpose to the life in which we presently are.*[55]

As one reads these pages, one feels in a field of magnetic force, set between poles. Calvin's deep religious insight was born in controversy. Constantly he strove to find a middle, Scripturally informed ground between extremes: here it lies between Roman Catholic and Anabaptist. When we study Calvin, we can never flatten out his thought, excerpt it, generalize from it. We must read it in its totality, and within the historical, Biblical, and theological context out of which it came. Our own view and practice of the Christian life, in like manner, must issue from pondering on the deep antinomies of the faith in our own time. Yet there is a great deal that Calvin can say to us about the conduct of the Christian life in this last quarter of the twentieth century. Right in this section, for example, he enunciated a principle of Christian stewardship of nature and of style of living that speaks to our present ecological crisis.[56] Before the great technological advances of recent centuries, before the present age of extraterrestrial exploration, Calvin knew the planet Earth was what we today call a "closed eco-system." Here and elsewhere in his writings he tells us how the creation is to be used by man.

> Moses now adds, that the earth was given to man, with this condition, that he should occupy himself in its cultivation. Whence it follows, that men were created to employ themselves in some work, and not to lie down in inactivity and idleness. This labour, truly, was pleasant, and full of delight, entirely exempt from all trouble and weariness; since, however, God ordained that man should be exercised in the culture of the ground, he condemned, in his person, all indolent repose. Wherefore, nothing is more contrary to the order of nature, than to consume life in eating, drinking, and sleeping, while in the meantime we propose nothing to ourselves to do. Moses adds, that the custody of the garden was given in charge to Adam, to show that we possess the things which God has committed to our hands, on the condition, that being content with a frugal and moderate use of them, we should take care of what shall remain. Let him who possesses a field, so partake of its yearly fruits, that he may not suffer the ground to be injured by his negligence; but let him endeavour to hand it down to posterity as he received it, or even better cultivated. Let him so feed on its fruits, that he neither dissipates it by luxury, nor permits [it] to be marred or ruined by neglect. Moreover, that this economy, and this diligence, with respect to those good things which God has given us to enjoy, may flourish among us; let every one regard himself as the steward of God in all things which he possesses. Then he will neither conduct himself dissolutely, nor corrupt by abuse those things which God requires to be preserved.[57]

Calvin believed too, as we have said, in gradual growth in the Christian life.[58] Does not the very writing of this section illustrate his own growth, not to be complete until his death in 1564?

How may we sum up, for our own use, Calvin's teaching on *pietas,* on Christian discipleship? From Calvin's experience, as we have just reviewed it, and from our own experience of trying to live the Christian life in these times, we may infer a few general principles that may assist us in our search of a style of living commensurate with the gospel.

1. One cannot really understand a particular Christian's view of discipleship apart from his times and apart from his own distinctive experience of Christ.

2. Also, certain tacit assumptions which we make in our daily living must be identified, and at least momentarily set aside, if we are to understand a classic theologian's teaching: for example, (1) the myth of human self-sufficiency and of scientific-technological supremacy; (2) the treatment of God as a shadowy concept, not very important for daily life; (3) the notion of the Scriptures as a human book, rather like other books; (4) the rejection of an afterlife and the concentration of all human attention and effort on the present life; (5) the emphasis on the production of goods and the notion of man as a consuming animal; and (6) the view of man as a creature whose wants are to be satisfied.

3. Conversely, to understand Calvin's view of Christian discipleship, we must for the moment open our minds to certain basic assumptions that he makes: (1) man's total dependence upon God; (2) nature's being ours to use and enjoy, but with moderation and accountability; (3) God's providential care; (4) the contrast between philosophers and Scripture; (5) the afterlife's being not only the goal of the present life, but its nourishment in hope; (6) all goods as the gifts of God's kindness to us; and (7) the account we will at the end render to God of their use.

Obstacles to Piety According to the Polemical Tracts

One thing that has marked all great theologians, from Paul the apostle onward, is that their finest theology has been called forth by specific requests for help. At bottom, then, true theology and true exegesis are an exercise of the pastoral office. Calvin claimed a double pastoral intent for the *Institutes:* (1) to introduce neophytes to the study of the Scriptures; (2) to justify the French evangelicals before a hostile government and (if we may add its corollary) to hearten these evangelicals in their effort to lead a Christian life under harsh circumstances.

Also for the heartening of beleaguered Christians, but even more pointed than Calvin's theological and exegetical works, are selected polemical works from his pen, most of them undertaken in response to anguished cries for help from evangelical Christians. This class of writings is virtually unknown except to specialists, yet they carry the teaching of *pietas* that necessary further step: to overcome the obstacles that commonly stand in the way of leading the Christian life for members of churches in the Reformed tradition. From this rich store of pastoral instruction, we have selected three tracts for a brief perusal: *On Scandals* (1550),[59] *Excuse to the Nicodemites* (1544),[60] and *What a Faithful Man...Ought to Do Dwelling Amongst the Papists* (1543).[61]

On Scandals (1550). Reformed Christians, especially Frenchmen, underwent great vexations on account of the faith. Calvin for a long time pondered writing a tract to amplify the spiritual advice he had already given in the *Institutes.* Many persecuted evangelicals sought refuge in Geneva; extensive correspondence also kept Calvin informed of the plight of his countrymen who remained at home. In September 1546 Calvin wrote to Farel that he was suspending work on such a tract because of labors on the *Commentary on Galatians;* the tract was completed in August 1550. The occasion for it was the misfortune of his friend, Laurence de Normandie, who after accepting the Reformed faith gave up his country and social position in favor of the gospel, and in the space of a year lost his father, wife, and little daughter. It is understandable that Laurence was tempted to read in these events the curse of God attendant upon his change of religion. Calvin took up his pen both to console Laurence in his great loss and to strengthen him in the faith.

The gospel teaches that Christ Himself is a scandal, and we cannot follow the gospel apart from scandal. The danger of this rock of offense has turned four classes of men away from the gospel: those who are so naturally modest as to be horror-struck at the scandal, and dare not even taste the gospel; those who are too lazy or sluggish or unteachable to bother with the gospel; those who reject the gospel because they are arrogant and perversely convinced of their own wisdom; and finally those who maliciously and deliberately collect all sorts of scandal and even invent many to deform the gospel out of hatred for it.

Calvin saw three sorts of scandals on which men stumble: those intrinsic to gospel-teaching itself; those "annexed" scandals that arise out of the preaching of the gospel; finally those "adventitious" scandals that spring from moral depravity, hypocrisy, the ingratitude and vanity of worldly professors of the faith.

"Intrinsic" scandals characterize those who take offense at the gospel because of the simplicity of its language. The Christian doctrines, in Calvin's view, that commonly stir disgust in men's minds include: the two natures of Christ, salvation obtained from Christ's sufferings alone, His becoming a curse for us and thus blessing us, our righteousness being in God only and not in ourselves, Christ's cross, our self-denial, and constancy in time of persecution. Here Calvin eloquently summarized the long chronicle of the church's sufferings.[62] Finally he noted the scandals of those who ascribe their sins to God or stumble at the doctrine of predestination.

The "annexed" scandals that arise when the gospel is preached lead to sects and controversies among Christian teachers. Some men are offended because the gospel often gives rise to strife and war. Calvin replied that war is justified if it is for souls; Christ foretold wars. The "cultured despisers" of the gospel (such as the circle of Rabelais) raise a scandal by converting Christian freedom into licentiousness.

Wicked ministers of the gospel living among the good are the cause of scandal; the gospel is not chargeable with their guilt; throughout its history offenses appear; the commingling of the wicked with the good is intended to prove the faith of the latter. Another source of offense is the easy enticement of some people from the profession of the truth. Over against this, Calvin set the courage of the women of Artois and the Netherlands.

"Adventitious" scandals spring from moral depravity, hypocrisy, and the ingratitude and vanity of worldly professors of the faith. Among the calumnies hurled at Reformed Christians by opposing preachers were the charges that the Reformed had abrogated auricular confession, condemned fasting, abandoned celibacy, and opened marriage to all.

Calvin closed the treatise with an eloquent admonition, translated here in the colorful language of the Elizabethan Age, to unity under Christ, the sole foundation. Christians

> . . . being armed with the remedies by me showed, they rather keep Christ still for their foundation, than by their rash and ignorant running against Him, make Him to themselves a stone to stumble at, and a rock to dash against. It cannot otherwise be but that in this world, many occasions of offense must from time to time be fathered upon the faithful. From these not even Christ himself was free. Rather, it is scarcely to be hoped for, that they should step one pace, but that the devil cast some stumbling block in their way. So must they walk through innumerable offenses. But albeit the variety of them be manifold, and the heap thick packed, yet shall none be a Christian, but he that wadeth through them with victory.[63]

Excuse to the Nicodemites (1544).[64] Laodicean lukewarmness, ever a problem in the Christian church, seems today one of the chief plagues of the old-line denominations in affluent America. Calvin had a name for the general class of such persons, "Messrs. the Nicodemites." They received their sobriquet from the well-known inquirer in John's Gospel. Calvin first encountered such people at the court of Marguerite at Ferrara, which he visited in 1536 on the eve of his detention by Farel in Geneva. Calvin directed several tracts against these siren prophets of religious compromise and sweet reasonableness. We shall look only at the *Excuse*.

Calvin's basic argument was that God is the Lord of the body no less than of the soul of the elect. Therefore the believer must honor God by public worship, upright life, and abstention from idolatrous conformity to the papal church. He directed his critique of religious lukewarmness against four kinds of "Nicodemites." There are evangelical priests and bishops who preach from Catholic pulpits the evangelical message but give their congregations the impression that they have thereby made acceptable the whole superstition-encrusted ecclesiastical shell in which the unreformed church hobbles. The second Nicodemite sect he found in the "delicate prothonotaries" who play religion with the ladies of the court and beguile them with sweet theological niceties, all of them condemning with one voice the too-great austerity of Geneva. This is the religion of the theological salon. A third group is comprised of the men of letters, given to philosophy and the tolerance of the foolish superstitions of the Papacy. For them it is enough to know God by books and contemplation in their ivory towers, without becoming strained or sullied by involvement in the organization of the community of faith, worship, and Christian action. These men half-convert Christianity into philosophy. In a rather extremely worded condemnation of them, Calvin said: "I would prefer that all human sciences were exterminated from the earth, than for them to be the cause of freezing the zeal of Christians and turning them from God."[65] The last group will raise a respondent chord in American hearts. This includes the merchants and common people, who would prefer that their pastors or priests not become so much involved in the fine points of doctrine and thereby disturb commerce and the workaday tasks and satisfactions.

What a Faithful Man ... Ought to Do Dwelling Amongst the Papists (1543). A basic issue in the two works already examined is what a Reformed Christian is to do when pressed to conform to the religious practices and beliefs of the unreformed church that dominates his native place. Calvin was indeed aware of the bitter prospect of losing body and goods, of stirring the world to opprobrium against oneself, and of forsaking the ease of life in one's own country for harsh exile in a foreign land. (Here one is reminded of the impassioned lines at the close of the dedicatory letter to Francis I of France that introduces the *Institutes of the Christian Religion.*)[66] This is the very route Calvin himself had taken. Many had been asking him how they should live and worship in accord with their own conscience when law and custom work against this. The tract was a detailed answer to them; it is also an extended application of *pietas*.

What shall men do? Calvin replied: We must not measure our duty to God according to our own advantage or physical convenience. We are not to rely on our own brain but rather to trust God's own providence, that He will keep us even in the midst of a thousand deaths.

What should be the general principles of Christian behavior? If God declares His will to us through His Word, we should follow it and not debate with God.

The first lesson in Christ's school is that if we are ashamed of Him or His Word, He will be ashamed of us when He comes in judgment. God is not satisfied that we acknowledge Him secretly in our hearts; we are to profess outwardly that we are His. Or to put it in the language of the treatise "On the Christian Life," with which we have already dealt, "We belong to God."[67] Should everyone declare himself openly, whether or not anybody ask him about his faith? Only those called thereto should preach openly, but everyone should witness according to his gifts, inviting his neighbor to join in true worship and Christian instruction. Since we have no definite rule for all, let every man ask our Lord to direct him in true wisdom to his duty, and then let him do it with all his power.

The chief question to which Calvin addressed himself in this tract is this: "Should a truly Christian man go to mass when he is among the Papists? Should he worship images, relics (and such like ceremonies)? A prior question which must be answered is: what is idolatry? Idolatry is of two sorts: first, when a man through a false fantasy conceived in his heart or spirit corrupts and perverts the spiritual balm of the one only God; second, when a man gives or transfers the honor which belongs to God only, to any creature." (Parenthetically, this would confirm our earlier postulation that the Romans passage underlying this view of idolatry is in fact the key verse that triggered Calvin's conversion.)

What duty do we owe God? Is it not enough to hold God in secret within our hearts? Calvin answered with a resounding no! God must be glorified in both our hearts and our bodies as well, for the latter too are redeemed by Jesus' blood. Therefore, we must not prostitute our bodies, which are the very temple of the Holy Spirit, before an idol. When we kneel before an idol we derogate God's majesty. All this is, once more, the familiar call to holiness before the all-holy God.

But can we really label the Mass as pagan idolatry? Surely, though it may be corrupt, it is still men's intention by it to worship God and not a humanly devised idol; consequently, such calling upon God's name, though perhaps idolatrous, is not perilous, is it? This argument did not impress Calvin. He responded: If you go about worshiping God in a perverse and unlawful manner, you are worshiping an idol.

What then about the practice of the Mass in Calvin's own day? One does not condemn all papal rites, but only those that are completely bad. No evangelical Christian can submit to daily mass, for this is manifest idolatry. What then about high mass? Is this not better since it is a memorial of the Lord's Supper? No, this is a corruption of the Lord's Supper and as such is idolatrous; also the priestly absolution that follows is a violation of God's authority.

Calvin then sketched the cultic acts that mark the daily life of an unreformed Christian, from birth to death, labeling them abominations to be avoided by faithful believers. But still a crowd of excuses for conformity to such practices must be dealt with. Of course it is wrong to participate in these rites, but if one does them out of fear of men, is this not a light fault? Surely far worse crimes than this are committed? Calvin replied that such hypocrisy is no light fault, for it runs clean counter to God's requirement that man sanctify and consecrate himself to God—both in body and in spirit, but the spirit as chief takes the principal place.

Another excuse: What good would come of it if everyone declared he would serve God purely? To this Calvin rejoined: If it pleases God, the faithful man will undergo persecution, flight, prison, banishment, and even death itself.

Still another excuse: Suppose everyone wished to leave idolatry; then all the countries under Antichrist's reign would be deprived of the faithful. Having thus departed, where could they settle, since the regions where God is purely called upon cannot absorb any more population. To this Calvin replied: If this happened, our Lord would provide for His faithful in some way—either convert the hearts of the princes and magistrates, moving them to put down idolatry and establish the true worship of God, or at least soften them so they would not force the faithful to defile themselves against their consciences or would not act cruelly against them.

The supply of excuses is not yet exhausted. If those capable of following the gospel take themselves away, how, if the seed is removed, can the doctrine of the gospel be multiplied? Calvin's answer is sharp: If all who have been given knowledge of the truth did but half their duty, there would not be one corner of the world not filled with it. Lack of courage is the fault. Have faith that if one man moves away, God will raise up four in his place.

The final excuse is a taunt thrown at Calvin: It is very well for you to talk from your safe place! If you were in our place, you would do as we do! Calvin answered: I speak as my conscience prompts, without boasting. If I were in a place where I thought I could not avoid idolatry without danger, I would pray the Lord to strengthen me and give me constancy to prefer His glory over my own life.

After a call to martyrdom, Calvin gave his final advice to evangelical Christians. If you live in a land where you cannot worship purely, go into exile if you can. If you cannot flee, abstain from idolatry while purely worshiping God in private. But suppose one has not the strength or constancy or is held back by parents, family, or the like? As far as your infirmity permits, follow the surest and soundest counsel. Insofar as you depart from the right way out of fear of men, confess your sin to God. Try daily to be sorry in order that you may obtain God's mercy. Then ask your Father to draw you out of bondage or to establish a right form of the church throughout the world so you can duly honor Him.

Thus do these tracts pastorally apply *pietas* to the troubled, perplexed lives of those who longed to work out the renewal that had already touched their hearts. It has been said that Calvin is a theologian for hard times. Though too often curtained over by affluence, the church is living in a hard time. All the forces contrary to a truly Reformed faith that stood in the way in the sixteenth century have their late-twentieth-century counterpart. Lukewarm Nicodemites and learned scoffers are in the very bosom of the church, and—I may say—the seminaries. It will not take much imagination to find the category of obstacle-makers to which each of us in our failure to follow Christ belongs. Deny self! Follow God! Bear your cross! Let the hope of the life to come give meaning for your present life. What excuses do we give for not following this way of *pietas*?

It remains for us to summarize the teaching of Calvin on *pietas*. What better passage to do this is there than the hymn to Creation which is included in chapter 7 of this volume and to which you, the reader, are invited to turn.

Notes

1. Ed. and trans. Ford Lewis Battles (Pittsburgh: Pittsburgh Theological Seminary, 1972), p. 2.

2. McNeill-Battles, 1.2.1.

3. Ibid., 1.2.2.

4. OC, 32:249; cf. *Institutes* 3.2.26.

5. *Institutes* 3.2.27.

6. OC, 38:96.

7. 2.6.4.

8. *Commentary on Acts* (on Acts 18:22), in OC, 48:435.

9. *Commentary on the Psalms* (on Ps. 119:78f.), in OC, 32:249.

10. OC, 40:426.

11. See renderings of *ḥāsîd, mansuetus*, etc., where piety is related to the kindness of man (Ps. 16:10, etc.).

12. OC, 26:312.

13. Ibid. This is the habitual twofold division (God and man) that Calvin applied to the Decalogue (*Institutes* 2.8.11) and the Lord's Prayer (3.20.35). See below, chap. 2, lines 125ff., 202ff.; also chap. 3, lines 281ff. (note).

14. *Commentary on John* (on John 4:36), in OC, 47:96.

15. *Commentary on Acts* (on Acts 17:28), in OC, 48:417.

16. Ed. and trans. Ford Lewis Battles and André Malan Hugo (Leiden: Brill, 1969), pp. 226–29.

17. Compare Justinian's comment: "For the power of the father ought to consist in piety, not cruelty." *Digest* 48.9.5.; cited by Calvin in *Commentary on "De Clementia,"* pp. 254–57.

18. 1.3–13 (1253 bl–1260 b25); cf. *Nicomachean Ethics* 8.11 (1160 cl). Note is from Calvin, *Commentary on "De Clementia,"* pp. 170f.

19. Calvin, *Commentary on "De Clementia,"* pp. 236–39.

20. Ibid., pp. 252–55; cf. pp. 308f.

21. OC, 45:324f.; cf. *Institutes* 1.4.4, where Calvin contrasted true and false *pietas*.

22. Walter Bauer, *A Greek-English Lexicon of the New Testament,* ed. and trans. William F. Arndt and F. Wilbur Gingrich, 4th ed. (Chicago: University of Chicago, 1952), p. 326.

23. In my introduction to *Institution of the Christian Religion . . . 1536,* trans. and an. Ford Lewis Battles (Atlanta: John Knox, 1975), pp. xvi ff.

24. Ibid., pp. xvii f.; cf. chap. 2, lines 1–4 (note) below.

25. See chap. 1 below.

26. See my introduction to *Institution,* pp. xxiii ff. T. H. L. Parker rejected the passage from Calvin's *Reply to Cardinal Sadolet* as a "source." *John Calvin: A Biography* (Philadelphia: Westminster, 1975), p. 162.

27. Battles, "Introduction," *Institution,* pp. xxiv f.

28. The word *subita* ("sudden, unexpected") has spawned a considerable literature. For discussion see chap. 1, line 257 (note) below.

29. Calvin called the law the perfect guide to all duties of piety and love. *Institutes* 2.8.51.

30. Cf. *Institutes* 3.9.4; 3.10.6. See chap. 3, lines 2197 (note), 2215 (note) below.

31. Beza, *Vita Calvini*, in OC, 21:125.41ff.; English translation (hereafter ET) by Henry Beveridge in John Calvin, *Tracts and Treatises in Defense of the Reformed Faith*, 3 vols. (Grand Rapids: Eerdmans, 1958), 1:xxix.

32. See chap. 1, line 445 (note) below.

33. See chap. 1, line 469 (note) below.

34. *Institutes* 2.10f.

35. Translated in chap. 3 below.

36. Section 3.8.1ff. of the 1559 edition of the *Institutes* is hinted at in the 1536 edition. *Institution*, p. 55. See chap. 3, lines 906ff. below.

37. See John Calvin, *Theological Treatises*, ed. and trans. J. K. S. Reid, LCC, vol. 22 (Philadelphia: Westminster, 1954), pp. 47–55.

38. See "Letter" in *Catechism*, pp. vii ff.

39. See chap. 6 below.

40. Cf. Ford Lewis Battles, "Against Luxury and License in Geneva," *Interpretation* 19 (1965): 186ff. Further on this, see chap. 3, lines 2008ff. (note) below.

41. See chap. 3 below.

42. McNeill-Battles, p. 3.

43. See my preface to *Catechism* (p. x) and the comparative table at the end of that volume.

44. Cf. *Institutes* 1.15.8. The crucial place of man's fall, not understood by the philosophers, was recognized by Calvin in his understanding of the soul in its present state (1.15.6–8; this is apparent mainly in the 1559 edition but to some extent in the 1539 edition), a reflection of Calvin's conversion insight. Cf. chap. 3, lines 34, 1309ff., 1473ff., 1860ff., and notes, below.

45. On Calvin's teaching on frugality and its relation to the "blue laws" of Geneva, see Battles, "Against Luxury," pp. 182ff. See also chap. 3, lines 1953ff. below.

46. Referring to the tenth commandment, Calvin said, "It was Augustine who first opened the way for me to understand this commandment." *Institutes* (McNeill-Battles) 2.8.50. See chap. 3, lines 6 (note) and 18 (note) below.

47. Cf. chap. 3, line 558 (note) below.

48. See chap. 3, lines 1–280 below.

49. In his *Reply to Cardinal Sadolet* (1539) Calvin confessed that his own Christian nurture (under the Romanism into which he had been born) was quite inadequate for right worship, hope of salvation, or duties of the Christian life. See *Institution*, pp. xix f. But cf. note 26 above.

50. See *Institution*, pp. 375f. (note on line 34, p. 152).

51. See chap. 3, lines 281–905.

52. Ibid., lines 906–1505.

53. Ibid., lines 1506–1952.

54. Ibid., lines 1953–2255.

55. See ibid., line 1662 (note) below.

56. See ibid., lines 2133ff. (note) below.

57. *Commentary on Genesis* (on Gen. 2:15), trans. John King, 2 vols. (Edinburgh: Calvin Translation Society, 1847–1850), 1:125.

58. See notes 48 and 49 above.

59. OC, 8:1–64; OS, 2:162–340. Translated into English by Arthur Golding (London: Seres, 1567).

60. OC, 6:589–614. For critical text see Francis M. Higman, ed., *Three French Treatises* (London: Athlone, 1970).

61. OC, 6:537–88. Translated into English by R. G. in 1548.

62. See "The Church as Pilgrim" in epilogue below.

63. P. 109.

64. See chap. 3, lines 171ff. (note) below.

65. OC, 6:600; cf. George H. Williams, *The Radical Reformation* (Philadelphia: Westminster, 1962), pp. 603f.

66. Cf. *Institution*, pp. 17f.

67. See chap. 3, lines 281ff. below.

Chapter 1

The Spiritual Pilgrimage of Calvin

It is hard to express in words
What varied and shining riches
This treasure contains:
Whatever I am about to say
5 I know will fall far short
Of the worth of the Book of Psalms.
But because it is better to give a taste,
However slight, to my readers
Than to remain utterly silent,
10 Permit me to touch briefly
On a matter whose importance
Cannot be completely explained.
Not without reason, it is my custom
To call this book
15 *An Anatomy of All the Parts of the Soul*
Since there is no emotion
Anyone will experience
Whose image is not reflected
In this mirror.
20 Indeed, here the Holy Spirit
Has drawn to the life
All pains, sorrows, fears, doubts,

Hopes, cares, anxieties—
In short—all the turbulent emotions
25 With which men's minds
Are commonly stirred.
The rest of the Scriptures contains
The commandments that God
Enjoined upon His servants
30 To announce to us.
But here the prophets themselves
Speaking with God
Uncover all their inner feelings
And call, or rather drag,
35 Each one of us
To examine himself.
Thus is left hidden
Not one of the very many infirmities
To which we are subject,
40 Not one of the very many vices
With which we are stuffed.
A rare and singular achievement it is
When, all recesses laid bare,
The heart, purged of hypocrisy
45 (Most baneful infection of all),
Is brought into the light of day.
In short, if calling upon God
Is the greatest bastion of our salvation,
Since in no other place
50 Can one seek
A better and surer rule for it
Than in this book,
It follows that,
As each man best advances
55 In understanding it,
He will attain a good part
Of heavenly doctrine.

True prayer is born
First from our own sense of need,

60 Then from faith in God's promises.
Here will the readers be best awakened
To sense their ills,
And, as well, to seek
Remedies for them.
65 Whatever can stimulate us
When we are about to pray to God,
This book teaches.
Not only are God's promises presented to us there,
But often there is shown to us
70 Someone, girding himself for prayer,
Caught between God's invitation
And the hindrance of the flesh.
Thus are we taught how,
If at any time
75 We are plagued with various doubts,
To fight against them
Until the mind, freed,
Rises to God.
And not that only:
80 But amid hesitations, fears,
Trepidations, we are still
To rely on prayer
Until some solace comes.
Although unfaith may shut the gate
85 To our prayers,
Yet are we not to yield
Whenever our hearts waver
Or are beset with unrest,
Until from these struggles
90 Faith emerges victorious.
In many passages we are shown
God's servants so wavering
In the midst of prayer
That, almost overwhelmed
95 By alternate despair and hope,
They gain the prize
Only by hard effort.

On the one hand the infirmity of the flesh
Reveals itself,
100 On the other, the force of faith
Is manifested.
If it is not as vigorous
As might be desired,
Yet is it prepared to struggle
105 Until little by little
It acquires perfect strength.
But since the principles
Of proper prayer will be found
Scattered through the whole work,
110 I shall not burden my readers
With needless repetition
Nor hold up their progress.
Only, it was worthwhile in passing
To show that in this book
115 Something no less desirable
Is furnished to us:
Not only does intimate access to God
Lie open to us,
But infirmities that shame forbids us
120 To confess to men,
We are permitted and free to lay open
Before our God.
Here also is precisely prescribed
The proper way to offer
125 "The sacrifice of praise,"
Which God declares
Is most precious and sweet-smelling
To Him.
Nowhere else does one read
130 More shining tidings
Of God's singular kindness to His Church
And of all His works.
Nowhere else are related so many deliverances,
Or shine so brightly
135 Proofs of His fatherly providence

And care for us.
Nowhere else, to sum up,
Is set forth a fuller reason
To praise God,
140 Or are we more sharply pricked
To perform this duty of piety.

Moreover, although this book is crammed
With all sorts of precepts
Capable of shaping our life
145 Holily, piously, justly,
Still especially does it instruct us
To bear the cross.
Here is the true proof of obedience,
Where, bidding farewell to our own affections,
150 We subject ourselves to God
And allow our lives
To be so governed by His will
That things most bitter and harsh to us—
Because they come from Him—
155 Become sweet to us.
Finally, here not only general praises
Of God's goodness are recounted
To teach us to rest in Him alone,
So that godly minds may await
160 Some help from Him in all necessity;
But also freely given forgiveness of sins,
Which alone both reconciles us to God
And obtains for us quiet repose with Him,
Is so commended
165 That utterly nothing is lacking
To our knowledge of eternal salvation.

Calvin's Identification with David

Moreover, if my readers should happen
To feel some benefit and profit
From the labor I have put

29

170 Into writing this commentary,
I want them to know
That the experience I have had
Through the struggles in which
The Lord has exercized me,
175 Even though it has not been of the highest degree,
Has nonetheless served me greatly.
I have benefited
Not only in being able to fathom
How one must apply
180 And put into practice
All the teaching one could gather from the Psalms,
But also in opening up more fully
To my understanding
The intention of each of the writers
185 Who composed the Psalms.

And because David is the chief among them,
I was greatly helped to understand more fully
The laments he made concerning the afflictions
The church had to bear within itself,
190 By the fact that I suffered
The same or similar troubles
From the enemies of the church
Within her household.
For although I am far away
195 From following David
And fall far short
Of being his equal—
Or, to put it better,
Although aspiring slowly
200 And with great difficulty
To the many virtues in which he excels—
I still feel so tied to the opposing vices;
Yet, if I have some things
In common with him,
205 I am content to examine these
And make some comparison
Between us.

Thus, therefore, when I read
The evidences of his faith,
210 Patience, ardor, zeal, uprightness,
I am often compelled to groan and sigh
That I am so far
From approaching him.
Yet it is a very useful thing
215 For me to contemplate in him,
As in a mirror,
Both the beginning of my calling
And the continued course of my office.
From this I recognize most certainly
220 That all that this most excellent king and prophet
Has suffered and borne
Is set before me by God
As an example to imitate.

Calvin's Education

True it is that my condition
225 Is inferior and more humble
(And I do not need to stop
In order to point this out!),
But just as he was taken
From tending sheep
230 And raised to the highest degree
Of royal dignity,
So God, from my small, humble beginnings,
Has advanced me to the point
Of calling me to this very honorable post
235 Of minister and preacher of the gospel.
From my early childhood
My father had destined me
For theology:
But after a time,
240 Having considered that the knowledge of the law
Commonly enriches those who follow it,

This hope suddenly made him change his mind.
That was the reason
I was withdrawn
245 From the study of philosophy
And was put into the study of law,
To which, although, in obedience to my father,
I tried to apply myself faithfully,
God nevertheless by His secret providence
250 Finally made me turn
In another direction.

Calvin's Conversion

And first, since I was
So obstinately devoted
To the superstitions of the Papacy
255 That it was difficult to pull me
Out of that very deep morass—
By a sudden conversion
God tamed and brought to teachableness
My heart, which, despite my youth,
260 Was too hardened in such matters.
Having therefore received
Some taste and knowledge
Of true piety,
I was suddenly fired
265 With such a great desire to advance
That, even though I had not forsaken
The other studies entirely,
I nonetheless worked at them
More slackly.
270 But I was utterly amazed
That before a year had passed,
All those who yearned
For pure doctrine
Were coming again and again to me

275 To learn it,
Even though I was still a novice,
A mere recruit.
For my part, being of a nature
Somewhat unpolished and retiring,
280 I always longed for repose and quiet.
Hence I began to seek
Some hiding place
And way to withdraw from people.
But, far from attaining my heart's desire,
285 All retreats and places of escape
Became for me like public schools.
In short, although I always cherished
The goal of living in private, incognito,
God so led me and caused me to turn
290 By various changes
That He never left me at peace in any place
Until, in spite of my natural disposition,
He brought me into the limelight.
Leaving my native France,
295 I departed into Germany
With the express purpose
Of being able to live
At peace in some unknown corner,
As I had always longed.

Calvin's Sojourn in Basel

300 But it happened that while I was dwelling at Basel,
Hidden there, as it were, and known only to few people,
Many faithful, holy men were burned in France,
And reports of this having spread to foreign countries,
A great part of the Germans
305 Reacted with grave disapproval
So as to conceive a hatred
Toward the authors of that tyranny.

In order to quiet things down,
It was arranged to circulate
310 Certain shameful pamphlets
Full of lies, to the effect
That only the Anabaptists and seditious persons
Were being treated so cruelly,
Who by their dreams and false opinions
315 Were overturning not only religion
But the whole political order.
It appeared to me that these tools of the court
Were by their disguises trying
Not only to keep this shameful shedding
320 Of innocent blood
Buried under false charges and calumnies
Brought against the holy martyrs after their death,
But also that thereafter they might have a means
Of proceeding to the ultimate extremity
325 Of murdering the poor faithful
Without anyone having compassion for them.
Unless, then, I strongly opposed them
To the best of my ability,
I could not justify my silence
330 Without being found lax and disloyal.
This was the reason that roused me
To publish my *Institutes of the Christian Religion:*
First, to answer certain wicked charges
Sowed by the others
335 And to clear the memory of my brethren
Whose death was precious
In the presence of the Lord;
Second, as the same cruelties
Could very soon thereafter
340 Be exercized against many poor people,
That foreign nations might at least
Be touched with some compassion
And concern for them.
For at that time I did not publish
345 The book as it now is,

Full and laborious,
But it was only a little booklet
Containing in summary form
The principal matters.
350 I had no other purpose
Than to acquaint others
With the sort of faith
Held by those
Whom I saw
355 These wicked and faithless flatterers
Villainously defaming.

Calvin's First Sojourn in Geneva

But to show that it was not my purpose
To acquire prominence and notoriety,
I would have it known
360 That, directly afterward, I left Basel,
And even while I was there
No one knew
I was the author of the book.
Also in other places I kept
365 The matter secret and determined
To continue to do so
Until finally Guillaume Farel
Kept me at Geneva,
Not by advice and urging,
370 But by a dreadful curse
As if God from on high
Had stretched out His hand
Upon me to arrest me.

Because the most direct road to Strasbourg,
375 Where I wished to retire,
Was closed on account of hostilities,
It was my plan

To pass through Geneva
Without stopping more than one night
380 In the city.
A little earlier
Popery had been driven out
By the fine person I just named
And by Pierre Viret:
385 But conditions were not yet settled,
And evil, dangerous factions
Divided the city.
Thereupon an individual
Who has since basely revolted
390 And returned to the Papists
Discovered me and identified me
To the others.
At this point Farel
(Burning with a wondrous zeal
395 To advance the gospel)
Suddenly set all his efforts
At keeping me.
After having heard
That I was determined
400 To pursue my own private studies—
When he realized
He would get nowhere by pleas—
He came to the point of a curse:
That it would please God
405 To curse my leisure
And the quiet for my studies
That I was seeking,
If in such a grave emergency
I should withdraw and refuse
410 To give aid and help.
This word so overwhelmed me
That I desisted from the journey
I had undertaken.
Still, feeling my shame
415 And my timidity,

I would not undertake
To discharge any particular function.

After that, scarcely four months passed
Before we were assailed on one side
420 By the Anabaptists
And on the other by a wicked apostate
Who, being secretly sustained
And supported by certain prominent persons,
Was able to cause us a good deal of trouble.
425 During this time an incredible number
Of seditions afflicted us.
And so, though I recognize myself
As being timid, soft, and fainthearted
By nature, I had, from the very beginning,
430 To bear these violent waves.
Even though I did not succumb to them,
Yet I was not sustained
By sufficient greatness of heart
As not to rejoice more than I ought when,
435 As a consequence of certain troubles,
I was banished.

Calvin's Sojourn in Strasbourg

Then free, released by this means
From my calling,
I had planned to live quietly
440 Without undertaking any public responsibility,
Until that excellent servant of Christ,
Martin Bucer, making use
Of a curse
Similar to that of Farel's,
445 Removed me to another post.
Terrified therefore by the example of Jonah
That he set before me,

I continued to function in teaching.
And even though I continued
450 As always to keep to myself,
That is, not to wish to appear at
Or to participate in
The great assemblies,
Yet was I led as it were by force—
455 I know not how!—
To the imperial assembly.
There, willy-nilly, I was thrust
Into a great crowd of people.

Afterward the Lord, having pity
460 On this city, had calmed
The dangerous emotions and troubles
That had prevailed here
And by His wonderful power
Had defeated both the wicked plots
465 And the bloody efforts
Of the disturbers of the republic.
Then, contrary to my desire and inclination,
The necessity was laid upon me
Of returning to my first post.
470 For although the welfare of this church
Was so much on my conscience
That for her I would not have hesitated
To lay down my life,
Yet my timidity gave me
475 All kinds of reasons
To excuse myself
For not reshouldering straightway
Such a heavy burden.
But finally regard for my duty,
480 Which I considered reverently and conscientiously,
Won me over
And made me agree to return
To the flock from which I had,
As it were, been torn away.

485 This I did with sadness,
Tears, great care, and distress—
The Lord is my best witness—
And several good people
Who had desired to see me clear
490 Of this trouble,
Had it not been that what I feared
And had made me consent,
Restrained them
And shut their mouths.

Calvin's Subsequent Years in Geneva

495 A long history it would be
Were I to recount the various conflicts
With which the Lord exercized me
Since that time;
With what trials He tested me.
500 But to avoid boring my readers
With useless words, I'll now briefly repeat
What I touched on a little while ago:
In considering the whole course of David's life,
It seems to me that at his every step
505 He showed me the way.
This was for me
A marvelous solace.
For although with continual wars
This holy king was troubled
510 By the Philistines and other foreign nations,
His enemies,
Still more grievously was he stricken
In the midst of his own people
By the ill will
515 Of certain disloyal, vicious men.
I can say similarly of myself:
On all sides have I been assailed,

Scarcely even for a moment
Experiencing repose;
520 Always the brunt of some attack
Either from without or from within.
Satan has often tried by his plots
To overthrow the whole structure
Of this church.

A Five-Year Trial

525 Once it came to such a pass
That, feeble and fearful as I am,
I was nevertheless compelled,
In order to break and quiet
His deadly attacks,
530 To put my life in danger
And expose myself to his blows.
Afterwards, for five years
Some wicked good-for-nothings
Got too much power,
535 Gained authority,
While a part of the common people,
Corrupted by the allurements
And wicked schemes
Of these fellows,
540 Longed for an unbridled license;
Therefore it became necessary
To fight ceaselessly
In order to defend and maintain
The church's discipline.
545 For these profane folk, despisers
Of the heavenly teaching,
Cared not at all if the church
Fell into ruin,
Provided they could attain
550 The power they demanded:
To do entirely as they pleased.
Many there were also

Whom poverty and hunger hounded;
Others were pressed by insatiable ambition
555 Or by avarice and desire of dishonest gain.
All of these persons were so enraged
That they preferred while ruining us
To ruin themselves,
Rather than restrain themselves somewhat
560 By living peaceably and honestly,
That whole long length of time
I believe they did not overlook
A thing that could be forged
In Satan's workshop
565 To gain their end.
And the final outcome
Of their cursed machinations
Could not be anything else
Than ignominious destruction
570 Upon their heads.
Even to me was this
A painful and pitiable spectacle.
For even though they very much deserved
Great torments,
575 Yet always I desired
They might prosper
And live at ease.
This would have happened
If they had not remained
580 Ever incorrigible and rebellious
To all good warnings.

Theological Conflicts

This five-year trial
Was very painful
And hard to bear.
585 Yet I experienced
No less pain
From the ill-will of those

Who ceased not to assail me
And my ministry
590 With their poisoned slanders.
For even though a good part of them
Are so blinded with a passion
To slander and backbite
That, to their great dishonor,
595 They betray at once their shamelessness,
The others, crafty and cunning as they are,
Cannot so cover up or disguise
As not to remain convicted;
Yet when a man has a hundred times
600 Been cleared of the charge of blasphemy
And still the charge is repeated against him
Without cause or any occasion,
It is an outrageous villainy
And very hard to bear.
605 Because I affirm and maintain
That the world is directed and governed
By a secret providence of God,
A heap of arrogant people rise up
Croaking that by this reckoning
610 God would become the author of sin.
A ridiculous slander, this,
One that would easily vanish of itself
Were it not that it meets folk
With giddy ears who take pleasure
615 In drinking up such gossip.
But several of them there are
Whose hearts are so filled
With envy and spite,
Or ungratefulness, or ill will,
620 That there is no lie so far-fetched,
Even monstrous,
That they do not receive
If some one speaks to them of it.
Others try to overturn
625 God's eternal predestination

Whereby He distinguishes
Between the reprobate and the elect;
Others defend free will.
It is not ignorance
630 But some sort of perverse zeal
That draws many at once
Into their ranks.
If it were only open enemies
Who brought these troubles on me,
635 The matter would be somewhat bearable.
But that those who pose as brothers,
Who not only eat
The holy bread of Christ,
But even administer it to others,
640 In short, who at the top of their lungs
Boast of being preachers of the gospel,
Wage this unhappy war against me—
What horror is this?
In this matter I have every right
645 To complain, after David's example:
"My intimate friend,
Who ate bread with me,
Has raised his heel against me."
Again: "My close friend, my colleague
650 Who used to go to the temple of God with me,
With whom I used to converse intimately,
Has, like an enemy,
Assailed me with insults."

False Charges and Rumors

Some scatter abroad ridiculous rumors
655 Concerning my wealth;
Others, concerning my limitless power;
Others talk of my luxury
And magnificence.
But when a man contents himself
660 With scanty fare and common garb,
And of the humblest persons

36

Does not require
More frugality
Than he himself shows,
665 Shall it be asserted
Such a one lives too high?
As for the power
For which they envy me,
I should like to unload
670 Some of it upon them,
For they think
The heavy load of work
Weighing me down
Is a "kingdom"!
675 And if there is any one of them
I can't persuade, while alive,
That I am not rich,
My death will at last show it.
Certainly, since I seek no more
680 Than I already have,
I admit I am not at all poor.
But even though in all these fictions
There is no plausibility,
Many folk there are,
685 Nonetheless, who approve them.
The reason is
That the majority
Think the only way
To cover up their evil deeds
690 Is to mix black and white.
For them the best shortcut
To impunity and license
Is for the authority
Of Christ's servants
695 To fall into ruin.
Besides all these
There are also
Cake-eating dandies
Of whom David complains:

700 I do not mean only
The epicures of the table,
But all those
Who by false reports
Are currying favor with the great.

Attacks from Lutherans

705 Being long accustomed
To swallowing such indignities,
I was nearly hardened to them,
But when the insolence of such persons
Was ever growing and increasing,
710 I could not help being stricken
By some pangs of bitterness.
But to be thus inhumanly treated
By my neighbors
Was not enough—
715 Also out of the icy sea
Some sort of frenzy
Was stirring a troop
Of evilly idle men
Against me.
720 I am still speaking
Of the domestic enemies of the church,
Men who stoutly boast
Of the gospel of Christ,
But because I do not embrace
725 Their gross fiction
Concerning the physical eating of Christ,
They rush against me with an impetuosity
Greater than that of open enemies.
Against these I can protest
730 After the example of David:
"While I am seeking peace,
They are rushing into war."
But the barbarous ungratefulness
Of all these shows itself
735 In that they are attacking

37

From flank and rear
A man who works hard
To maintain a cause
They have in common
740 With him,
And to whom they should give
Their help.
Surely if these fellows
Had had a drop of humanity,
745 The fury of the Papists unleashed upon me
With such unbridled intensity
Would soften whatever very great hatred
They bear me.

David's condition was such
750 That, deserving his people's esteem,
He was nonetheless
Groundlessly hated by many
(As he complained that
"He had paid back
755 What he had not taken away").
No small consolation for me it was—
When assaulted by the unwarranted hatred
Of those who should have put their efforts
Into helping me—
760 To conform myself
To such a great and excellent pattern.

And this very knowledge and experience
Was a great help to me
In understanding the Psalms,
765 To keep me from wandering as it were
In a strange land.
And actually my readers (I am sure)
Will recognize that when I recount
The inner feelings
770 Both of David
And of others,

I am speaking of them as things
With which I am intimately acquainted.

L'Envoi

Moreover, since I have labored conscientiously
775 To communicate this treasure
To all faithful people,
Even though I haven't achieved what I wished,
Yet this effort of mine
Deserves a favorable reception.
780 Still, all I ask of others
Is that each one judge my labor frankly and fairly,
In accordance with the profit and benefit
He derives from my book.
In reading this commentary
785 One can see at a glance
That I have done this
Not only to please
But to profit as well.
Therefore, not only have I kept
790 To a simple style of teaching throughout;
But also, in order to separate myself the more
From all ostentation,
I have refrained from refuting others
Even though I had ample occasion
795 Thus to win the applause
Of those who might read my book.
I have never touched on contrary opinions
Unless there was danger
That in remaining silent
800 I might leave my readers in doubt.
I am quite aware
How much more attractive
Many would have found it
Had I, out of this complex pile,

805 Produced a dazzlingly ambitious piece.
But of greatest importance to me
Was to see to the upbuilding of the church.
May God, who has given me the mind to do this,
Grant that the result also
810 Will correspond!

At Geneva, 22 July 1557

Notes

Note: This English translation of the preface to the *Commentary on the Psalms* is based on the Schipper edition of the Latin text (tom. 3, fol. *2ʳ line 22–fol. *3ᵛ line 27).

3. The Book of Psalms.

6. See John R. Walchenbach, "The Influence of David and the Psalms on the Life and Thought of John Calvin" (Th.M. thesis, Pittsburgh Theological Seminary, 1969), passim.

15. Ἀνατομὴν omnium animae partium.

19. In 3.2.17 of the *Institutes* Calvin rehearsed the varied emotional states that David had revealed in his Psalms.

31. Compare this statement from the *Institutes:* "I include the psalms with the prophecies, since what we attribute to the prophecies is common to them." McNeill-Battles, 4.8.6. Calvin habitually referred to David as "the prophet," presumably on the basis of Matthew 13:25 and Acts 2:29f.

58ff. Cf. chap. 4, lines 1ff. below. Calvin forcefully asserted: "But for the saints the occasion that best stimulates them to call upon God is when, distressed by their own need, they are troubled by the greatest unrest, and are almost driven out of their senses, until faith opportunely comes to their relief." *Institutes*, McNeill-Battles, 3.20.11.

70. In a section of the *Institutes* entitled "Faith in the Struggle Against Temptation" (3.2.17), Calvin cited Psalms 42:5; 43:5; 31:24; 77:7, 9, 10; 116:27.

90. Cf. Ps. 92:12; 27:14.

95. On the alternation between despair and hope in the life of the believer, see *Institutes* 3.2.16–28. This passage is mainly based on one in the edition of 1539.

109. E.g., Ps. 5:8; 7:7; 22:3; 23:1, 7, 15, 18; 33:22; 38:3; 39:9; 44:20; 65:2; 79:10; 91:15; 106:48; 115:1; 119:10. Also note in *Commentary on Psalms* Calvin's comments on Psalms 10:13; 17:8f.; 18:6; 25:8; 28:1f.; 38:9; 50:15; 55:16f.; 61:1f.; 66:17ff.; 85:1; 102:17; 107:6; 118:26; 140:6; 145:18f.

122. On Calvin's doctrine of confession, see *Institutes* 3.4.

125. On "sacrifice of praise" see Ps. 50:23 (cf. 51:19); Heb. 13:15; *Institutes* 4.18.17 (cf. 3.20.28).

147. On bearing the cross see chapter 3, lines 906ff. below.

176. Cf. lines 256ff. below. There is a copious literature on Calvin's conversion. See chap. 2, lines 1ff. (note) above. Also, on the character but not the dating of that conversion, see John T. McNeill, "Introduction," *Institutes*, McNeill-Battles, pp. xxix ff. McNeill also gave a clear reconstruction of Calvin's conversion in *The History and Character of Calvinism* (New York: Oxford University, 1967), pp. 107–18. Calvin's most recent biographer, T. H. L. Parker, examined the evidence once more in *John Calvin: A Biography* (Philadelphia: Westminster, 1975), pp. 162–65.

186. The parallel that Calvin drew between his spiritual experience and David's, here sketched, is examined in detail in Walchenbach, "The Influence of David." The parallels are summarized in Ford Lewis Battles, *An Analysis of the "Institutes of the Christian Religion" of John Calvin*, 2nd rev. ed. (Pittsburgh: Battles, 1972), pp. 18*–21*.

229. I Sam. 16:11ff.

238. Beza, *Vita Calvini*, in OC, 21:121.27f.; ET by Henry Beveridge in John Calvin, *Tracts and Treatises in Defense of the Reformed Faith*, 3 vols. (Grand Rapids: Eerdmans, 1958), 1:xxii.3f.

242. Ibid., in OC, 21:121.43ff.; ET in Calvin, *Tracts*, 1:xxii.18ff.

243–77. For a detailed commentary on these crucial lines, see Parker, *John Calvin*, pp. 163f. The fullest philological treatment of this passage is in Paul Sprenger, *Das Rätsel um die Bekehrung Calvins* (Neukirchen Kreis Moers: Neukirchener, 1960).

246. Beza, *Vita Calvini*, in OC, 21:121.51ff.; ET in Calvin, *Tracts*, 1:xxii.30ff.

251. Ibid., in OC, 21:122.43ff.; ET in Calvin, *Tracts*, 1:xxii.20ff.

257. *Subita conversione*. Calvin noted in his *Commentary on Seneca's "De Clementia"* (1532) that "*subita* means not only 'sudden' but also 'unpremeditated' " (ed. and trans. Ford Lewis

39

Battles and André Malan Hugo [Leiden: Brill, 1969], pp. 56f.), or, as Parker has suggested, "unexpected" (*John Calvin,* p. 163).

275. Wrote Beza: "Meanwhile, however, he [Calvin] diligently cultivated the study of sacred literature and made such progress that all in that city [Orléans] who had any desire to become acquainted with a purer religion often called to consult him, and were greatly struck with both his learning and his zeal." *Vita Calvini,* in OC, 21:122; ET in Calvin, *Tracts,* 1:xxiii.

276f. *Ad me novitium adhuc et tyronem.* On *tyro (tiro)* see chap. 3, line 387 below.

294. With Louis du Tillet, Calvin "set out to Basel, by way of Lorraine; but when not far from the town of Metz," one of the accompanying servants made off with the money and the stronger horse. Calvin and his companion were forced to borrow ten crowns from the other servant and proceeded with difficulty first to Strasbourg, then to Basel, finally arriving there in early 1535. Beza, *Vita Calvini,* in OC, 21:124; ET in Calvin, *Tracts,* 1:xxvi f.

295. "There he lived on intimate terms with these two distinguished men, Simon Grynaeus and Wolfgang Capito, and devoted himself to the study of Hebrew." Beza, *Vita Calvini,* in OC, 21:124; ET in Calvin, *Tracts,* 1:xxvii.

300. See Beza, *Vita Calvini,* in OC, 21:123; ET in Calvin, *Tracts,* 1:xxv f.

302. Etienne de la Forge, in whose house Calvin lived while writing the *Commentary on "De Clementia,"* was a devout Waldensian from Piedmont, imbued with Lutheran ideas and hospitable to the poor and to religious refugees. McNeill, *Character of Calvinism,* pp. 109, 120, 242. He was burned alive on 15 or 16 February 1535. According to Beza, "Francis . . . ordered thirty-two martyrs to be burned alive (eight at each of the four most public places of the city). . . ." *Vita Calvini,* in OC, 21:124.8–25; ET in Calvin, *Tracts,* 1:xxvi.9–27.

307. See Beza, *Vita Calvini,* in OC, 21:124.49–125:1; ET in Calvin, *Tracts,* 1:xxvii. For a recent study of the diplomatic history of that time, see K. J. Seidel, *Frankreich und die deutschen Protestanten* (Münster: Aschendorff, 1970).

310. See Battles, "Introduction," in Calvin, *Institution of the Christian Religion . . . 1536,* trans. and an. Ford Lewis Battles (Atlanta: John Knox, 1975), p. xxxii; see also pp. 313–17 (note on p. 4, line 11).

316. Münster, A.D. 1534–1535. See George H. Williams, *The Radical Reformation* (Philadelphia: Westminster, 1962), pp. 362–86.

317. *Aulici artifices.* Josef Bohatec included among these, Robert Ceneau. *Budé und Calvin* (Graz: Böhlaus, 1959), p. 128. See also Battles, "Introduction," *Institution,* pp. 313–17 (note on p. 4, line 11).

336f. Cf. Ps. 116:15.

392. This individual is usually identified as Louis du Tillet. Parker more cautiously identified the "individual" as du Tillet "or another friend." *John Calvin,* p. 52. Du Tillet, a wealthy friend of Calvin's presumably from their days as students in Paris, afforded the latter, who had fled from Paris after the incident of the rectorial address of Nicholas Cop (1 November 1533), asylum at his home in Claix, Angoulême. Ibid., pp. 31f. After the affair of the placards (see appendix 1 in *Institution,* pp. 437–40) and the following official persecution of evangelical Christians in France, du Tillet accompanied Calvin in fleeing to Basel, which they reached in January 1535. A year later they set out together for Italy. Parker, *John Calvin,* p. 51. The incident here mentioned occurred on their return from Italy, when, bound for Strasbourg, they had to make a detour through Geneva and were spending the night there at an inn. Du Tillet in 1538 returned to France, forsaking the evangelical cause; their former friendship was terminated in an exchange of letters in which du Tillet suggested that Calvin's banishment from Geneva (in 1538) was a sign of God's displeasure. Ibid., pp. 70f.

420. In March 1537 two Dutch Anabaptists, Herman of Gerbihan (Liege) and Audry Benoit of Anglen in Brabant, visited Geneva. Calvin debated with them on the 16th and 17th (a Friday and Saturday) before the Council of Two Hundred, fearing that a full public debate might prove too dangerous. After deliberating on the 18th and 19th, the council voted against the Anabaptists and ordered them out of the city. *Annales,* in OC, 21:208–10; cf. McNeill, *Character of Calvinism,* p. 141.

423. Pierre Caroli, a scholar from Paris who converted twice to Protestantism but who finally returned to Roman Catholicism, was at this time pastor of the church in nearby Lausanne. Calvin drew Caroli's ire when he went to Lausanne to defend Viret, whom Caroli had attacked. Caroli then turned on Calvin, accusing him of Arianism because of both the absence of the word *Trinity* from Calvin's first *Catechism* (1537–1538) and Calvin's reluctance to use the so-called Athanasian Creed with its anathemas. After long deliberations, Calvin was finally cleared of the charge, which was of course groundless. For a summary see McNeill, *Character of Calvinism,* pp. 141, 155. The entries in the *Annales* covering the Caroli quarrel begin in April 1537 (OC, 21:210).

Calvin alluded to the incident in his prefatory letter to the *Catechism* of 1538 (ed. and trans. Ford Lewis Battles [Pittsburgh: Pittsburgh Theological Seminary, 1972], p. iv). For Calvin's final refutation of Caroli, see OC, 7:312–406.

445. Strasbourg. Calvin was pressed, after his expulsion from Geneva, to accept a post at Strasbourg. So Bucer wrote to him at Basel about 1 August 1538 (Herminjard, no. 729). Calvin wrote to Farel at Neuchâtel on 20 August (Herminjard, no. 736) and to du Tillet at Paris on 20 October (Herminjard, no. 754): "But when the most moderate persons threatened me that the Lord would seek me out just as He did Jonah (Jonah 1), and when they came even to these words: 'Imagine a church lost by your fault alone; what better sort of repentance would there be than for you to give yourself over completely to the Lord? Endowed with these gifts, how can you in good conscience spurn the proffered ministry?'—I did not know what to do, apart from setting forth my reasons for turning them down, in order to pursue my own plans [i.e., to stay in Basel] with their consent." Herminjard, 5:164. Beza (see next note) associated the Jonah story with Calvin's recall to Geneva in 1541. *Vita Calvini,* in OC, 21:131.10ff.; ET in Calvin, *Tracts,* 1:xxxvii.21ff.

469. Calvin, writing on 1 March 1541 to Jacques Bernard, pastor at Geneva, explained his scruples about leaving Strasbourg: "My conscience holds me bound to my present calling and does not let me leave it easily. For it is lawful and holy: that is what my spirit attests before God and what many godly men attest before the world. For after that catastrophe [Calvin's exile from Geneva] when my ministry appeared to me unhappy and unfortunate, I had resolved, on my part, never again to accept any church position unless the Lord Himself called me with a clear voice, that is, unless He presented a need I could not resist. As I obstinately held to that resolution, the Strasbourgers did not cease to batter at me with various rams until they overcame me. But they did not make a breach at their first attack. As they realized they were not making great progress, they had recourse at last to threats, saying that it would be as impossible for me, as it had been for Jonah, by my evasions to flee from God's hand. The sentry post where the Lord has stationed me—it is no wonder that I am not abandoning it lightly." Herminjard, no. 949, 5:39.

482. Calvin returned to Geneva from the Strasbourg sojourn on 13 September 1541. Beza, *Vita Calvini,* in OC, 21:131.24f.; ET in Calvin, *Tracts,* 1:xxxviii.1f.

498. Beza resumes the chronicle of Calvin's tribulations in 1542, the year following the latter's return to Geneva. Ibid., in OC, 21:133ff.; ET in Calvin, *Tracts,* 1:xli ff.

511. II Sam. 1ff.

515. E.g., Absalom (II Sam. 15) and Ahithophel (II Sam. 17).

524. Among the external enemies of Calvin's work at Geneva in the 1540s were the Sorbonne, Pierre Caroli, and Albert Pighius. Among the internal enemies (in Calvin's view) were at this time, Sebastian Castellio, and later the faction led by Ami Perrin. Beza, *Vita Calvini,* in OC, 21:133ff.; ET in Calvin, *Tracts,* 1.xli ff.

531. Is this a reference to the struggle of 1546–1547, which culminated in the confrontation at the Hotel de Ville in Geneva and of which Calvin despairingly wrote: "My influence is gone, believe me, unless God stretch forth His right hand"? In OC, 12:612f. (epistle 977).

532. See line 582 (note) below.

540. See Ford Lewis Battles, "Against Luxury and License in Geneva," *Interpretation* 19 (1965): 133ff.

566. In the dedicatory epistle to Francis I that heads all editions of the *Institutes,* Calvin contrasted Satan's strategy in past ages of the church with his strategy in the sixteenth century. He said, in effect: "For centuries Satan kept the church asleep in worldly luxury. When, however, it started to wake up, in this new Apostolic age so to speak, he countered with a new strategy. He raised up contentions of all sorts, prompted religious strife, especially centering his ingenious new strategy on those Calvin called the 'Catabaptists.'" Battles, "Introduction," *Institution,* p. xli; cf. pp. 15f.

581. In a general way Calvin seems to refer in these lines to, among others, Servetus. There is apparently, however, no explicit reference in the preface of the *Commentary on the Psalms* to Calvin's chief theological opponent.

582. If 1549–1550 were considered years of comparative tranquillity (Beza, *Vita Calvini,* in OC, 21:142.9ff.; ET in Calvin, *Tracts,* 1:liv–lvi), the "five-year trial" would be dated 1543–1548, i.e., the five years following the first full year of this second sojourn in Geneva. After the two years of comparative calm, 1549–1550, Calvin seems to speak also, in the following lines, of difficulties that arose in subsequent years.

607. Cf. *Institutes* 1.16–18; *Against the Sect of the Libertines* (1545), chap. 14, in OC, 7:149–248. Calvin stated in the *Institutes:* "Also they rail at us with as much wantonness as they can; because we, not content with the precepts of the law, which comprise God's will, say also that the universe is ruled by his secret plans." McNeill-Battles, 1.17.2. I have suggested that the

critic of Calvin's teaching was Sebastian Castellio or some advocate of Castellio's cause. Ibid., p. 212 (note 3).

608. Calvin would seem, by the phrase *protervi homines* ("arrogant people") to be speaking of the Libertines, led by Quentin and Pocquet, against whom he directed in 1545 his tract *Against the Sect of the Libertines.* In 1555, however, a faction of local ministers, led by André Zébédée and instigated by Jerome Bolsec, alleged that Calvin "made God the author of evil, by excluding nothing from his eternal providence and ordination." Beza, *Vita Calvini,* in OC, 21:151; ET in Calvin, *Tracts,* 1:lxix f.

627. Calvin here probably referred to the former Carmelite monk Jerome Bolsec, who stirred up controversy over Calvin's teaching on predestination, 16–23 October 1551. See Ibid., in OC, 21:143ff.; ET in Calvin, *Tracts,* 1:lvi ff.

628. In the controversy over freedom of the will, Calvin's chief opponent was Albertus Pighius of Campen. Ibid., in OC, 21:135; ET in Calvin, *Tracts,* 1:xliii. Against Pighius, Calvin addressed his *Defense of the Doctrine of the Bondage of the Will* in 1543 (in OC, 6:225–404).

642. See line 608 (note) above.

646ff. Ps. 41:10. Lit., "the man of my peace." Calvin glossed this HebrVersionism as "my companion," one of "my greatest friends, nay even those with whom I was most intimate." *Commentary on the Psalms.*

649ff. Ps. 25:16.

655. Beza, in refuting the charge that Calvin had been a hoarder of wealth, noted that his personal effects, including his library, had been sold for scarcely 300 gold pieces. Beza quoted Calvin's refutation of this impudent charge, for which see lines 675–78 below. *Vita Calvini,* in OC, 21:170f.; ET in Calvin, *Tracts,* 1:xcix f.

658. "... some are not ashamed to say and to write that he [Calvin] reigned at Geneva, both in church and state, so as to supplant the ordinary tribunals." Ibid., in OC, 21:171f.; ET in Calvin, *Tracts,* 1:c.

659. Against this charge Beza stated: "As to indulgence in delicacies and luxury, let his labors bear witness." Ibid., in OC, 21:171; ET in Calvin, *Tracts,* 1:c.

663. Cf. chap. 3, lines 2096ff. below.

674. Beza, in rehearsing the various charges against Calvin, noted that some critics asserted that "he even aspired to a new popedom—he who, above all things, preferred this mode of life, this republic, in fine, this Church, which I may with truth describe as the abode of poverty." Ibid., in OC, 21:170; ET in Calvin, *Tracts,* 1:xcix.

697. *Placentarii scurrae.* In his comment on Psalm 35:16, here alluded to, Calvin offered as one meaning of *mā'wôg,* "a cake or tart"; eaters of these are those persons of finicky taste who frequent the courts of princes.

715. I.e., Germany. The reference is presumably to the Lutheran controversialist Joachim Westphal, against whose attacks on Calvin's eucharistic doctrine Calvin wrote, in 1555, 1556, and 1557, three refutations.

733f. Ps. 120:7.

754f. Ps. 69:5.

765. The interrelationship of *experientia* and *Scriptura* in Calvin's thought is frequently attested. For example, when Calvin dealt in the *Institutes* with the self-authentication of Scripture, he remarked, "I speak of nothing other than what each one of the faithful experiences within himself...." McNeill-Battles, 1.6.5.

773. Frequently Calvin, on the verge of making a personal testimony, turned to the Psalms and couched it in the words of David. This is what we called in the preface "a kind of *imitatio Davidis.*"

790. Cf. Calvin's dedication to Simon Grynaeus of his *Commentary on Romans.*

793. For an appreciation of the pastoral, nonpolemic character of Calvin's Biblical commentaries, see John R. Walchenbach, "John Calvin as Biblical Commentator: An Investigation into Calvin's Use of John Chrysostom as Exegetical Tutor" (Ph.D. dissertation, University of Pittsburgh, 1974), pp. 197ff.

810. Or 10 August 1557, the date given in Schipper, tom. 3, fol. *3^v, line 27.

Chapter 2

The Kernel of Calvin's Faith

Knowledge of God
And knowledge of ourselves:
These two make up
Almost the whole of sacred doctrine.

Knowledge of God

5 Of God what should we now learn?
With sure faith we ought first to hold
He is wisdom infinite;
Is righteousness, goodness, mercy,
Truth, power, and life.
10 For utterly no other wisdom there is;
No other righteousness and goodness,
No other mercy and truth,
Power and life.
Wherever seen, all these
15 Come from Him alone.
Second, we must learn that for His glory
Have all things in heaven and on earth been made.

Right requires we serve Him
For His nature's sake alone;
20 Keep His rule;
Accept His majesty;
In obedience own Him Lord and King.
Third, we must learn He is a just judge,
Taking harsh vengeance on those
25 Who turn aside from His precepts;
Who in all things follow not His will;
Who think, say, do what
Pertains not to His glory.
Fourth, we must learn
30 Merciful and gentle is He,
Kindly receiving the miserable and poor
Who flee to His mercy and trust in Him.
If you ask a favor of Him,
Ready He is to spare and pardon;
35 If you ask His help,
Willing He is to succour and give aid;
If you put all trust in Him,
Cleave to Him;
Eager to save is He.

Knowledge of Ourselves

40 How are we to reach
A sure knowledge of ourselves?
First, grasp we must the fact
That Adam, parent of us all,
Was created in God's image and likeness.
45 This means: he was endowed
With wisdom, righteousness, and holiness;
So clinging was he by these gifts
Of grace to God
That, had he stood fast
50 In his God-given uprightness,
In God he could have lived forever.

But when Adam slipped into sin,
This image, this Godlikeness,
Was cancelled, effaced:
55 Lost were all benefits of grace divine,
Gifts that could have led
Him back into the way of life.
Far removed from God,
Made a complete stranger
60 Man was by this;
Stripped, deprived of all wisdom,
Righteousness, power, life—
Gifts he could hold in God alone.
What then was left to man?
65 Nothing save ignorance,
Iniquity, impotence,
Death, judgment:
The fruits of sin.
And not upon Adam himself
70 Alone calamity fell:
It flowed down into us,
His seed and offspring.
Born of Adam are we all,
Ignorant and bereft of God,
75 Perverse, corrupt,
Lacking every good.
Our hearts are turned to every sort of evil;
Are stuffed with, addicted to, depraved desires;
Are obstinate toward God.

80 Suppose, however, we display some bit of good:
The mind yet wallows in its inner filth,
Its crooked perversity.
Not according to appearance does God judge;
Rather He gazes upon the secrets of the heart.
85 However dazzlingly, then, we may
Make show of holiness on our own,
In God's sight it is naught
But hypocrisy, even an abomination;

For lurking beneath the show
90 Are the mind's thoughts,
Ever depraved, ever corrupted.

Born we have been with no power
To do what is acceptable
Or pleasing to our God—
95 Yet the very thing we cannot supply
We do not cease to owe.
God's creatures, we should serve
His honor and His glory,
Obey His commandments.
100 Excuse ourselves we cannot
By claiming, like impoverished debtors,
We are unable to pay our debt.
For our very own is the guilt that binds us;
From our very own sin arises,
105 Cuts off our will, our power
To do the good.
Since God justly avenges crimes,
Recognize we must that we
Are subject to the curse,
110 Deserve the judgment of eternal death.
Not one of us there is who has the will,
Is able to do his duty.

And so by Scripture we are called
"The children of God's wrath,"
115 Hurtling to death, destruction.
To us is left no reason to seek in ourselves
Our righteousness, power,
Our life, salvation;
For in God alone are these.
120 By sin cut off, separated
From God, we find within
Ourselves naught but unhappiness, weakness,
Wickedness, death—in short,
Hell itself.

The Written Law

125 And so, not to let man go
Ignorant of these facts,
The Lord engraved, nay stamped,
Upon all hearts the law.
Yet what is the law but conscience,
130 To us the witness within
Of what we owe God?
Before us it sets good and evil;
Thus does it accuse, condemn us,
Conscious as we are within ourselves
135 That we have not discharged our bounden duty.
And still with arrogance, ambition swollen,
With self-love blinded,
We cannot see ourselves,
Cannot descend into ourselves,
140 Cannot confess our misery.

God sees our sorry state
And so provides for us a written law.
Teach us through this He will
The perfect righteousness,
145 How it is to be kept:
Fixed firmly in God,
Turn we must our gaze to Him alone;
To Him aim our every thought,
Yearning, act, or word.
150 How far we have strayed from the right path
This teaching of righteousness clearly shows.
To this end also look all promises
And curses, set forth for us
In the law itself.
155 For the Lord has promised that
If anyone should by his own effort
Perfectly and exactly fulfill
Whatever is commanded,
Receive he will the reward

160 Of life eternal.
By this—there is no doubt—
God points out to us
That the perfection of life taught in the law
Is truly righteousness;
165 Is so considered with Him;
And would be worthy of such a reward
If among men any could be found.
On the other hand,
Upon all who do not fully
170 And without exception keep
The whole righteousness of the law,
God pronounces a curse,
Announces the judgment of eternal death.

All men that ever were,
175 Are, or will be, assuredly
By this punishment of God's
Are constrained.
Not one among them can be pointed out
Who is not a transgressor of the law.
180 The law teaches us God's will
(Which we are constrained to fulfill
And to which we are in debt).
The law shows us unable to carry out
A shred of what God has commanded us.
185 So is the law a mirror wherein
We may discern and contemplate
Our sin and curse,
Just as in a glass we see reflected
The scars and blemishes of our faces.
190 This very written law is really
But a witness of the natural law,
A witness to arouse our memory,
To instill in us what natural law
Failed sufficiently to teach us.

195 What then are we to learn from the law?
God is the Creator, our Lord and Father.

Hence to Him we owe
Glory, honor, love.
Since, however, not one of us performs
200 These duties, we all deserve the curse,
Judgment—eternal death.

Forgiveness of Sins

Seek we must then
Another way to salvation,
Another path than our own works-righteousness.
205 What is this way?
Forgiveness of sins.
What we owe the law
We have not the power to carry out:
Hence despair of ourselves we must
210 And seek help from another quarter.
Once we descend to this humility,
This submission, the Lord
Will shine upon us;
Will show Himself lenient,
215 Kindly, gentle, indulgent.
For of Him it is written:
"He resists the proud;
Gives grace to the humble."
And first, if we pray to Him to avert His wrath,
220 If we ask His pardon,
Doubt there cannot be
He will give it to us.
Everything our sins deserved
He will forgive, receive into grace.

225 Then if we implore His helping hand,
Assurance will be ours that,
Equipped with His protection,
We will be able to do all things.
According to His own good will

230 He bestows a new heart upon us
That we may will;
A new power whereby we may be enabled
To carry out His commandments.
All these blessings He showers upon us
235 For the sake of Jesus Christ our Lord,
Who—though He was one God with the Father—
Put on our flesh to enter with us
A covenant; to join us
(By our sins far separated from God)
240 Closely to Him. Also,
By the merit of His death
He paid our debts to God's justice,
Appeased God's wrath.
From the curse and judgment
245 That bound us He redeems us;
Bears in His body the punishment of sin,
Thus to absolve us from it.
Descending to earth,
He brought with Him
250 All the rich heavenly blessings;
With a lavish hand
Showered them upon us.
These are the Holy Spirit's gifts.
Through Him we are reborn,
255 Wrested from the power
And chains of the devil,
Freely adopted as God's children,
Sanctified for every good work.
Through Him also—so long
260 As we are held in this mortal body—
Dying there are in us
The depraved desires,
The promptings of the flesh,
Everything the twisted,
265 The corrupt perversity
Of our nature brings forth.
Through Him renewed we are

From day to day, that we
May walk in newness of life,
270 May live for righteousness.

In Christ our Lord, God offers us,
Gives us all these benefits:
Free forgiveness of sins,
Peace and reconciliation with God,
275 Gifts and graces of the Holy Spirit.
Ours these are if with sure faith
We embrace them, receive them,
Utterly trusting and leaning upon
Divine goodness, not doubting that
280 God's Word (which promises us all these things)
Is power and truth.
If, in short, we partake of Christ,
We shall in Him possess
All heavenly treasures,
285 All gifts of the Holy Spirit
That lead us into life and salvation.
Except with a true and living faith,
Never will we grasp this.
But with such faith
290 Recognize we will
All our good to be in Him,
Ourselves to be nothing apart from Him;
Hold as certain we will
That in Him we become God's children,
295 Heirs of the heavenly kingdom.
On the other hand,
Those who have no part in Christ—
Whatever their nature,
Whatever they may do or undertake—
300 Depart into ruin and confusion,
Into the judgment of eternal death;
Cast away from God they are,
Shut off from all hope of salvation.

47

What then are we taught
305 By this knowledge of ourselves,
Of our poverty and ruin?
From it we learn to humble ourselves,
Cast ourselves before God,
Seek His mercy.
310 Not from ourselves comes forth
The faith that furnishes us
A taste of divine goodness and mercy,
Wherein God in His Christ
Has to do with us.
315 Rather God it is whom we
Are to ask to lead us,
Unfeignedly repentant,
To the knowledge of His gentleness,
His sweetness, which He
320 Shows forth in His Christ.
And so will Christ, our leader,
The only Way to reach the Father,
Bring us into eternal blessedness.

Notes

Title. The compressed passage translated in strophic form in this chapter has been titled "The Kernel of Calvin's Faith" because here, in a passage from chapter 1 of the first edition of the *Institutes*, Calvin's theological reflection on his conversion is found in a more connected form than in any of the subsequent editions. In later editions the materials of this passage were distributed to various contexts. If my speculations are correct, Calvin twice in 1535 summarized the history of his salvation: once in French in his preface to Pierre Robert's French translation of the New Testament; and again in Latin in the *Institution*. "Introduction," *Institution of the Christian Religion ... 1536*, trans. and an. Ford Lewis Battles (Atlanta: John Knox, 1975), pp. xxiv–xxvii.

1–4. This key sentence, which heads all editions of the *Institutes*, is noted in *Institutes*, McNeill-Battles, at 1.1.1 (with full bibliography), and in *Institution* at 1.1 (p. 327, note on p. 20, line 2n).

This sentence appeared in the following revised form in the 1539 and subsequent editions: "Nearly all the wisdom we possess, that is to say, true and sound wisdom, consists of two parts: the knowledge of God and of ourselves." The Scriptural passage that may have "triggered" Calvin's conversion, Romans 1:21 (or perhaps the larger context of Romans 1:18–25), seems to underlie this account of the two knowledges: "They know God, but they do not give Him the glory that belongs to Him; nor do they thank Him." Cf. Introduction, note 4, above.

13. Bar. 3:12–14; James 1:17. On the *virtutes Dei* see chap. 4, lines 870ff. below.

15. Prov. 16:4.

17. Ps. 148:1–14; Dan. 3:59–63.

22. Rom. 1:20.

28. Ps. 7:9–11; Rom. 2:1–16.

39. Ps. 103:3f., 8–11; Isa. 55:6; Ps. 25:6–11; 85:5–7, 10.

44. Gen. 1:26f.

57. Gen. 3.

67. Rom. 5:12–21; cf. Calvin, *Commentary on "De Clementia"* 93.30ff.

68. Gal. 5:19–21.

79. Jer. 17:9.

84. I Sam. 16:7; Jer. 17:10.

106. John 8:34–38; Rom. 7:15–25.

115. Eph. 2:1–3; Rom. 3:9–20.

121. Hos. 13:4–9.

128. Rom. 2:1–16.

139. The classical phrase "to descend into oneself," which for Calvin signifies the intense examination of self that discloses our sinful state, is widely used in his writings. E.g., *Institutes* 1.1.2; 2.8.3; 3.20.6; 4.17.40; *Reply to Cardinal Sadolet* (as quoted in Battles, "Introduction," *Institution*, pp. xx, xxvi). For classical and contemporary uses of the expression, see *Institutes*, McNeill-Battles, 1.5.3 (note 11); and *Institution*, trans. and an. Battles, p. 373 (note on p. 150, line 25).

160. Lev. 18:5.

173. Deut. 27:26; Gal. 3:10.

184. Rom. 3:19; 7:7–25.

185. The mirror was one of Calvin's favorite figures of speech. On the law as mirror, see *Institutes* 2.7.7; 3.18.9 ("... the law ... is a perfect mirror of righteousness").

203. Cf. chap. 4, line 5 below.

211. Cf. line 139 (note) above.

217f. James 4:6; I Peter 5:5 (quoting Prov. 3:34).

233. Ezek. 36:26.

236. John 1:1−14.

240. Isa. 53:4−11.

247. Eph. 2:3−5; Col. 1:21−22.

252. John 1:14−16; 7:38; Rom. 8:14−17.

268. II Cor. 4:16.

269f. Rom. 6:4.

281. Rom. 3:21−26; 5:1−11.

295. John 1:12; Rom. 8:14−17.

303. John 3:18−20; I John 5:12.

309. Jer. 31:18−20.

323. Phil. 1; John 14:6; Rom. 5:1−11.

Chapter 3

Calvin on the Christian Life

In undertaking to shape the life of the Christian man
I am entering a vast matter,
One that would fill a large tome
If I wished to pursue it at length.
5 For we see how wordy are the ancient doctors' exhorta-
    tions
That treat only a single virtue.
This does not arise out of mere talkativeness:
For each virtue one sets out to praise and commend
Will entail such an abundance of material
10 That, without using many words,
One will not seem to have properly discussed it.

My intent, however, is not to extend
The instruction in living I wish to set forth
To the point of elucidating each virtue individually
15 And of making long exhortations.
One can get such from others' books,
And especially from the ancient doctors' homilies—
Their popular sermons.
Enough for me will it be to show
20 Some order whereby the Christian man

51

May be led and directed
To order his life aright.

As I just said, I'll content myself
With briefly setting forth a general rule
25 To which the Christian can refer all his acts.
Perhaps we shall sometime have occasion to make
　　exhortations
Like those in the ancient doctors' sermons.
The task now in hand, however, demands
That we put forth simple teaching
30 With the greatest brevity possible.
Just as the philosophers postulate
Certain ends of honesty and right from which
They derive individual duties
And all acts of virtue,
35 So also Scripture has, in this respect,
Its way of working, a way much better
And surer than the philosophers'.

Only this difference lies between them:
The philosophers, ambitious men, have tried
40 As best they can to articulate
The order and disposition they are using
To show their subtlety.
The Holy Spirit, by contrast, because
He teaches unaffectedly and unpompously,
45 Has not always kept so narrowly
A definite order and method;
Yet when He has, He clearly lets us know
Not to neglect it.

Motives for the Christian Life

Two parts there are to the Scriptural order
50 Of which we speak.
One is to press upon our hearts

The love of righteousness to which
By nature we are not at all inclined.
The other is to give us a clear rule
55 To keep us from wandering to and fro
Or misestablishing our life.
On the first point: Scripture has
Many and excellent reasons to bind our heart
To love the good.
60 Several of these we have in divers places noted
And will touch once more upon them here.

God's Command to Be Holy

With what foundation could one better begin
Than to admonish us to be made holy
Even as our Lord is holy?
65 To this He adds the reason:
Like stray and scattered sheep
We have been dispersed throughout
The labyrinthine world.
Yet has He collected us
70 To join us to Himself.
When we hear Him speak of
The conjoining of God with us,
He must be reminding us that the bond
Of this conjoining is holiness.
75 Not that by the merit of our own holiness
Do we come into company with our God—
Since we must first cleave to Him
To be made holy, so He may
Pour His holiness upon us.
80 Rather, because it is the very nature
Of His glory to have nothing to do
With iniquity and uncleanness,
We must be like Him in this
Since we are His.

85 Scripture teaches us this is the end
Of our calling to which we must ever look

If we answer our God.
For what point is there in rescuing us
From the filth and pollution in which
90 We were plunged if we desire
To wallow therein our whole life long?
Scripture accordingly advises us that
If we wish to be in the company
Of God's people, we must dwell
95 In Jerusalem, His holy city.
It too, being hallowed and set apart
For His honor, cannot lawfully
Be befouled and stained
By unclean, profane inhabitants.
100 From this have come such texts as these:
"He who walks unblemished
And sets out to live uprightly
Will dwell in the Lord's tabernacle."

God's Redemptive Act in Christ

To rouse us even more, Scripture shows us
105 God is reconciled to us in His Christ
And has in Him
Established for us pattern and patron
To which we must conform.

Some think philosophers have well
110 And duly treated moral doctrine.
Let such show me a scheme
As good as that I have just recounted.
When they, with all their force, intend
To exhort us to virtue, the only thing
115 They cite is that we should live
In accord with nature.

From a better fountain Scripture draws for us
Its exhortations:
Not only bids us refer

120 Our whole life to God its author,
But, after warning us we have
Sunk down from the true origin of our creation,
Adds that Christ, reconciling us to God
His Father, has given us an example
125 Of innocence to image in our life.
What thing more forceful, more effective can one say?
What more than this can one require?
For if God adopts us as His sons
Only on the condition that Christ's image
130 Appears in our life,
If we do not give ourselves to righteousness and holi-
ness,
Not only are we with crass disloyalty
Abandoning our Creator,
But also we are renouncing Him our Savior.
135 Consequently, from all God's benefits
And from all parts of our salvation,
Scripture takes occasion to exhort us.
For example, when it says:
Since God gave Himself as Father to us,
140 We prove our gross ingratitude
If we do not act as sons.
Since Christ has cleansed us by the washing
Of His blood and through baptism
Has shared this cleansing,
145 It is not fitting for us in new filth
To soil ourselves.
Since He has joined and grafted us
Into His body, we, His members,
Must carefully keep ourselves
150 Unspotted.
Since He, our head, has risen into heaven,
We must dismiss all earthly loves,
Must wholeheartedly aspire to heavenly life.
Since the Holy Spirit consecrates us to be
155 God's temples, we must take care
That in us God's glory be exalted;

And, conversely, we must guard ourselves
Against receiving any pollution.
Since our souls and our bodies are destined
160 For the immortality of God's kingdom
And the incorruptible crown of His glory,
We must strive to keep them both
Pure and unspotted, to the day of the Lord.

Here are the good and proper foundations
165 On which to set our life.
Ones like these you'll never find
In all the philosophers.
For they never rise higher than to show forth
Man's natural dignity,
170 When they should be showing
What is his duty.

The Necessity of Striving for Holiness

Here I must address my words to those
Who of Christ have naught but title,
Yet wish to be considered Christians.
175 How shameless indeed are they to boast
About His sacred name
When no one has anything to do with Him
Save one who by the gospel word
Knows Him in truth!
180 But St. Paul denies any man has received
True knowledge of Him
Save him who has set out
"To put off the old man corrupt
In disordered desires," to be clad
185 With Christ.
Under false banners, then, it seems,
Such people pretend to know the Christ.
Great injury to Him they do in this,
Whatever they may babble on their tongues.
190 No doctrine of tongue the gospel is,
But of life itself;

Not to be grasped in understanding and memory only
As other disciplines are, it must
Entirely grip the soul;
195 Must have its seat and dwelling
Deep in the heart—
Else it has not been in truth received.
Well, then, let them stop boasting
Of what they're not,
200 Or show themselves disciples
Of the Christ.

To this doctrine wherein our religion is contained
We have given first place,
Because here our salvation begins.
205 But to make itself useful and fruitful
It must reach the inmost recess of our heart
And show its power in our life—
Even transform us into its nature.

Rightly the philosophers rage against those
210 Who profess their art, which should be
The mistress of life, yet turn it
Into sophistical chatter.
With even better reason we detest those chatterers
Who are content to roll the gospel
215 On tip of tongue, yet misprize it
In their whole life!
For its workings ought to penetrate
The deepest heart, be rooted in the soul—
A hundred thousand times more
220 Than all philosophic exhortings
With their puny power!

I do not require that the morals of the Christian man
Be pure and perfect gospel (although
Such consummation is to be desired
225 And striven for).
No, I do not require so strictly,

54

So rigorously, a Christian perfection
That I would recognize as Christian
Only him who has attained it.
230 For thus measured, all human beings
Would be excluded from the church,
Since one will not find any of them
Not still far removed.
Although he has profited greatly,
235 The majority has still scarcely advanced at all.

What then? We must surely have this end
Before our eyes to which our every act
Is aimed: to strive toward the perfection
The Lord requires of us. Necessary it is,
240 I say, to strive and to aspire to reach it.
Not lawful for us is it to divide
Things with God so as to receive
A part of what He has required of us
In His Word, leaving the rest behind
245 According to our fancy. For always
Chiefly He requires of us
Uprightness. This means a pure simplicity
Of heart: devoid, free, of all feigning,
The opposite of double-mindedness.
250 But while we dwell
In this earthly prison, none of us
Is strong and determined enough to hasten
On this path with the eagerness he ought;
In fact the greater part of us is so weak and feeble
255 As to waver and limp and be unable
Much to advance.

So let us each one go at his feeble pace,
Not ceasing to pursue the journey once begun.
None will so feebly journey as not to advance
260 Some little daily, to reach his homeland.
Let us then not cease to strive thither
That we progress unceasingly

In the Lord's way.
Let us not lose courage even though
265 Our progress is but slight.
For even though the actuality may not correspond
To our desire, when today outstrips
Yesterday, all is not lost.
Only let us look with pure and true simplicity
270 Toward our goal; let us strive
To reach our end, not fondly puffing up ourselves
With vain adulation, not excusing our vices.
Let us strive unceasingly to make
Ourselves become from day to day
275 Better than we are, until we reach
The sovran goodness, which throughout our lives
We've sought and followed, to grasp it
When, freed of the weakness of our flesh,
We shall become full participants in it,
280 When God receives us into His fellowship.

A Rule for the Christian Life

Seeking God's Wisdom

Now we come to the second point.
Although God's law provides an excellent method
And a well-disposed order to establish our lives,
It seemed fitting to the heavenly Teacher
285 To shape His people by a more perfect doctrine
Than the rule He had given in His law.
The plan He has adopted begins as follows:
The duty of believers is "to offer
Their bodies to God as living sacrifice,
290 Holy, acceptable; and herein consists
The lawful service we are to render to Him."
Thereafter comes this exhortation:
Believers are in no wise to conform themselves
To the pattern of this world,

295 But are to be transformed by a renewal
Of their understanding, to seek out
And know the will of God.
It is already a weighty point to say
That we are hallowed and set apart for God,
300 So hereafter we may neither think, speak,
Meditate upon, nor do anything
Save for His glory.
For not lawful is it to apply
A sacred thing to profane use.
305 If then we are not our own
But belong to the Lord, thence
Can one see what we must do
To avoid erring, and whither
We must direct all actions of our life.
310 We are not our own: accordingly
Let not our reason and our will
Lord it over our counsels and our tasks.
We are not our own: then
Let us not set ourselves this end—
315 To seek out what is expedient
According to the flesh.
We are not our own: let us then,
As much as in us lies,
Forget ourselves and all that hems us in.
320 Conversely, we are the Lord's:
Let us live and die to Him.
We are the Lord's: may His will, then,
And wisdom rule all our acts.
We are the Lord's: may every part
325 Of our life be referred to Him
As to their only goal.
Oh, how much that man has profited
Who, recognizing himself not to be his own,
Has deprived his own reason of dominion and rule,
330 Resigning it to God!
For, as to please themselves
Is the worst plague men have

To ruin and destroy them—
So the sole haven of safety is not to be
335 Wise in oneself, to will nothing of oneself,
But to follow the Lord alone.

The first step then is for us
To withdraw from ourselves
And put the whole force of our understanding
340 At God's service. "Service" I call
Not only what lies in obedience
To His Word, but that by which men's understanding,
Void of its own sense, turns completely
And submits to God's Spirit.
345 This transformation, called by St. Paul
"The renewal of the understanding," is
To all philosophers unknown,
Though it is the first entrance into life.
For they teach that reason alone
350 Must rule and control man, and think
That it alone is to be heeded and followed,
And hence entrust to it alone
The government of life.
The Christian philosophy, though,
355 Would have reason yield, retire,
Give place to the Holy Spirit,
Subject itself to His direction:
So that man may no longer live
To himself alone, but have within himself,
360 And suffer, the living, reigning Christ.

Seeking God's Glory

From this derives the second part we have set forth:
We are not to seek what pleases us
But rather that which pleases God,
Exalts His glory.
365 Here too is great virtue that,
Almost forgetting ourselves, we apply
And faithfully devote our zeal

To follow God and His commandments.
For when Scripture forbids us particularly to have
370 Concern for self, not only does it erase
From our heart all greed, desire to rule,
To attain great honors or alliances,
But also would it have us root out
All ambition, craving for human glory,
375 And other hidden plagues.
The Christian man indeed must be
So disposed that he thinks it is with God
He has to deal throughout his life.
This will he ponder: as to God
380 He knows he must render account
For all his works, so will he direct
To God his whole intention,
Holding it fixed in Him.

For whoever looks to God in all his works,
385 Easily turns his spirit from all vain thought.
This is the denial of ourselves
That Christ so earnestly requires
For their first apprenticeship
Of all His disciples.
390 This it is that, when once it occupies man's heart,
First pride, arrogance, ostentation
Are extinguished; then also greed,
Intemperance, luxury, and all delights,
With the other vices engendered
395 By love of ourselves.
Conversely, where self-denial does not reign,
Shamelessly man breaks into every villainy,
Or else—if there is some seeming virtue,
It is corrupted by a wicked lust for glory.
400 Show me a man who, without denying self
According to the Lord's command,
Freely exercises goodness among men.
For those without this feeling have,
In following virtue, at least

405 Been seeking praise.
Even the philosophers (who have striven most
To show that virtue is to be sought
For its own sake) have been so puffed up
With arrogance and pride
410 That one can see they have pursued
Virtue for no other reason than to have
Occasion to be proud.
But so necessary is it that ambitious men
Who seek worldly glory, or people puffed up
415 With inner presumption, should be able
To please God, who declares that the first
Have received their reward in this world;
The second class are further from the kingdom
Of God than publicans and adulterers.
420 Not yet have we clearly explained
How many obstacles hold back
A man from devoting himself to good deeds
If he has not denied himself.
A truly ancient saying, this:
425 That in the soul of man is hid
A world of vices.
And no other remedy we'll find for it
Save in self-denial and disregard
For what is pleasing to us.
430 Now we train and devote our understanding
To seek the things that God requires of us,
And to seek them only because
They please Him.

Self-Denial and Our Fellow Men

We must note that this denial of ourselves
435 Refers partly to men,
Partly (and chiefly) to God.
For when Scripture bids us so act
Toward men as to prefer them
In honor to ourselves and to try
440 Faithfully to advance their good,

57

It gives us commandments that our minds
(Unless emptied of their natural feeling)
Are unable to keep.
For so blind, so carried away with love
445 Of ourselves are we all, that there is no one
Who does not consider he has good reason
To elevate himself over all and to despise
All others in comparison to himself.
If God has given us some gift
450 To be proud of, once under the pretext of it
Our heart soars up.

Not only puffed up, but almost bursting
Are we with pride. The very vices
Of which we are full we carefully hide
455 From others, make believe they're small and slight,
Or even sometimes take for virtues.
When there are any gifts, highly we esteem
Them in ourselves, even to the point
Of holding them in admiration.
460 If such appear in others,
Even if greater ones than ours,
To avoid having to yield place to them,
As much as is in our power
We cover up or belittle them.
465 Conversely, if in our neighbors any faults appear,
Not content to note them strictly,
We hatefully exaggerate them.
Hence comes forth such insolence
That each of us, as if exempt
470 From the common lot, yearns to tower
Above the rest and without exception
Belittles all as his inferiors.
The poor yield to the rich;
The common folk to the nobles;
475 Servants to their masters;
The uneducated to the learned.
But not one there is who in his heart

Does not dream that he is worthy
To be held excellent above all others.

480 Thus each in his place, flattering himself,
Nourishes a kingdom in his heart.
For, claiming as his own what pleases him,
He censures the character and morals of others.
If one comes to the point of conflict,
485 Then the venom bursts forth and shows itself.
Many there are who appear gentle and moderate
So long as they see all goes according to their liking.
But how few there are who keep gentleness and modera-
     tion
When pricked and irritated!
490 Actually there is nothing else to do
With this mortal plague of loving
And exalting self than to rip it out
From the heart's depths, as Scripture too
Would rip it out. For if we listen
495 To its teaching, we must remember
That all the gifts that God has given us
Are not our own goods, but freely given
Gifts from His bounty.

Thus if anyone is proud, in this he shows
500 His own ungratefulness; conversely, diligently
Recognizing our faults, to humility we must once more
Betake ourselves. Thus nothing will remain in us
To puff us up, but much cause will there be
To overrule and cast us down.
505 Moreover, we are commanded to hold in such honor
And reverence all gifts of God we see in our neighbors
That, because of these, we should honor
The persons wherein the gifts reside.
Great depravity would it be to wish
510 To despoil a man of the honor
God has done him. Anew we are bidden
Not to look at faults but to overlook them—

58

Not to embrace them with flattery,
But not to revile one who has committed some fault,
515 Since to him we should bear love and honor.
Thus will it come about that toward each one
With whom we have to deal, we will conduct
Ourselves not only modestly and moderately,
But in gentleness and friendship as well.
520 Conversely, by no other path will one arrive
At true gentleness than with heart
Disposed to humble itself
And honor others.

To do our duty in seeking our neighbor's good—
525 How difficult it is!
Unless we lay aside consideration of self,
Clear ourselves of all carnal affection,
We will accomplish nothing.
For who can discharge all the duties
530 St. Paul demands, unless he denies himself,
To devote himself wholly to his neighbors?
"Charity," the apostle says, "is patient,
Humble, not jealous or boastful;
Is not puffed up or envious;
535 Seeks not its own," etc.
If this alone is required—
That we are not to seek our own advantage—
Then in order to look after others' welfare
(Or rather to renounce our right,
540 Yielding it to our neighbors)
We must treat our nature with no little harshness:
For this it is that draws us into self-love,
Not letting us lightly neglect our own advantage.
But Scripture, to lead us to this reason,
545 Warns us that all we have received
At the Lord's hand has been entrusted to us
On condition that we transfer it
To the church's common good.
Therefore, the lawful use of it is

550 A kindly, liberal sharing with our neighbors.
No better, surer rule for practicing such sharing is there
Than when 'tis said: All our goods God has given
Into our keeping on the one condition
They be distributed to benefit others.

555 Scripture, however, goes further still:
Compares the gifts each holds to the functions
Each member of the human body possesses.
No member has this power for itself alone
Nor applies it to its own private use;
560 But each uses it to benefit the others.
Nor does it take any profit therefrom save what proceeds
From the common advantage of the whole body.
In this way the faithful man must lay out his whole power
For his brothers, not looking after his own interest,
565 Without at the same time ever turning his eyes
To the church's common good.
Let us then hold to this rule
In doing our acts of goodness and humanity:
Of everything the Lord has given us
570 To help our neighbor
We are the stewards, having one day to render account
Of how we have discharged our task.

Moreover, the only good and just stewardship
Is that governed by the rule of love.
575 Thus will it come about that not only will we join
Our care to benefit our neighbor
With solicitude for our own profit,
But also will we subordinate
Our profit to that of others.
580 And actually the Lord, to show us
This is the way to administer skillfully,
Devoutly, what He has given us,

Of old required it of the Israelites,
When for the least gift given by Him
585 Ordained that the first fruits thereof
Be offered to Himself, so that by this
The people might testify it was not lawful
To receive for themselves any fruits
That had not been already consecrated to Him.
590 But if God's gifts are finally sanctified to us
Only after we have from our own hand
Consecrated them to Him,
Clearly what is not yielded up to that consecration
Is a damnable abuse.
595 Yet it would be folly to try to enrich
Our God by sharing with Him the things we have in
    hand.
Since then our benefits cannot come to Him
(As the prophet says),
We must share them with His servants
600 Who dwell on earth.

Furthermore, to avoid slackening in well-doing
(Which otherwise would happen at once)
We must remember likewise what the apostle adds:
"Love is long-suffering and not easily irritated."
605 The Lord commands us to do good to all men,
Of whom the majority are unworthy—
If we judge them by their own merit.
But Scripture helps by admonishing us
Not to consider what men merit of themselves;
610 Rather we should look to the image
Of God in all, to which we owe
All honor and affection.
Especially must we recognize it
Among members of the household of faith,
615 Insofar as it has been renewed and restored
By the Spirit of Christ.
Whatever man presents himself to us,
Seeking our help, we will have no reason

To refuse it to him.
620 If we say, "He is a stranger,"
The Lord has stamped him with a mark
That must be familiar to us.
If we claim him to be contemptible and worthless,
The Lord replies, showing us He has honored him
625 By setting upon him His image.
If we say that we are in nothing
Beholden to him, the Lord says
He has put him in His place,
So we may recognize in him
630 The blessings He has given us.
If we say he is not worth our taking
A single step in his behalf,
The image of God on which in him
We must needs gaze, is worth
635 Our staking everything we are and have.
Even when he is such a man as has
Not only deserved nothing at our hand,
But also has heaped injury and insult upon us,
Still is this not cause enough for us
640 To leave off loving, pleasing, serving him.
For if we say he has not deserved this of us,
God can ask who has deserved it of Him.
For when He bids us forgive men
The offenses they have done us,
645 He takes these upon Himself.

Only one way there is to reach
What is not only difficult
But utterly repugnant for human nature:
To love those who hate us,
650 Repay good for ill,
Pray for those who speak ill of us.
We will, I say, come to this point
If we remember not to concentrate
On men's evil intent, but rather to contemplate
655 In them God's image, which by its excellence

And worth can and must move us
To love them and rub out all defects
That could turn our eyes away.

This mortification will take place in us
660 When we have fulfilled love.
This consists not in accomplishing only
All duties that belong to love,
But in doing them with true and friendly affection.
For it could happen that some one
665 Discharges for his neighbor all required of him
In outward duty, yet is far away
From doing the duty laid upon him.
One sees many who wish to seem
Most liberal, yet bestow nothing without reproach,
670 Either by haughty mien or proud word.
At present we have come into the sorry state
That most of us cannot give alms without contempt.
Even among the pagans
Such perversity was intolerable.
675 But of Christians the Lord requires
Something far different: a joyful, cheerful face
To make their gift pleasing
Through humanity and gentleness.
First must they put themselves in the place
680 Of the one who needs their help,
That they may pity his ill fortune
As if they felt and bore it themselves,
And that they may be touched with the same feeling
Of compassion to go to his aid
685 As if they were giving help to themselves.
He who so good-heartedly assists his brothers
Will neither sully his kindness with any arrogance
Or reproach nor despise their neediness
Or try to put them under obligation.

690 We would not more upbraid one of our members
That the rest of the body labors to restore

Or fail to think that it is specially obligated
To its fellow members,
Because it has caused them more trouble
695 Than it has taken for them.
For what the members share among themselves
Is not considered a free gift but rather payment
And satisfaction of what is due
By law of nature.
700 By this means also we shall gain another point:
Not to think ourselves free and released from obligation
When we have done our duty in some respect,
As one commonly understands it.
For when a rich man has given something of his away,
705 He leaves behind and neglects all other responsibilities
As if they did not belong to him.
Conversely, each one will realize
That in all he has and can do he is a debtor
To all his neighbors, and that he must not limit
710 His obligation to do them good except
As his resources fail, which as far
As they can extend must be limited by love.

Self-Denial and God

Now let us discuss the other part
Of denial of ourselves, which has to do with God.
715 Of this we have already spoken here and there;
It would be superfluous to repeat
All that has been said of it.
Suffice it to show how it should
Draw us to patience and gentleness.
720 First, then, in seeking the means to live
Or to repose at our ease,
Scripture ever leads us to resign to God
Ourselves and all our belongings,
Put down our heart's affections
725 To tame and yoke them.
A mad uncontrol, unbridled greed
To seek recognition and honor,

61

To grab for power, amass wealth,
Heap up all that seems to make
730 For pomp and magnificence—
These are our overmastering passions.
On the other hand, how marvelous
Our fear and hatred are of poverty,
Low birth, and ignominy.
735 These we flee with all our strength.
This shows what restless spirits
Are all those who order their lives
To their own plan. We see how they
Try every means, torture themselves
740 In every way to reach the goal
To which their ambition and greed sweep them—
All to avoid poverty and abjection.

Faithful Christians, to keep from falling
Into such traps, will have to hold to this path:
745 First, they must not desire, hope, or imagine
Another way of prospering than by God's blessing
And accordingly must surely lean and repose on it.
The flesh seems sufficient of itself to attain
Its aim, when by its own effort it aspires
750 To honors, wealth, or when helped by men's favor.
Yet all these things are nothing;
We can never even slightly advance
Either by our skill or by our effort
Except the Lord enable them both.
755 Conversely, His blessing alone will find
Its way through the midst of all obstacles
To give in all things happy issue.
Moreover, when it so happens that without God's bless-
ing
We can yet acquire some honor or opulence
760 (As we daily see the wicked come to great wealth
And high estate), nevertheless
Since where God's curse lies
One cannot know even a drop of happiness,

We'll get nothing that does not turn to ill
765 Unless God's blessing is upon us.
But great madness would it be indeed
To seek what can only bring us misery.

Suppose, therefore, we believe that every means
Of prospering lies solely in God's blessing
770 And that without it every misery
And calamity await us.
Then our duty is not to aspire
With excessive greed to riches, honors,
Relying on our own skill or diligence
775 Or men's favor, or fortune; but to look
Always to God, so that by His leading
We may be led to that state
That seems good to Him.
Thence will it come to pass that we
780 Will not try to rake in wealth,
To steal honors by right or wrong,
By force or craft, and other devious ways,
But only to seek the good that will not
Turn us away from innocence.

785 For who will ever hope God's blessing
Will help him commit fraud, robbery,
Or other wickedness?
For as that blessing helps only those
Who think right thoughts and do right deeds,
790 So the man who desires it must thereby
Be withdrawn from all iniquity
And evil thought.
Moreover, it will be like a bridle
To restrain us from what we burn
795 With inordinate yearning to enrich ourselves
And try to get ahead.
What shamelessness would it be to think
God must aid us to get the things
We want against His Word!

800 Impossible that God would advance
By the gift of His blessing
What He curses with His mouth!

Lastly, when things do not go
According to our hope and wish,
805 By this consideration we'll be restrained
To curb our impatience and loathing of our state.
For we will recognize that this will be
To murmur against God, by whose will
Poverty and wealth, contempt and honors
810 Are dispensed. To sum up:
Whoever rests upon God's blessing
(As has been said) will not aspire
By evil, devious ways toward things
That men with crazed greed seek after,
815 For he will realize this way
Will profit him nothing.
And if any prosperity befalls him,
Neither to his diligence, his industry,
Nor to his fortune will he impute it,
820 But will recognize it to be from God.
On the other hand, if he scarcely advances,
Even goes backward, will he not bear
His poverty more patiently and modestly
Than a faithless man bears middling wealth
825 That's not as great as he had hoped.
For he will have a solace far better
Wherein to repose than all
The riches and honors of this world
Heaped in one great pile:
830 His solace is that he will deem all things
Ordained of God, as is expedient,
For his salvation.

Not only in this respect are believers
To maintain such patience and moderation;

835 They are to extend it as well
To all the chances to which
This present life is subject.
He alone has duly resigned himself to the Lord
Who willingly lets his whole life
840 Be governed at God's pleasure.
He who is thus composed in mind,
Whatever may happen, never will deem himself un-
happy,
Will not complain of his condition
As if obliquely taking God to task.

845 How necessary this disposition of mind is,
Will appear if we consider to how many
Accidents we are subject.
A thousand maladies there are that beat
Incessantly upon us, one after another.
850 Now the plague tortures us, now war,
Now ice or hail strikes down our crops
And threatens us with poverty;
Now through death we lose wives, children,
Other relatives; sometimes our houses
855 Are set afire. Such things
Cause men to curse their life,
Loathe the day of their birth,
Abominate heaven and the light of day,
Rail against God and, being eloquent
860 At blasphemy, accuse Him
Of injustice and cruelty.

But even in these events
The faithful man must look to
God's mercy and His fatherly kindness.
865 If he sees himself bereft by the death
Of all his kinsfolk, his house forsaken,
Even then he will not cease to bless God.
Rather will he turn to the thought that
Since God's grace dwells in his house,

870 It will not leave him desolate.
If his crops and vines are blasted and destroyed
By frost, hail, or other storms,
And from this he foresees peril of famine,
Still will he not lose courage
875 And become displeased with God.
Rather will he stand fast, firm in faith,
Saying in his heart: We still
Are in the Lord's keeping, the sheep of His feeding.
Whatever barrenness may come, the Lord
880 Will ever give us food.
Stricken by disease, he will not be
So unmanned as to break into impatience
And complain of God.
Rather, thinking on the righteousness
885 And goodness of our heavenly Father,
Out of the chastisement itself he will
Betake himself to patience.

In short, whatever befalls him,
Knowing that all comes forth from the Lord's hand,
890 He will receive it with a peaceful, grateful heart
In order not to resist the command of Him
To whom he once gave himself over.
Let the pagans' foolish, miserable consolation
Be banished from the Christian's breast:
895 To blame on Fortune their adversities
And make them thus more bearable.
For the philosophers used the reason
That it would be folly to rage against Fortune,
Unthinking, blind, throwing her darts at random,
900 To break both good and bad men indiscriminately.
On the contrary, here is the rule of godliness:
God's hand alone governs fortune good or bad,
Acts not with unthinking rashness,
But by an ordered justice
905 Dispenses good and bad.

The Christian Life and the Cross

Still must the faithful Christian's mind mount up:
To know whither Christ calls all His own.
His own cross each should bear.
For all whom the Lord has adopted and received
910 Among His children must equip themselves
For a hard life, toilsome, full of labor
And endless sorts of evil.
The heavenly Father's will is so to exercise
His servants and season them.
915 This order He began in Christ, His first-born Son,
And now practices it toward all others.
For though Christ was His beloved Son
In whom He was well-pleased,
We see however that in this world
920 Christ was not pampered.
Not only can one say He was unceasingly afflicted;
His whole life in fact was but a sort
Of endless cross.
How can we be spared this condition
925 To which even Christ our head had to submit?
Especially since He submitted to it
For our sake, to give us
An example of patience!
Accordingly the apostle announces
930 That God has set this end
For all His children:
To shape them to His Christ.

Thence comes to us a great consolation.
Enduring all miseries
935 (Called adverse and evil things),
We cleave to the cross of Christ
So that, as He has passed through an abyss
Of all evils to enter the heavenly glory,
We too, passing through divers tribulations,
940 Reach that place.

For St. Paul teaches us that
When we feel within ourselves the sharing
Of His sufferings, at the same time
We grasp the power of His resurrection.
945 And when we become sharers in His death,
This is a preparation to reach His glorious eternity.
How much power that has to soften
All bitterness the cross may hold:
It is that the more affliction, misery we undergo,
950 The surer is our fellowship with Christ.
When we share with Him, adversities to us
Not only are blessed but are also helps
Greatly to advance our salvation.

Affliction Brings Us to Trust in God

Besides, the Lord Jesus had no need
955 To bear the cross, endure trials,
Except to attest and prove His obedience
Toward God His Father.
But necessary for us is it, for several reasons,
To be ceaselessly afflicted in this life.
960 First, as we are by nature inclined
To exalt ourselves and claim
All things for ourselves, if our frailty
Is not set before our very eyes,
We immediately value our own virtue
965 Beyond measure, unhesitatingly deeming itself
Unconquerable against all troubles
That could beset it.
From this it comes to pass that we
Are puffed up in empty, foolish confidence in flesh,
970 Which later rouses us to haughtiness
Against God as if our own strength
Suffice without His grace.
This arrogance He best restrains
In showing us by experience how in us
975 There lies not only stupidity—but also frailty.
Therefore He afflicts us either by disgrace,

By poverty, disease, bereavement,
Or other calamities to which—
Resist them as we will—directly we succumb,
980 Not having the power to bear them.
Thus humbled, we learn to call upon His power,
Which alone makes us stand firm, unflinching
Under the weight of such burdens.

Even the most holy, although they recognize
985 Their firmness is founded on the Lord's grace
And not on their own virtue, still would have
Too much assurance of their strength and constancy
If the Lord did not lead them
Into a surer knowledge of themselves,
990 Testing them by the cross.
When things are peaceful, they are puffed
With self-esteeming firmness and constancy,
But directly tribulation strikes they recognize
This feeling is nothing but hypocrisy.
995 This then is the way the faithful must be
Warned of their diseases, in order to advance
In humility and to slough off
All perverse confidence in flesh,
Betake themselves completely to God's grace.
1000 But once in His care they feel His present power,
In which they possess strength enough.

This it is that St. Paul means in saying,
"Tribulation engenders patience;
And from patience comes proof."
1005 To help His faithful in tribulations
The Lord has promised;
This they truly feel when in patience
They stand, sustained by His hand,
Something by their strength they could not do.
1010 Patience then is proof to the saints
That God truly gives the help
He promised, when there is need of it.

65

By it also their hope is strengthened,
Because it would be gross ingratitude
1015 Not to expect that, for the future,
God's truth will be as firm and unchangeable
As it has already proved to be.

Now we already see how much benefit
Comes from the cross, as from an endless thread.
1020 For it, reversing the false opinion
Naturally conceived by us
Of our very own virtue
And uncovering our hypocrisy
(Which flatteringly seduces and abuses us),
1025 Reduces the reliance on our flesh
(A most pernicious influence on us).
After, it teaches us thus humbled
To rest in God, who, being our foundation,
Does not let us succumb or lose courage.
1030 Hope follows this victory.
Moreover, the Lord, in fulfilling His promise,
Establishes His truth for time to come.
Surely if these were the only reasons,
How necessary is the training of the cross
1035 Would still appear.
No small profit is it to us
To be cleansed of our blinding self-love
So we may straightway recognize our weakness;
To feel our weakness so we may learn
1040 Distrust of self; distrusting ourselves,
To transfer our trust to God;
To lean on God with trusting heart
So that by His help we may persevere
Unto the victorious end;
1045 To stand in His grace so we may know
Him true and faithful in His promises;
To have unquestioned assurance in His promises
So our hope may thereby be strengthened.

Affliction Teaches Patience and Obedience

Still another reason the Lord has
1050 To afflict His servants:
It is to prove their patience,
Teach them obedience.
Not that they could have another obedience
Than that He has given them.
1055 But it pleases Him so to show,
Attest the gifts sent to His faithful ones,
That these may not lie idle, hidden within.
Therefore when He brings into the open
The virtue of patience He has given His servants,
1060 'Tis said He is proving their patience.
Hence arise such expressions:
"He tried Abraham and proved his piety
When he did not refuse to sacrifice his son
To please Him."
1065 St. Peter likewise says our faith
Is proved by tribulation just as gold
Is assayed in a furnace.

But who will deny it expedient
That a gift so excellent which the Lord has made
1070 To His servants, be put to use to make it known
And manifest? Never would it otherwise be esteemed
As it deserves. If the Lord has just reason
To give substance to the virtues
He has bestowed upon His faithful,
1075 To stir them up that they may not
Remain hidden, even stay unused,
We see that there is point
To His sending afflictions,
Without which their patience would be nil.
1080 I also say that by this means
He instructs them in patience,
Since by it they learn not to live
As they please but at His pleasure.

Obviously if all things they ask
1085 Came to them, they would not know
What it is to follow God.
Seneca, a pagan philosopher, quotes
An ancient proverb:
When one wishes to urge a man
1090 To endure adversity with patience,
This expression is used:
"You must follow God."
In this the ancients meant that a man
At last submits to the Lord's yoke
1095 Only when he lets himself be chastised
And willingly presents his hand and back
To the Lord's lash.
But if it is reasonable for us
In every way to render obedience
1100 To our heavenly Father,
It is not ours to refuse His accustoming us
In every way possible to that obedience.

Still we fail to see how needed
This obedience is unless we ponder
1105 How our flesh pants to reject
The Lord's yoke the moment
We ever so gently favor our failing.
The same thing happens to mettlesome horses
After being for some time left idle
1110 And pampered: they cannot be tamed
And will not obey their masters,
Whose commands they previously obeyed.
In short, what the Lord complains
Of happening to the Israelites
1115 Is commonly seen in all men.
It is that, fattened with too gentle nurture,
They kick against Him
Who has nourished them.
It is true that God's beneficence should have
1120 Drawn us to prize and love His goodness.

But since our ungratefulness is such
That we are corrupted by His kindness
Rather than aroused to good,
He has to checkrein us and keep
1125 Us under discipline, lest we
Break forth into such wantonness.
For this reason, in order that we may not
By too abundant good become proud;
In order too that honors may not puff us up;
1130 In order that our adornments of body
Or of soul may not arouse insolence in us—
The Lord confronts us and puts in its place,
Reining and taming by the remedy of the cross,
The folly of our flesh.
1135 This He does in various ways
As He knows to be expedient
And salutary to each one.
For the illness of some of us
Is not as severe or even the same
1140 As that which strikes the rest;
Hence the same remedy cannot apply to all.
That is why the Lord tests some
With one kind of cross, others with another.
Yet in wishing to minister to the health of all,
1145 On some He uses a gentle medicine,
A harsher, more rigorous one on others,
Leaving no one untouched,
For He knows that all men are sick.

Affliction Is a Sign of God's Love

Besides, it is needful that our good Father
1150 Should not only anticipate our future weakness
But also oftentimes correct
Our past faults, to keep us in obedience to Him.
Directly any affliction strike us,
We ought to be mindful of our past life.
1155 So doing, we will doubtless find
We have committed some faults

67

Deserving of such chastisement,
Although from the recognition of our sin
We must take the chief reason
1160 To exhort ourselves to patience.
For Scripture puts in our hands
A far better consideration, saying,
"The Lord corrects us by adversity
To keep us from being condemned with this world."
1165 Therefore we must recognize our Father's pity
And kindness amid the bitterest trials,
For even in these He does not cease
To advance our salvation.
For He afflicts us not for our ruin
1170 Or perdition, but to deliver us
From the condemnation of this world.
This thought will lead us to what
Scripture elsewhere teaches:
"My son, reject not the Lord's correction;
1175 Do not grow weary when He corrects you.
For God corrects those He loves
And embraces them as His children."
When we hear these corrections called
"Fatherly rods," is it not our duty
1180 To show ourselves teachable children
Rather than, resisting, imitate
Desperate persons, hardened in their crimes?
The Lord destroys us if we do not
Return to Him through correction
1185 When we have failed.
And, as the apostle says, we are bastards,
Not legitimate children,
If we do not keep under discipline.
Too perverse then are we
1190 If we cannot bear the Lord
When He declares to us
His benevolence and the care
He has for our salvation.
Scripture notes a difference

1195 Between unbelievers and believers:
The first, like ancient serfs,
Perverse of nature,
Only worsen and harden under the lash;
The second benefit by repentance
1200 And amendment, like freeborn sons.
Let us now choose which we prefer to be.
But since this matter has been treated elsewhere,
Enough it is to have touched upon it lightly.

Affliction Is an Honor

But highest consolation of all is
1205 When we endure persecution
For the sake of righteousness.
We must remember what honor
The Lord has done us in giving us
The badge of His militia.
1210 By "persecution for righteousness"
I mean our suffering not only
To defend the gospel but also
To maintain any rightful cause.
Whether in defending God's truth
1215 Against the lies of Satan,
Or else in sustaining the innocent against the wicked
And in preventing wrong or injury from being done
    them—
We must encounter the hatred, indignation of the world,
To the peril of our honor,
1220 Our possessions, or our life.
Let us not begrudge spending ourselves for God;
Let us not think ourselves unhappy
When with His own mouth
He declares us happy.
1225 True it is that poverty valued for its own sake
Is misery. Likewise exile, contempt,
Disgrace, prison; lastly, death
Is the ultimate calamity.

But when God breathes His favor,
1230 None there are of these things
That do not turn out for us
To be happiness, felicity.
With Christ's witness, not with the false
Notion of our flesh, let us be content.
1235 From this it will come about that
At the apostles' example we'll rejoice
Whenever and how much He will count
Us worthy to endure
Dishonor for His name.
1240 For if, being innocent and of good conscience,
We are deprived by the wickedness of evil men
Of our possession,
We are impoverished before men,
But thereby toward God our true riches increase.
1245 If we are hounded and banished from our homeland,
All the more are we received
Into the family of the Lord.
If we are vexed and despised,
All the more are we strengthened in our Lord
1250 To take our refuge there.
If branded with disgrace and ignominy,
All the more are we exalted in God's kingdom.
If slain, entrance to the blessed life
Will open for us.

1255 Ashamed then should we not be to value less
The things the Lord has highly prized
Than the delights of this world,
Which pass away like smoke?

Since Scripture then so comforts us
1260 In all disgrace and calamity we must endure
For the defense of righteousness,
We are ungrateful indeed if we do not,
With patience and cheerful hearts, bear these.

Especially is this sort of cross appropriate,
1265 Above all others, for faithful Christians;
By it Christ wills to be
"Glorified in them," as St. Peter says.

Christians Express Pain and Sorrow

Yet God does not require of us
Such cheerfulness as to remove
1270 All bitterness of pain.
Otherwise the patience of the saints
Would not be in the cross
Unless they were tormented by pain,
Felt agony, when someone
1275 Caused them trouble.
Likewise, if poverty were not harsh and bitter for them,
If they did not endure some torment in disease,
If disgrace did not stab them,
If dread death did not hang over them,
1280 What fortitude or moderation would there be
In scorning all these things?
But since each of these has a bitterness attached
That by nature stabs all our hearts,
Therein is proved the fortitude
1285 Of a faithful man, if tried by a feeling
Of such harshness, yet valiantly resisting,
He strives constantly to resist,
Surmount, and rise above them.
In this is his patience shown
1290 If, pricked by this same feeling,
He is at all times restrained
By fear of God, as by a bridle,
Which will not let him break forth
In any intemperate act.
1295 In this appears his joy and cheerfulness,
If being struck by sadness and sorrow,
He nonetheless gives himself
To God's spiritual consolation.

The combat that the faithful, following patience
1300 And moderation, wage against the natural feeling of
    sorrow
Is well described by St. Paul:
"Tribulation we endure in all things,
But we are not in distress.
Poverty we endure, but are not left destitute.
1305 Persecution we endure, but are not deserted.
Cast down we are, but perish not."

We see that to bear one's cross with patience
Is not to be utterly stupefied, deprived of all feeling,
As the Stoic philosophers long ago foolishly described
1310 "The great-souled" man who,
Having cast off his humanness,
Was equally untouched by adversity and prosperity,
By things sad or joyful—or rather
Was senseless as a rock.
1315 And what have they profited
With this high wisdom?
They have painted a picture of patience
Never yet found among men,
Utterly impossible to realize;
1320 Even in desiring to have such perfect patience,
They have banished its use among men.
Now also among Christians their like is found,
Men who consider it a vice not only to groan
And weep, but even to be sad
1325 And ridden with cares.
Such harsh notions arise from idle folk
Who, busying themselves with speculation
Rather than putting hand to work,
Produce nothing but fantasies like these.

1330 For our part, we have nothing to do
With this harsh and rigorous philosophy,
One condemned by our Lord Jesus
Not only in words but also by His own example.

For He groaned and wept out of His own pain
1335 And out of pity for others as well,
And taught His disciples to do the same.
"The world," He says, "will rejoice,
But you will be in sorrow;
It will laugh, you will weep."
1340 And, that no one might turn it into a vice,
He declares those who weep to be blessed.
And no wonder! For if all tears
Be condemned, what will we judge
Concerning Lord Jesus, from whose body
1345 Trickled down drops of blood?
If one brands all terror as unbelief,
What opinion will we have of the dread
With which our Lord was so wondrously stricken?
How will we approve His confession:
1350 That His soul is sorrowful
Even to death?

These things I intended to say
To draw all good hearts back from despair
So they might not renounce
1355 The pursuit of patience,
Though not freed utterly
From the natural feeling of sorrow.
But this is what happens to those
Who make patience into insensibility,
1360 A strong, steadfast man into a block of wood:
Their courage falters and they despair
When they would like to apply
Themselves to patience.
Scripture, on the other hand, praises the saints
1365 For their forbearance;
When they are so stricken by the harshness
Of their misfortune, they are not broken,
Do not fail; when pricked by bitterness,
They feel a spiritual joy;
1370 When pressed with agony, catch their breath,

Rejoicing in God's consolation.
Yet a loathing still agitates their heart:
This is the natural sense fleeing from
And holding in horror
1375 All that is opposed to it.

Christians Remain Obedient and Patient

On the other hand, the disposition
To godliness draws them to obedience
To God's will through the midst of these hardships.
This loathing Jesus Christ has described
1380 In speaking to St. Peter:
"When you were young,
You girded yourself as you pleased
And walked where it seemed good to you;
When you become old, another
1385 Will gird you, lead you
Where you do not wish to go."
It is unlikely that St. Peter,
When he had to glorify God in death,
Was drawn to it by force and against his will;
1390 Otherwise his martyrdom would not
Have been greatly praised.
Yet even though he obeyed God's command
With free and cheerful courage,
Because he had not put off his humanness,
1395 He was distracted with a double will.
When he realized the cruel death
He had to suffer, overcome by horror of it,
He would willingly have escaped.
On the other hand, when he pondered
1400 That he had been called by God's command,
He presented himself willingly, even joyfully,
Thrusting all fear underfoot.

Now if we would be Christ's disciples,
We must take care that our hearts

1405 Are filled with such reverence
And obedience to God as is able to tame and yoke
All affections contrary to His will.
Hence it will come about that in whatever trial
We may be, in the greatest distress of heart
1410 We can possibly experience, we will not slacken
Our firm grip on patience.
For adversities will always have
Their bitterness to gnaw us.
For this reason, afflicted by disease,
1415 We will groan, complain, long for health;
Pressed by poverty, will feel
Some pricks of perplexity and care.
Equally, disgrace, contempt, and every injustice
Will rend our hearts.
1420 When one of our relatives dies, we shall pay
To nature the tears we owe.
But always we shall come back to this conclusion:
"Yet the Lord has willed it; let us follow His will."
Even amid the pricks of pain, tears, groans,
1425 This thought must intervene
To lead back our heart to bear
Cheerfully the things that sadden it.

Because we have taken the prime reason
For bearing the cross from the contemplation
1430 Of the will of God,
We must briefly distinguish
Christian patience from philosophical.
Few philosophers indeed have mounted up so high
As to understand that through God's hand
1435 Men are aroused by afflictions,
And at this point to know that we
Must obey God's will.
Still, those who have come this far
Adduce no other reason except
1440 That it is necessary.
What is this but to say

71

That one must yield to God
Because it would be vain
To try to resist Him?
1445 For if we obey God because it's necessary,
When we can escape
We cease to obey Him.

But Scripture would have us look
At something else in God's will:
1450 Namely, first His justice and equity;
Then the care He takes for our salvation.
Such are Christian exhortations:
Whether poverty, banishment, prison,
Insult, disease, bereavement,
1455 Or other adversity plagues us,
We must ponder that none of these things
Happens save by the Lord's will and providence;
Moreover, that He does nothing
Save with a well-ordered justice.
1460 What then? Do not the sins we commit
Each day deserve a hundred thousand times
Harsher dealing than He is wont
To mete out to us?
Is it not right indeed that our flesh be tamed,
1465 Accustomed to the yoke, that it may not stray
Into the intemperance to which
Its nature bears it off?
Are not God's justice and truth worth
What we endure for them?
1470 If God's equity clearly appears
In all our afflictions, we cannot
Without iniquity murmur or rebel.
The cold song of the philosophers
We do not hear: "Yield we must
1475 Because it is necessary";
Rather, a lively and efficacious warning:
"Obey we must, for it is not lawful
To resist."

Patience we must grasp, for impatience
1480 Would be insolence against the will of God.
But because nothing is right pleasing to us
Save what we recognize to be
Good and salutary for us,
The Father of mercies also consoles us here,
1485 Affirming that in the afflictions He brings us
By cross, He is providing
For our salvation.
But if these tribulations are not salutary,
How can we not receive them
1490 With composed and grateful heart?
And so, in patiently enduring them,
We are not giving in to necessity
But consenting for our own good.
These thoughts, I say, will bring it about
1495 That, although our heart is imprisoned
In the cross by the very bitterness of its nature,
Yet it will be filled with spiritual joy.
Thence also comes thanksgiving—
Which cannot be joyless!
1500 But if the praise of the Lord and thanksgiving
Can only come forth from a happy, cheerful heart—
And nothing at all ought to hinder this—
From this appears how necessary it is
That the bitterness which is in the cross
1505 Be tempered with spiritual joy.

The Christian Life, Earthly Life, and Eternal Life

The Vanity of Earthly Life

Moreover, whatever sort of tribulation
May afflict us, we must ever look
To this end: accustom ourselves to despise the present
    life
And so by this to be aroused

1510 To meditate upon the life to come.
For because the Lord well knows
How prone we are to a blind—even brutish—love
Of this world, He uses a right proper means
To draw us back, shake off our sluggishness,
1515 So our hearts will no more be so much attached
To such a foolish love.
Not one of us there is who does not wish
To seem, throughout his life, to aspire
To heavenly immortality
1520 And strive to reach it.
For we are ashamed to be in no way
More excellent than brute beasts,
Whose condition would not be inferior to ours
If there did not remain in us
1525 Some hope of eternity after death.
But, if one examines the plans,
Deliberations, schemes, and works of anyone,
One will see there nothing but earth.
But this stupidity of ours arises
1530 Because our understanding is, so to speak,
Dazzled by the empty glitter
Of riches, honors, powers,
In their outward appearance;
Thus can it see no farther.
1535 Likewise our heart, gripped with greed,
Ambition, and other wondrous lusts,
Is so attached to earth
That it cannot look upward.
Lastly, the whole soul, enveloped
1540 And, as it were, enmeshed
In allurements of the flesh,
Seeks its happiness on earth.

The Lord, then, to counter this evil,
Instructs His servants concerning the vanity
1545 Of the present life, continually
Exercising them in divers miseries.

That they may not promise themselves
Peace and repose in the present life,
He permits them often to be troubled
1550 And plagued by wars, tumults,
Robberies, or other injuries.
That they may not with too much greed
Aspire to fleeting wealth or repose
In what they have,
1555 Sometimes by barrenness of earth,
Sometimes by fire,
Sometimes by other means
He reduces them to poverty—
Or at least confines them
1560 To a moderate condition.
In order that they may not get
Too much pleasure in marriage,
He either gives them uncouth, hot-headed wives
To torment them, or gives them evil offspring
1565 To humble them, or afflicts them
By taking away their wives and children.
But if in all things He gently treats them,
Yet to keep them from becoming puffed up
In vainglory or exulting in unbridled confidence,
1570 He warns them by disease and peril
And, as it were, sets before their eyes
How frail and short-lived are all the goods
That are subject to mortality.
Only then do we benefit by the discipline
1575 Of the cross, when we learn that the present life,
Esteemed for itself, is full of disquiet, trouble,
Entirely miserable, in no respect clearly happy;
That all its goods, so highly esteemed,
Are fleeting, uncertain, fickle,
1580 Mixed with infinite miseries.
Thus from this we conclude
That here we must look for, hope for
Nothing but warfare;
If we are concerned about our crown,

1585 We must raise our eyes to heaven.
A sure fact it is that our heart
Is never seriously aroused to desire
And meditate upon the life to come
Without first being touched
1590 By contempt for earthly life.

Between these two extremes there is no middle ground:
Either the world must be worthless to us
Or it holds us bound by unchecked love of it.
Accordingly, if we have any concern for immortality,
1595 Diligently we must strive to strike off
These evil fetters.
But because the present life has strong allure
To entice us, great show of pleasantness,
Of grace, of sweetness to wheedle us,
1600 It behooves us to be drawn back from time to time
So we may not be abused and, so to speak,
Bewitched by such flatteries.
For what will happen to us, I ask you,
If here we enjoy such unending happiness,
1605 Seeing that being constantly pricked
With so many spurs,
We cannot be sufficiently awakened
To weigh our misery?
That life is like a shadow, smoke—
1610 Not only is this a fact known to the learned,
But also it is among the people a common proverb.
And since men saw it to be
Something useful to know,
They spread it abroad
1615 In many striking sayings.
Yet nothing there is that we consider
More negligently or remember less.
For we undertake everything as if
We were setting up immortality
1620 For ourselves on earth.
If a dead man is being buried

Or we are among the graves in a cemetery,
Because we have before our eyes
The image of death,
1625 I confess, brilliantly we philosophize
Upon the frailty of this life.
Yet this does not always happen to us,
For sometimes these things
Scarcely move us at all.
1630 But when it happens, ours is
A transitory philosophy that vanishes
The minute we turn our backs,
So no memory of it remains.
Forgetful not only of death
1635 But also of our own mortality,
As if we had never heard tell of it,
We lapse once more into carefree,
Foolish assurance of earthly immortality.
If someone, however, quotes to us
1640 The ancient proverb,
"Man is the creature of a day,"
We admit it, but do so
Without thinking about it,
While this thought always remains
1645 Firm-fixed in our mind:
That we have to live here forever.
Who then will deny
That it is very necessary—
I do not say to be admonished—
1650 But by all experiences that can possibly happen
To be convinced
How unhappy man's condition is
With respect to this earthly life:
Since, even when convinced, we scarcely stop
1655 Holding it in admiration and are so stunned by it
As if in itself it contained all happiness?
But if the Lord has so to instruct us,
Our duty is to heed His remonstrances
By which He is waking up our carelessness,

1660 So that we, despising the world,
May wholeheartedly aspire to meditate
Upon the life to come.

Gratitude for Earthly Life

Yet faithful Christians must become accustomed
To such a contempt of present life
1665 As does not engender hatred of it
Or ungratefulness toward God.
For although this life is full of countless woes,
Still is it numbered among God's blessings,
Which are not to be despised by us.
1670 However, if in it we recognize no grace of God,
We are guilty of great ingratitude.
For the faithful especially it must be
A witness to the Lord's benevolence,
Wholly destined as it is
1675 To further their salvation.
For the Lord, before plainly revealing to us
The inheritance of immortal glory,
Would show Himself our Father
In lesser things, that is, in His benefits
1680 That daily we receive from His hand.
Since, therefore, this life serves us
In understanding God's goodness,
Should we despise it as if it had
No good in itself?
1685 We must, accordingly, be so disposed
In mind and feeling as to count it
As a gift of the divine kindness
That is not to be rejected.
For if Scriptural testimonies were lacking
1690 (Which nevertheless are not lacking),
Still nature itself exhorts us
To give thanks to God,
Since He has created us, put us in this world,
Preserves us in it, and ministers to us

1695 All things necessary for us
To remain in it.

Moreover, a still greater reason it is
If we reflect that He is preparing us
For the glory of His kingdom.
1700 For He has once ordained that those
Who are to be crowned in heaven
First must fight on earth,
In order that they may not triumph
Until the press of war is overcome
1705 And victory obtained.
But the other reason also has weight:
It is that we here begin to taste
The sweetness of His bounty in His benefits,
In order to whet our hope and desire
1710 To seek after the full revelation.
After we have come to know
That the earthly life is a gift
Of God's mercy,
For which we are beholden to Him,
1715 Also that we should be cognizant of this
When the time comes to consider
Its unhappy condition,
We may be extricated
From this excessive desire,
1720 To which (as we have shown)
We all are by nature inclined.

Desire for Eternal Life

But all we take away from uncontrolled love of this life
Transfer we must to the heavenly life.
I admit that, according to their human sense,
1725 Those reasoned well who judged our highest good
Would be never to be born;
The next, to die as quickly as possible.
For since they were pagans,
Destitute of God's light and of true religion,

1730 What else in earthly life could they discern
Than poverty and dread?
Not without point is it that the Scythians
Weep at the birth of their children;
But when one of their kin dies,
1735 They rejoice and make holiday.
But this profited them nothing.
For because they lacked the true doctrine
Of the faith, they could not see
How what is neither happy nor desirable of itself
1740 Turns into salvation for the faithful.
Thus their judgment ended in despair.
Let God's servants then always pursue this goal
In weighing this mortal life:
Seeing in it naught but misery,
1745 They should be more eager, ready
To meditate upon the eternal life to come.
When they come to compare the two,
Not only will they be able to neglect
The first, but also despise it
1750 And hold it of no value
In comparison with the second.
For if heaven is our homeland,
What else is earth but an exile, banishment?
If leaving this world is entering into life,
1755 What else is this world but a tomb?
And what else to remain in it
Than to be plunged into death?
If it is freedom to be delivered from this body,
What else is the body but a prison?
1760 And if our highest happiness is to enjoy
The presence of God,
Is it not misery not to enjoy it?

But until we leave this world,
"We are away from God."
1765 Therefore, if the earthly life is compared
To the heavenly, there is no doubt

It can be despised, valued as smoke.
True it is, however, that we must never hate it
Unless it hold us in subjection to sin,
1770 Which is, however, properly not to be imputed to it.
Be that as it may, we must be so wearied,
Vexed by it that, yearning to see its end,
We are, however, prepared to dwell in it
At God's good pleasure,
1775 So that our weariness may be far away
From all murmuring and impatience.
For the present life is like a sentry post
At which the Lord has stationed us
And which we must man
1780 Until He recalls us.

St. Paul, feeling himself too long bound in the prison
Of his body, laments his lot
And sighs with fervent desire
To be delivered from it.
1785 Nevertheless, to obey God's will,
He asserts he is ready for one or other
Because he knows he owes it to God
To glorify His name,
Whether through death or life.
1790 But it is for the Lord to determine
What makes for His glory.
Therefore, if it befits us to live and die
Unto Him, let us leave to His decision
Our life as well as our death,
1795 But in such a way that we ever
May desire our death and continually
Meditate upon it,
Despising this mortal life
In favor of the coming immortality,
1800 Desiring to renounce this life
Whenever it pleases the Lord,
Because it keeps us in sin's bondage.

No Fear of Death

A monstrous thing it is, however,.
That many who boast themselves Christians,
1805 Instead of longing for death,
Hold it in such dread that, directly
They hear it mentioned, tremble
As if the greatest misfortune possible
Has overtaken them.
1810 No wonder is it if natural sense
Is moved, astonished
When we hear it said our body
Must be separated from our soul;
But it is utterly intolerable
1815 That in a Christian heart there is not
Light enough for it to master
And suppress this fear,
Great as it is, by a greater consolation.
For if we consider that this bodily tent of ours—
1820 Weak, defective, corruptible, fleeting,
Rotting—is undone, shattered,
So that afterward, restored to perfect glory,
Firm, incorruptible, heavenly,
Will not faith constrain us
1825 Eagerly to seek what nature flees
And holds in horror?
If we ponder that by death
We are recalled from miserable exile
To dwell in our homeland,
1830 Our heavenly country,
Must we not from this get
Singular consolation?
But someone will object that all things
Crave to persist in their being.
1835 I admit it. For this very reason
I contend that we must aspire
To future immortality,
Where a firm condition will be ours
That nowhere appears on earth.

1840 Is it right that the brute beasts,
Even inanimate creatures—
To the point of wood and stone—
Having some inkling of their vanity, corruption,
Should "long for the day of judgment
1845 To be delivered from it":
While on the other hand we,
Having first some light of nature,
Moreover, being illumined with God's Spirit,
When our very being is at stake,
1850 Should not lift our eyes beyond this earthly decay?

But here it is not my intention at length
To dispute against such great perversity.
Actually at the very beginning
I stated that I did not intend to treat
1855 Each item in the form of exhortation.
Persons of timid heart I would advise
To read St. Cyprian's book
Entitled *On the Mortality,*
Unless they deserve to be sent off
1860 To the philosophers, with whom they'll find
A contempt of death that ought
To make them ashamed.
We must, however, hold to this maxim:
No one has progressed in Christ's school
1865 Except the man who awaits in joy and gaiety
The day of death and of the final resurrection.
For St. Paul describes all the faithful
By this mark, and to it Scripture
Habitually recalls us,
1870 Whenever it would set forth
Reason to rejoice: "Rejoice,"
Says the Lord, "and raise up your head,
For your redemption nears."

Is it reasonable, I ask you, that
1875 What Jesus Christ has thought

Proper to our rejoicing, engenders
In us nothing but sorrow and dismay?
If this is so, why should we boast
Of being His disciples?
1880 Let us then return to better sense
And, although the desire of our flesh
(As it is blind and stupid) resists,
Let us not hesitate to long for
The Lord's coming as the happiest thing of all.
1885 Let us do this not only with simple longing,
But even to the point of groans and sighs.
For He our Redeemer will come to us
To lead us into the inheritance of His glory,
After He has rescued us from this abyss
1890 Of all evils and miseries.

Consolation of Eternal Life

All faithful men so long as they dwell on earth
Must be "as sheep destined for slaughter,"
That they may be shaped
To Jesus Christ, their head.
1895 Desperately unhappy would they have been
If they had not directed their minds upward
To surmount all that is in this world
And pass beyond the contemplation
Of present things.
1900 Conversely, if they have once raised
Their thought above the things of earth,
When they see the wicked flourishing
In wealth and honors, enjoying deep repose,
Having everything as they wish,
1905 Living in luxury and pomp;
Even when they see themselves
Inhumanly treated by the wicked;
When they bear their insults;
When they are robbed or harried
1910 With all manner of outrage—
Still will it be easy for them

To bear up under these evils.
For they will ever have before their eyes
The last day, on which they know
1915 The Lord must gather His faithful ones
Into the repose of His kingdom,
Wipe the tears from their eyes,
Crown them with glory,
Clothe them with rejoicing,
1920 Fill them with infinite sweetness of His delights,
Elevate them into His loftiness;
To sum up—make them sharers
In His happiness.
On the contrary, those wicked ones
1925 Who have flourished on earth
He must cast into utter disgrace,
Change their delights to dreadful torments,
Their laughter and joy to weeping and gnashing of teeth;
Break their peace with dire torment of conscience;
1930 To sum up—plunge them into eternal fire
And put them in subjection to the faithful
Whom they have so wickedly treated.

Here truly is our sole consolation:
Taken away, either we must needs lose heart
1935 Or else be soothed, allured
By the vain and futile solace
That will turn us to destruction.
For the prophet himself confesses
That he has wavered, his feet almost slipping,
1940 While he has stopped too long
To dwell upon the present happiness
Of the wicked; that he could scarcely stand
Until he redirected his thought
To contemplate God's sanctuary, that is,
1945 To consider what will one day
Be the end of good and evil men.
In a word, I am saying that the cross of Christ
Will in the hearts of the faithful

At last triumph against the devil,
1950 Flesh, sin, death, and the wicked,
If they turn their eyes to contemplate
The power of His resurrection.

Extreme Views of Earthly Goods

By this same lesson Scripture teaches us
The proper use of earthly goods—
1955 A matter we dare not neglect
When the right ordering of our life's at stake.
For if we are to live,
Also we must use the helps
Necessary for life.
1960 And also we cannot avoid the things
That seem more to serve pleasure than necessity.
We must therefore hold to some measure
So as to use them with a pure, clean conscience,
As much for our need as for our delight.
1965 This measure is shown to us by God
When He teaches that the present life
Is for His servants like a pilgrimage on which
They are pressing toward the heavenly kingdom.
If we must simply pass through this world,
1970 There is no doubt we ought to use its goods
Rather to advance our course
Than hinder it.
But because this is a troublesome matter
And there is danger of falling as much
1975 Into one extreme as into the other,
Let us try to give sure teaching
On which one can securely settle.
Some good and holy persons there have been
Who—seeing the intemperance of men
1980 (If not severly restrained)
Ever raging unbridled
And wishing to correct such a great evil—
Did not allow men to use physical goods
Except insofar as necessity required.

1985 This they did because they saw
No other remedy. Their plan came
From a good intent, but they went at it
With far too great severity.
For they did something very dangerous:
1990 They bound consciences more tightly
Than they are bound by God's Word.
On the other hand, there are several persons today
Who, wishing to seek an excuse
For all intemperate use of outward things
1995 And to slacken the bridle upon the flesh
(All too ready otherwise to break loose!),
Take for granted what I do not concede to them:
That this freedom is not to be restrained
By any limitation; rather one must leave
2000 To each man's conscience to use
As seems lawful to him.
I admit that we ought not, cannot,
Bind consciences in this matter,
Setting formulas and precepts.
2005 But since Scripture furnishes general rules
For lawful use, why should it not
Be limited in accordance with them?

Purpose of Earthly Goods

As to the first point, hold fast to this:
The use of God's gifts is not misdirected
2010 When referred to the end God created
And destined them for—since He created them
Not for our harm but for our good.
Accordingly no one will hold to a straighter path
Than he who earnestly looks to this end.
2015 But if we ponder to what end
God created food,
We shall find He willed to provide
Not only for our need
But also for our pleasure and recreation.
2020 Thus for clothing, beyond necessity

He considered what was proper and appropriate;
For grasses, trees, fruits,
Beyond the various uses He has given to us for them,
He willed to gladden our sight by their beauty
2025 And give us still another pleasure in their odor.
For if that were not so,
The prophet would not have reckoned
Among God's blessings that
"Wine gladdens the heart of man,
2030 And oil makes his face shine."
Scripture would not have mentioned here and there,
To commend God's kindness,
That He has given all these goods to men.
And even the good qualities that all things
2035 Have by nature, show us how, to what end,
And even to what point, we ought to enjoy them.
Do we think that our Lord would have given
Such beauty to the flowers as meets the eye,
Yet make it unlawful for us to be touched
2040 With some pleasure in seeing that beauty?
Do we think He would have given them
Such good odor if He did not intend
Man to delight in smelling it?
Moreover, did He not so distinguish colors
2045 As to make some more lovely than others?
Did He not impart a loveliness to gold,
Silver, ivory, marble, to make them
More precious and noble than
The other metals and stones?
2050 Finally, has He not given us
Many things that we should prize
Apart from the fact that they
Are necessary for us?

Away then with that inhuman philosophy
2055 That concedes to man only the necessary use
Of God's creation; for this not only senselessly
Deprives us of the lawful fruits

Of God's kindness, but also cannot stand
Without despoiling man of feeling,
2060 Leaving him a block of wood!
On the other side, we must
No less diligently resist the lust
Of our flesh that, if not bridled,
Goes wild.
2065 Moreover, some of these men there are
(As I have said) who under pretext
Of freedom concede everything to flesh.
First, therefore, is it bridled by this rule:
All goods we have were created for us
2070 So we might in them recognize
The Author and magnify His kindness
With thanksgiving.

But where is your thanksgiving
If by gluttony you so gorge yourself
2075 With wine and food that you become
Stupid and are rendered useless
To serve God and the duties of your calling?
Where is your recognition of God
If the flesh, aroused by too great abundance
2080 To vile lust, with its filth
Infects the mind to the point
Of blinding and depriving it
Of its discretion between good and evil?
How can we thank God for the clothing we wear
2085 If it is so luxurious as to make us
Puffed up and scornful of others,
If it so glitters as to become for us
An instrument to adultery?
How, I say, will we recognize our God
2090 If our eyes are fixed to contemplate
The magnificence of our attire?
One can say the same of all other matters.
It therefore appears that leave
To abuse the gifts of God

2095 Is by this consideration somewhat restrained.

Aspiration to Eternal Life

Nor surer, shorter way there is
Than when a man is led
To despise the present life
And meditate upon heavenly immortality.
2100 From this derive two rules:
The first rule is that
Those who use this world
Must have as little affection for it
As though they used it not;
2105 Those who marry,
As if they did not marry;
Those who buy,
As if they did not buy—
According to St. Paul's rule.
2110 The second rule is that
We learn equally
To bear poverty with patient, peaceful hearts,
And to use affluence with moderation.
He who bids us use this world
2115 As if we used it not,
Not only suppresses all intemperance in eating, drinking,
All delights, too great ambition, pride,
Overfastidiousness in buildings, clothing, style of life;
But also corrects all care and inclination
2120 That divert or hinder us
From thinking on the heavenly life
And from decking our soul with its true ornaments.
Long ago Cato truly said:
"Where there is great care for dress,
2125 There is great neglect of virtue."
Also the old proverb bears it out
That those who are much occupied
With pampering and decking out their bodies
Do not take sufficient care of their souls.

2130 Therefore, although the freedom of the faithful
In outward matters must not be restricted
To fixed formulas, still it is subject to this law,
Namely, that they allow
Themselves as little as possible;
2135 On the other hand, that they be watchful
To cut back all superfluity
And vain show of affluence—
But not intemperately; and diligently
To guard against making hindrances
2140 Of the things that ought to help them.

The other rule will be that those
Who are in poverty learn in patience
To go without the things they lack,
Lest they be troubled with too much concern for these.
2145 Those able to observe this moderation
Have profited no little
In the Lord's school.
On the other hand, he who has not profited
In this regard can scarcely have
2150 Anything to prove himself a disciple of Christ.
For beside the fact that several other vices
Follow the desire of earthly things,
It almost always happens that he
Who bears poverty impatiently,
2155 In affluence betrays an opposite vice.
By this I mean that he who is ashamed
Of mean clothing will boast of costly;
He who, not content with a slender meal,
Troubles himself with the desire of a better,
2160 Cannot control himself when well supplied;
He who cannot keep himself in low, deprived condition
But is troubled and vexed by it,
Cannot, if any honors come his way,
Refrain from pride and arrogance.
2165 Therefore, all those who wish
To serve the Lord unflaggingly

Must study, by the apostle's example, "to learn
How to bear affluence and need":
This is to control oneself in affluence
2170 And have real patience in poverty.

Stewardship of Earthly Goods

Scripture has yet a third rule
To control the use of earthly things:
This we briefly treated
In dealing with the precepts of love.
2175 For it shows that all things
Have out of God's kindness so been given,
So destined for our benefit,
That they are, as it were, on deposit,
And we one day will have
2180 To render account of them.
We must therefore so manage them
That in mind we always have this statement:
We have to render account of all
Our Lord has entrusted to us.
2185 Moreover, we have to consider who it is
That calls us to account.
It is God, who, as He has commended abstinence,
Sobriety, temperance, and modesty,
Also abominates all intemperance,
2190 Pride, show, and vanity;
Who approves no management of our goods
Except one ruled by love;
Who with His mouth has condemned
Every delight that diverts man's heart
2195 From charity and purity
Or stupefies his mind.

The Lord's Calling and Earthly Life

Also with care we must observe that God
Bids each of us look to his calling
In all actions of his life.

2200 For He knows how man's understanding
Burns with restlessness,
With what fickleness
Is borne hither and yon,
With what ambition and greed
2205 Is set on embracing all at once
Several different things.
Therefore, lest through our folly and rashness
We stir up everything,
He has distinguished levels and styles of life,
2210 Ordaining for each man what he is to do.
And in order that no one may thoughtlessly
Transgress his limits, He has named
Such styles of life, "callings."
Each man therefore ought to consider his position
2215 As a sort of sentry post to which
God has assigned him,
So that he may not flit about
And wander here and there
Heedlessly throughout his life.
2220 But so necessary is this distinction
That all our works are judged before God by it,
And often otherwise than human reason
Or philosophy would judge them.
Not only the common folk but the philosophers as well
2225 Consider as the noblest and most excellent act
That man can do, to deliver
One's country from tyranny.
Yet a private citizen who lays his hand
Upon a tyrant is openly condemned
2230 By the voice of God.
However, I do not wish to stop to recount
All the examples one could bring forward.

Enough it is for us to know
That God's calling is for us
2235 Beginning and foundation of our right management of
    all things,

And that he who does not direct himself to it
Will never hold the right path
Duly to discharge his duties.
He can even do some deed
2240 Praiseworthy in outward appearance,
Yet will it not be accepted
At the throne of God,
However esteemed before men.
Moreover, if for us our calling
2245 Is not a perpetual rule,
There will be no harmony
Among the parts of our life;
While for him who directs his life
To that end, it will be well ordered indeed.
2250 From this to us will come
A singular consolation:
No work there is so vile or base
That will not shine before God,
Not be very precious in His sight,
2255 Provided in it we are serving our calling.

Notes

Note: "On the Christian Life," originally chapter 17 of the 1539 edition of the *Institutes,* was probably written in the spring of 1539 after Calvin returned to Strasbourg (he had accompanied Bucer to Frankfurt). Pannier, 4:348 (note). The first French edition of the *Institutes* in which it was included was that of 1541. Badius printed it separately at Geneva in 1545 (reprinting it in 1551) under the title *A Very Excellent Treatise on the Christian Life.* For an excellent modern study that utilizes material from both Calvin's commentaries and his sermons, see Ronald S. Wallace, *Calvin's Doctrine of the Christian Life* (Grand Rapids: Eerdmans, 1959).

6. The Vautrollier edition of the *Institutio,* published in London in 1576, lists at this point Basil the Great, Cyprian, Chrysostom, Ambrose, and other authors of such treatises.

18. Calvin was aware of the value of the homilies of the ancient fathers of the church. He himself at one time projected a French translation of the *Homilies* of John Chrysostom, intended both as a source of edification for the laity and as an exegetical guide for the clergy, many of whom were deficient in both Greek and Latin. The Latin text of Calvin's preface to Chrysostom's *Homilies* is in OC, 9:831–38. An English translation is in J. H. McIndoe, "Preface to the Homilies of Chrysostom," *Hartford Quarterly* 5 (1965): 19–26.

34. Calvin's rejection of the ancient philosophers as moral guides in favor of the Christian faith, clearly expressed in the *Institution* of 1536, becomes even more explicit in the final chapter ("On the Christian Life") of the 1539 edition. What he retained of their teaching is as significant as what he set aside. His use of Stoic teaching, for example, was already tempered by Cicero and Augustine when he wrote the *Commentary on Seneca's "De Clementia,"* but his thorough Christian reworking of Stoicism came, at his conversion, as a gradual growth. Cf. line 896 (note) below and the references to the philosophers scattered through this chapter (see lines 167, 347, 406, and 1428ff.).

For a summary of Calvin's study in his youthful classical period of pagan moralists, see *Commentary on Seneca's "De Clementia,"* ed. and trans. Ford Lewis Battles and André Malan Hugo (Leiden: Brill, 1969), pp. 3–4 (various views of ultimate happiness among Greek and Latin philosophers), 41 (the interconnection of the virtues, from Cicero and Seneca), and 149ff. (efforts to define clemency, rejecting the Stoic notion of the passionless wise man). Cf. lines 1309ff. below.

38ff. *Commentary on "De Clementia,"* p. 3, line 36.

53. By "nature" (*natura*) Calvin here meant "fallen nature."

64. Lev. 19:2; I Peter 1:15f.

68. Cf. *Institutes* 1.5.12.

95. Cf. Ps. 116:19; 122:2–9.

105. II Cor. 5:18.

107. Cf. Heb. 1:3.

115. Cicero, *On Duties* 3.3.13; *The Limits of Good and Evil* 2.11.34; 3.7.26; 4.15.41; Seneca, *Dialogues* 7: *On the Happy Life* 8.2.

141. Mal. 1:6; Eph. 5:1; I John 3:1.

146. Eph. 5:26; Heb. 10:10; I Cor. 6:11; I Peter 1:15, 19.

150. Eph. 5:23–33; I Cor. 6:15; John 15:3–6.

153. Col. 3:1ff.

158. I Cor. 3:16; 6:19; II Cor. 6:16.

161. I Peter 5:4.

163. I Thess. 5:23; cf. Phil. 1:10.

169. Cf. Cicero, *Tusculan Disputations* 5.15.45; *Limits* 2.21.68; 2.23.76; Seneca, *Epistles* 84.13.

171ff. The emphasis upon the inward disposition of the Christian calls to mind the *Institutes* 3.3.16; 3.4.10. Calvin's battle with nominal evangelical Christianity (Nicodemitism) is the theme of several of his tracts, notably *Excuse to the Nicodemites* (1544), found in OC, 6:589–614. See the introduction, note 63 above.

184. Eph. 4:22, 24.

190. Cf. chap. 4, line 555 below.

212. Cf. Seneca, *Epistles* 48; 108.23.

227. See line 275 (note) below.

247. Gen. 17:1; Ps. 41:12; etc.

249. *Cor duplex.* Cf. James 1:8; 4:8; Ps. 12:2; 1 Chron. 12:33; Ecclus. 1:36; 2:14 (Vulgate). Calvin commented on this in *Commentary on the Psalms* (on Ps. 12:3), in OC, 31:127; and in *Commentary on James* (on James 1:8 and 4:8), in OC, 55:387, 418.

251. Cf. line 1759 below.

275. The notion of life-time growth in the Christian life, with which Calvin (as well as Luther and Melanchthon) countered the perfectionism of the Anabaptists, is already stressed in the *Institution* of 1536. See edition trans. and an. Ford Lewis Battles (Atlanta: John Knox, 1975), pp. 367 (note on p. 133, line 11), 375 (notes on p. 152, lines 30 and 33), 420 (note on p. 266, line 12). Benoît has supplied additional references to this theme from other writings of Calvin. 3:164. The Reformers who espoused this view found rich materials in Augustine; he had already enunciated Christian growth in response to the claims of the Donatists. Also cf. *Institutes* 3.3.9.

281ff. Cf. chap. 2, lines 125–323 above. Wallace saw the Christological pattern worked out in the heart (denying self) and in the outward life (bearing the cross). *The Christian Life*, p. vi. Also one sees in the organization of lines 281–905 of this chapter the familiar, twofold Calvinian division between God and man, seen also in his analysis of the Decalogue and the Lord's Prayer: lines 281–433, self-denial and God; lines 434–712, self-denial and fellow man; lines 713–905, self-denial and God. On this scheme as applied to the Lord's Prayer, see chap. 4, lines 875ff. (first

three petitions–to God), 1040ff. (second three petitions–to God, through fellow man).

291. Rom. 12:1.

305. Cf. I Cor. 6:19.

310–26. Note the hymnic character of these lines, reflected in their intricate, interlocking structure. See chapter 7 below for a discussion of the "prose-poems" scattered through Calvin's writings. As laid out in our text, this passage has the form ABC/CAB. For a careful rhetorical analysis of Calvin's style, see Antoon Veerman, *De stijl van Calvijn in de "Institutio christianae religionis"* (Utrecht: Kemink, 1943). Veerman did not, however, note the hymn fragments found in the *Institutes*. Of the present lines Pannier commented: "Here is one of those harmonious periods, with well-balanced antitheses, which make Calvin–as A. Lefranc has said–'the master of modern French style.'" 4:349.

326. Rom. 14:8; cf. I Cor. 6:19.

345ff. Note the trinitarian character of this transformation: God the Father is the source and goal of the Christian life; Christ the Son is the pattern, assimilated within the believer, through the Holy Spirit.

346. Eph. 4:23.

354. The Erasmian phrase "the Christian philosophy" is the subject of a full note in McNeill-Battles, 20:6f. (referring to its use in "Subject Matter of the Present Work" from the 1560 French edition of the *Institutes*). It was first used in a work associated with Calvin in Nicholas Cop's rectorial address (ET in Calvin, *Institution*, trans. and an. Ford Lewis Battles, pp. 468f.). See also chap. 4, lines 20–24 below.

360. Gal. 2:20.

387. The Latin text has *"primo tyrocinio"*; the French, *"leur premier apprentissage."* Cf. *Institutes* 4.4.9: *"militiae tyrones. . . . haec tyronum rudimenta. . . ."* Cf. Charles A. M. Hall, *With the Spirit's Sword: The Drama of Spiritual Warfare in the Theology of John Calvin* (Richmond: John Knox, 1968). Hall examined at great length Calvin's use of the military analogy. The Latin version here more clearly hints at the initial training of the army recruit than does the French, although even in classical Latinity, *tirocinium* can have the more general meaning of "the first attempt" or even of "inexperience."

389. Cf. Matt. 16:24.

393. Cf. II Tim. 3:2–5.

408. Compare Calvin's discussion of virtue as the chief end of life in *Commentary on "De Clementia,"* pp. 24f. Also see Cicero, *Limits* 3.11.36; *Laws* 1.14–40; Seneca, *Dialogues 7: On the Happy Life; 9: On Peace of Mind* (chap. 4).

419. Matt. 21:31.

424ff. The French text has *"qu'il y a un monde de vices caché en l'âme de l'homme;* the Latin, *"mundum vitiorum esse reconditum in hominis anima."* This is possibly from Seneca: "Be assured . . . that there are as many vices as there are men" (*De ira* 2.8.1); "All vices exist in all, yet all are not prominent in each individual" (*On Benefits* 4.27.2f.). Calvin quoted these in *Commentary on "De Clementia,"* pp. 128f.

439. Phil. 2:3.

440. Rom. 12:10.

444ff. *Commentary on "De Clementia,"* p. 29, lines 15f.

535. I Cor. 13:4f.

557. Cf. I Peter 4:10.

558. In these lines are doubtless reflected Calvin's Strasbourg lectures on Corinthians, delivered in May 1539 after his return from Frankfurt. Pannier, 4:350; Beza, *Vita Calvini*, in OC, 21:248.36–41.

561. I Cor. 12:12ff.

589. Exod. 23:19; cf. 22:29 (Vulgate).

600. Ps. 16:2f.

601. Gal. 6:9.

605. I Cor. 13:4f.

606. Heb. 13:16.

614. Gal. 4:10.

640. Matt. 6:14; 18:35; Luke 17:3.

651. Matt. 5:44.

659. Compare Calvin's "interiorization" of the Decalogue in the *Institutes* 2.8.13–50, e.g., in sections 39–40 concerning the sixth commandment.

674. Calvin commented on the phrase "fling insultingly their alms": "Let the men of our times take heed of this, very many of whom are far, far away from this gentleness of the pagan philosophers: if at any time such persons come to give alms to a poor man, then as if it were beneath their dignity to hand it to him,

they fling it down by way of insult." *Commentary on "De Clementia,"* pp. 372f. Also see *On the Harmony of the Gospels,* sermon 63 (in OC, 46:792). Cf. lines 1860ff. below.

678. Cf. II Cor. 9:7.

699. Cf. Calvin's comments on Seneca's phrase "begotten for the common good" and similar passages from Lucan, Quintilian, and Juvenal. *Commentary on "De Clementia,"* pp. 84f.

823. Pannier noted that "at the end of March 1539–before composing this chapter, perhaps–Calvin wrote: 'I am in the situation of not being able to pay a farthing. I must accordingly live on what I have if I do not wish to become a charge of my brothers.' In April he wrote to Farel: 'I have decided not to use your generosity nor that of other friends, unless forced to do so by the greatest need. . . . For the future, the Lord will provide.' " 4:351; cf. OC, 106:339. On Calvin's modest circumstances, cf. chap. 1, lines 654ff. above.

862ff. One is here reminded of the experience of Job. Cf. *Institutes* 1.1.3.

876. Cf. Ps. 78:47.

878. Ps. 79:13.

896. See Calvin's rejection of fortune, chance, and fate (Stoicism) in the *Institutes* 1.16.8 (1539, 1543, and 1559). Cf. lines 1473ff. below.

900. Cf. Seneca, *Dialogues 1: On Providence* (chap. 5); *Epistles* 76:23; 107:7f.

906. Cf. lines 281ff. (note) above. For the corporate aspect of bearing the cross, see "The Church as Pilgrim" in the epilogue below. On Calvin's liturgical use of this theme, see chap. 5, lines 180ff. below.

908. Matt. 16:24.

918. Matt. 3:17; 17:5.

923. Compare Calvin's picture of the patriarchs' sufferings in the *Institutes* 2.10 (paralleling Heb. 11).

932. Rom. 8:29.

937f. This is an allusion to the descent into hell. Cf. *Institutes* 2.16.8.

940. Acts 14:22.

944. Phil. 3:10f.

950. In his note on this passage, Benoît commented: "Suffering

has no value in itself, but it draws us to Christ and deepens our communion with Him." In support of this, Benoît quoted Calvin's comment on Matthew 16:24 in *On the Harmony of the Gospels.* On the imitation of Christ, see the *Institutes* 4.2.3; 4.12.20; 4.17.40; 4.19.29.

975ff. God's method of dealing with His children, using affliction to bring us ultimately to Him, is here described by Calvin in Pauline terms in "six movements": (1) He afflicts; (2) we succumb; (3) we learn to call upon His power; (4) still we tend to lapse; (5) God therefore sends new afflictions; (6) at last all is resolved.

983. Benoît here cited Calvin's statement that "our Lord has to cleanse His believers and His children, thus taking away occasion for relying on their own prudence; and they must find themselves in such perplexities and anxieties that they can only learn to have recourse to Him." *On the Harmony of the Gospels,* sermon 21; in OC, 46:253.

1001. Benoît here cited two of Calvin's letters of spiritual counsel—one to Madame de Pons (OC, 14:669) and one to Madame de Seninghen (OC, 20:140)—noting the direct application Calvin had made of these principles to his correspondents. 3:179 (note 3).

1004. Rom. 5:3f.; cf. Vulgate.

1064. Gen. 22:1, 12.

1067. I Peter 1:7.

1075. "To stir" follows the Latin, *excitandis,* rather than the mistranslation in the French version, *exercitare* ("to exercise"). Benoît, 3:180 (note 5).

1092. Seneca, *Dialogues* 7: *On the Happy Life* 15.5; *Epistles* 16.5.

1118. Deut. 32:15.

1127f. For a summary of Calvin's use of medical analogies and his attitude toward medicine, see *Commentary on "De Clementia,"* pp. 66f. (notes 22–24). See also Ford Lewis Battles, "God Was Accommodating Himself to Human Capacity," *Interpretation* 31 (1977): 30f.

1134. Benoît here cited Calvin's letters to Pericel (OC, 12:636) and Admiral de Coligny (OC, 17:322). 3:182 (note 1).

1164. I Cor. 11:32.

1177. Prov. 3:11f.

1180. On teachableness compare Calvin's account of his own conversion in chapter 1, line 258 above.

1188. Heb. 12:8.

1202. Calvin elaborated on the distinction between the judgment of vengeance and the judgment of chastisement in the *Institutes* 1.17.8; 3.4.31–35.

1205. Cf. Matt. 5:10. The following lines reflect the teaching of the Beatitudes (Matt. 5:3–12).

1224. Matt. 5:10.

1239. Acts 5:41.

1240–54. Another short passage of hymnic form; cf. lines 310–26 above and pp. 167f. below.

1258. A proverb; cf. line 1609 below.

1267. I Peter 4:12ff.

1306. II Cor. 4:8f.

1309ff. Calvin's first comment on the Stoic ideal—passionlessness and serenity—was noncommittal: "Whether it is true that no emotions may touch the wise man at all is not part of our present purpose to discuss." *Commentary on "De Clementia,"* pp. 368f. (note 14). See also "Introduction," *Commentary on "De Clementia,"* pp. 50*–53*. But in these lines of Calvin's treatise on the Christian life and in other passages of his later writings, Calvin followed Augustine in rejecting this aspect of Stoic teaching.

1330ff. On the reality of Christ's own pain, see John Chrysostom, *Homilies on Matthew* 83(84).1 (in PG, 58:745f.). Benoît cited Calvin's *Homilies on I Samuel* (in OC, 30:670) and *Sermons on Job* (in OC, 33:93). 3:186 (note 9).

1339. John 16:20.

1341. Matt. 5:4.

1345. Luke 22:44; cf. *Institutes* 2.16.

1348. Matt. 26:37; Mark 14:33.

1351. Matt. 26:38.

1381ff. John 21:18.

1440. Cf. Seneca, *On Providence* 5.8.

1457. On providence compare the *Institutes* 1.16f.

1459. Benoît here commented: "On his deathbed Calvin expressed the assurance that his sufferings were expressly willed by

God." 3:187 (note 3). Benoît then quoted Beza: "From that point in his illness even to his death he was in continual prayer, despite his continual pain, with the words of Psalm 39 often on his lips: 'I have kept silent, O Lord, for thou hast done it.' At another time he quoted Isaiah 38:14: 'I have mourned like a dove.' On another occasion in speaking to me he cried out: 'Lord, thou crushest me, but it is enough that it is thy hand.' " *Vita Calvini,* in OC, 21:44.28–37.

1473ff. "The cold song of the philosophers" refers to the Stoic doctrine of fate, which Calvin explicitly rejected in the *Institutes* 1.16.8. Cf. line 896 (note) above.

1495ff. This dynamic tension between bitterness and sweetness is detailed in the *Institutes* 3.2.16ff., where Calvin cited Bernard of Clairvaux on the subject of the struggle between faith and fear in the life of the believer.

1505. Benoît cited other passages from Calvin's writings that express spiritual joy: *Commentary on I Thessalonians* (on 5:16); *Commentary on the Psalms* (on 32:11); *Homilies on I Samuel* (in OC, 29:286); *Commentary on the Psalms* (on 22:30); and a letter to Admiral de Coligny (in OC, 17:322).

1583. Compare Job 7:1, the chief traditional proof text for the warfare analogy as applied to human life. See line 387 (note) above. At this point Benoît cited a number of Calvin's letters that describe human life as a combat and Christians as soldiers. 3:190 (note 3).

1609. Ps. 102:11, 3.

1641. Plato, *Laws* 11.923.

1662. Cf. *Institutes* 3.25.2. Here Benoît cites similar teaching in several of Calvin's letters (in OC, 17:460; 18:732; 15:413). 3:191 (note 8). In these lines, with superb balance, Calvin anticipated the argument of lines 1953ff.: Our contempt for the present life (a gift of God's goodness to us) should not lead us to a hatred of it or ungratefulness toward Him; rather, hope of the future life should feed our present life and give it meaning and purpose.

1727. Cf. Eccles. 4:2f. Cicero related that Silenus, when captured by Midas, told the latter: "For man it were best never to be born; and the next best thing would be to die as soon as possible." *Tusculan Disputations* 1.48.114f.

1732. The French text here has *"le peuple des Scythes";* the Latin, only *"illi."*

1734. Cicero quoted from Euripides' *Cresphontes* that sorrow is the appropriate feeling of a family when a child is born, but that joy and happiness are the appropriate feelings when friends carry one to his last resting place.

1759. Plato, *Phaedo* 64A; Cicero, *Tusculan Disputations* 1.49.118.

1764. II Cor. 5:6.

1777. See line 2215 (note) below.

1784. Rom. 7:24.

1786. Phil. 1:23f.

1789. Rom. 14:8.

1794. Here Calvin eloquently rejected suicide.

1812f. On the separation of body and soul at death and the continued disembodied existence of the soul until the general resurrection, see Calvin's first theological work, *Psychopannychia,* which was directed against the French Anabaptist doctrine of soul-sleep or soul-death.

1833. Benoît cited Calvin's comments on II Corinthians 5:8 in his *Commentary on II Corinthians:* "It is a sign of unfaithfulness when in us dread of death lords it over joy and comfort and hope." Benoît also cited Calvin's letter to M. de Richebourg (in OC, 11:191, 193), who had lost his son. 3:194 (note 3).

1834. Compare Thomas Aquinas's statement, "Each substance craves, according to its own nature, the conservation of itself." *Summa Theologica,* 1.2.94.2.

1844f. Rom. 8:19.

1858. Cyprian, *On the Mortality* 3.1.

1860ff. In his contrasting of philosophers and Christians in "On the Christian Life," Calvin frequently had recourse to the *argumentum a minore:* "If even the philosophers do thus and so, how much more ought Christians . . ." Cf. lines 673ff. above.

1868. Titus 2:13; cf. II Tim. 4:8.

1873. Luke 21:28. Calvin said in his *Sermons on the Passion:* "Even in the midst of death we can come before God with lifted head. . . ." In OC, 46:842; cited in Benoît, 3:195 (note 3).

1891f. Augustine said: ". . . the saints are in this life blessed in hope." *City of God* 10.20; ET in *Nicene and Post-Nicene Fathers,* 2:414.

1892. Rom. 8:36. Benoît cited the following comments of Calvin: "The chief point is that God wills us to be conformed to the image of His Son, as it is right that there be conformity between the head and the body" (*To the Faithful of France,* in OC, 17:685); "To sum up, since the Lord Jesus is the head (*patron*) to whom it befits us to be conformed, see to it that you entirely look to Him" (*To a Persecuted Church,* in OC, 16:113). 3.195 (note 6).

1894. Cf. Rom. 8:29.

1899. Cf. I Cor. 15:19.

1917. Rev. 7:17; Isa. 25:8.

1919. Ecclus. 6:31.

1930. Cf. Isa. 66:24; Matt. 25:41; Mark 9:43, 46; Rev. 21:8. For spiritualization of these corporeal images, see the *Institutes* 3.25.12.

1932. This is reminiscent of the classic description in the final chapter of Tertullian, *On the Shows (De spectaculis).*

1942. Ps. 73:2f.

1946. Ps. 73:17.

1973. Lev. 25:23; I Cor. 29:15; Ps. 39:13; 119:19; Heb. 11:8–10, 13–16; 13:14; I Peter 2:11.

1984. On this ascetic view, see the *Institutes,* McNeill-Battles, 20:720 (note 2), where Augustine is cited.

1992. Here Calvin doubtless had in mind the Libertines and possibly also the Anabaptists. Against this extreme view he had already written his essay on Christian freedom, which constituted the first part of chapter 6 in the *Institution* (1536). Calvin elaborated on the mean between asceticism and Libertinism in its practical detail in *De Luxu,* to which reference is made at lines 2008ff. below.

2008ff. See *De Luxu* in OC, 10a:203–6. An annotated English translation of this small but significant work on frugality and sumptuary legislation in Geneva is Ford Lewis Battles, "Against Luxury and License in Geneva," *Interpretation* 19 (1965): 181–202. Cf. lines 2123ff. (note) below. Calvin elaborated on God's twofold intent for man in creation–for our need and for our delight–in *Commentary on Genesis.*

2025. Gen. 2:9.

2029f. Ps. 104:15.

2053. Benoît quoted the following passages at this point: "It is said in Psalm 104[:14] that not only has God given to men bread and water for the necessity of their life, but that he adds as well wine to comfort and gladden them. When we see that God out of

superabundance gives us beyond the exact necessity more than we need–well, then, let us enjoy His bounty and recognize that He allows us to use it in good conscience, with thanksgiving." (*Sermons on Deuteronomy,* in OC, 28:36). "Wine has been given not only to strengthen the heart of man, but to give him joy" (*Homilies on I Samuel,* in OC, 30:565). "I am not so austere as to condemn princes' festivals, nor the celebration accompanying their marriages" (letter to the Duc de Longueville, in OC, 17:532f.). Benoît commented: "Indeed Calvin was no ascetic." 3:199 (note 1).

2072. Benoît quoted Calvin's comment on Psalm 30:1 in *Commentary on the Psalms:* "There is nothing whose use would be pure and lawful without thanksgiving." 3:199 (note 3).

2108. I Cor. 7:29–31.

2109ff. Calvin claimed a similar frugality in his own life. See chap. 1, lines 660ff. above.

2123. Ammianus Marcellinus attributed this saying to Cato. *De rebus gestis* 16.5.2. Calvin commented: "Truer than I should like is that saying of the ancients that those who labor so much in developing the body are little concerned with the cultivation of the soul." *De Luxu,* in OC, 10a:204.

2133ff. The three rules Calvin derived from Scripture, and particularly the third, can serve as a sound basis for a Christian ecology and also will give the lie to the senseless affluence that marks so much of our life today.

2167. Phil. 4:12.

2184. Luke 16:2.

2197. Calvin wrote: "Quite rightly, then, Plato . . . makes God a sort of commander of the human race, assigning to each his station and military rank." *Commentary on "De Clementia,"* p. 6. See also line 2215 below, where the frequent "sentry post" image is used.

2215. Plato quoted Socrates as saying: "Wherever a man stations himself thinking it is best to be there, or is stationed by his commander, there he must, as it seems to me, remain and run his risks, considering neither death nor any other thing more than disgrace." *Apology* 28E. This analogy, found in Plato, Cicero, and Persius, was widely used by Calvin. See line 1777 above; *Institutes* 3.25.1. In commenting on Acts 13:36, Calvin wrote: "Plato learnedly teaches that it is fitting that only by God's decision do men depart from earth, by Whose hand they have for a time been placed, as at a sentry post." *Commentary on Acts,* in

OC, 48:304. In a sermon on II Samuel 17:23 Calvin said. "Here is a statement well worthy of noting: that this life is as if each human being were assigned to his watch, when God puts us here below. And who is the author of this saying? A poor pagan [Plato, in *Apology* 28C and *Phaedo* 62B]." SC, 1:513.33ff. On the military analogy in general, see lines 387 (note) and 1583 (note) above.

2225. I Sam. 24:7, 11; 26:9; cf. *Institutes* 4.20.25–30; Seneca, *On Benefits* 7.15.2; 20.3.

2228. Calvin spelled out the distinction between the public and private man in the *Institutes* 4.20.31.

2255. Here Calvin summed up his doctrine of calling, or in other words, of the "priesthood of all believers." Wallace said of this: ". . . the 'priesthood of all believers' in Calvin's teaching is not a doctrine which exalts the individual in his liberty before God apart from the Church. Rather it involves participating in and with the Church in the royal priesthood of the whole body." *The Christian Life*, p. vii.

Chapter 4

Calvin on Prayer

How bereft of every good,
How lacking help to save him,
Is man!
Where then can he go for help?
5 Only to some source outside himself.
Clearly we have seen this,
And in Christ we know
God freely reveals Himself.
Happiness for misery,
10 Wealth for poverty
He offers us in Christ,
Opens in Him the treasure-house
Of heaven.
Thus may our whole faith
15 Contemplate His beloved Son,
Our whole expectation
Wait upon Him,
Our whole hope cleave to Him,
Rest in Him.
20 No logic-bound philosophy, this—
Secret and hidden to all—
But those whose eyes,

God-opened, see it,
Learn it by heart.

25 Faith-taught to seek and find
Our every need
In God and in Jesus Christ our Lord,
In whom the Father willed
His whole bounty to abide,
30 Let us then seek in Him,
The overflowing spring,
Let us in prayer ask of Him,
What He has taught us
Is in Him alone.
35 Point out to a man a treasure
Hidden in the earth, yet he
Heeds not your finger:
Thus would it be for us,
Knowing God as master
40 And bestower of all,
And still not go to Him,
Still not ask of Him,
The good in His hand to give.

The Rules of Prayer

What then is the first rule
45 Of right prayer?
Leave behind all thought
Of our own glory,
Cast aside all notion
Of our own worth,
50 Put away all self-assurance,
Humbly giving glory to the Lord.
The prophet teaches this:
"Not on the ground of our own righteousness,
But on the ground of Thy great mercy,
55 We pour out our prayers to Thee.

Hear us, O Lord,
Kindly treat us;
Hear us, do what we ask,
For Thine own sake,
60 For over Thy people
And over Thy holy place
Is Thy name called upon."
Another prophet teaches:
"A soul sorrowful, desolate
65 In her great evil, feeble, bowed-down,
A soul hungering, her eyes failing,
Gives glory to Thee, O Lord.
Not on the strength of our father's righteousness
Do we pour out prayers to Thee,
70 Beg mercy in Thy sight,
O Lord our God.
No—because Thou art merciful,
Be Thou merciful unto us,
For before Thee we have sinned."

75 Our second rule of prayer is this:
Sense our insufficiency we must,
Earnestly ponder we must how much
We need the very things we seek
From God; let us then seek them
80 That we may attain them from Him.
For with a mind differently intending,
Feigned and foul our prayer would be.
Ask God for forgiveness of sins
Without knowing yourself
85 The sinner you truly are—
What is this but mocking God
In your pretending?
Ardently, eagerly, ceaselessly
Seek only what belongs
90 To God's glory.
You pray, "Hallowed be Thy name":
Do this hungering and thirsting

After that hallowing of God.
Pressed, belabored under the weight of sins,
95 Bereft of anything pleasing to God,
Let us not be terror-struck;
Rather let us betake ourselves to Him:
Approach Him we cannot
Unless we ponder and feel
100 Our misery.

God did not set forth prayer
Haughtily to puff us up before Him
Or greatly to value our own things.
Prayer is for us to confess, weep for
105 Our tragic state.
As children unburden their troubles
To their parents,
So it is with us before God.
This sense of sin spurs, goads,
110 Arouses us to pray.

We know our need to pray,
And yet our best of fathers
Gives us two things
To make us seek it more intently:
115 Command and promise.
Pray, and what you ask
You will receive.
Seek, come to me, ask me,
Turn back to me,
120 In day of need call on me.
Take not in vain
The name of the Lord.
Thus forbidden, we are bidden
To hold our God in glory,
125 To lay to His credit
All virtue, good, help, protection
As we ask of Him
These very blessings.

Unless when pressed by need
130 We flee to Him,
Unless we seek Him,
Beg His help—
We draw His anger just as much
As those who fashion foreign gods
135 Or idols.
When we despise all His commands,
We are despising His will.
But those who call upon Him,
Seek Him, and give Him praise—
140 Theirs is great joy and consolation,
For they know thus they render
Something acceptable to Him
And serve His will.

What is His promise?
145 Seek and you will receive,
It will be done for you,
I'll answer you, rescue you, refresh you,
Comfort, feed you abundantly;
You will not be confounded.
150 Surely all these, promised by God,
Will be fulfilled
If in staunch faith
We wait for them.
Prayer itself has no worth
155 To merit what it asks:
On these promises alone
Rests, depends the whole hope
Of prayer.
As Peter or Paul
160 Or any other saint
(Though outfitted with greater holiness
Of life than we)
Was answered when he prayed,
So in our heart of hearts
165 We too must resolve

93

Our prayer will be heard—
Provided in the same staunch faith
We call on God.
Equipped, armed
170 With the same command to pray,
With the same promise our prayer
Will be answered,
We know God weighs our prayer
Not by our worth
175 But by faith alone.
For in faith alone
We obey God's commandment
And trust His promise.

How goes it with those unsure
180 Of God's promise,
Who call His truth into question,
Doubt, hesitate over
Whether an answer will come?
Invoking God (as James says),
185 They get nothing.
They are waves wind-tossed.
Apart from faith
Nothing can happen to us,
For to each according to his faith
190 Is given what he asks.

Intercession of Christ

No man is worthy to come
Into God's sight.
Barred thus from His presence
Our hearts would be cast into despair
195 Had not our heavenly Father Himself
Set us free by giving us
His Son, Jesus Christ our Lord,
As Advocate, Mediator with Him.

Guided by Christ,
200 Confidently we come to Him.
Christ being our Intercessor,
We trust that
Nothing we ask in His name
Will be denied us,
205 Even as nothing is denied Christ
By the Father.
God's throne,
Throne of majesty,
Is also throne of grace:
210 In His name confidently we dare
Appear, receive mercy, find grace
In timely help.

Ordained is the way to call upon God,
Given is the promise that those who call
215 Shall be heard:
Bidden particularly we now are
To call upon our heavenly Father
In the name of Christ;
Promised is it to us that
220 What we have asked for
In Christ's name
We shall obtain.
Crystal clear then it is
That if in another name than Christ's
225 Men call upon God,
Obstinately they flout His commands,
Count as naught His will.
Such have no promise of obtaining anything.
In Him, says Paul, all promises
230 Of God find
Their yea and amen,
Confirmed, fulfilled.

One way, one access to God
We have been granted:

235 Turn aside from this way,
Forsake His access—
No way, no access remains
To God.
In His throne is nothing left
240 But wrath, judgment, terror.
The Father has set His Son
To be our head, our leader:
If we lean away,
Turn aside from Him,
245 We are doing all we can
To destroy, disfigure
Our God-imprinted mark.

Intercession of Saints

Dream not that the blessed saints
Who have died and live in Christ
250 Have any other way to petition God
Than Christ, who is alone the Way,
Or are by God accepted
In any other name.
Scripture calls us back
255 From every other way
To Christ alone;
Our heavenly Father wills
All be gathered together
In Christ alone.
260 Why then try access
Through the saints to God
When they even for themselves
Such access cannot gain?

The will of God alone
265 The saints desire and contemplate,
In it abide.
Well, then, only a stupid dolt

Would attribute to them
Any prayer but prayer
270 That God's kingdom will come.
How will that kingdom be fulfilled?
In the saving of the godly,
In the confounding of the reprobate.
So whatever the praying saints can do,
275 Their kingdom-prayers
Will not help us
Unless we too belong to Christ,
Belong to His kingdom.
As partakers in Christ,
280 We know that whatever
Through our efforts stands
Is from God;
We know that as the whole church
(Wherein the saints are members)
285 Prays, "Thy kingdom come,"
It prays for us.

Thus the saints do pray for us,
But it is not our part
To call upon them.
290 Yet we who dwell on earth
Can commend one another in prayer,
Thus fostering love among ourselves,
While sharing, bearing
In our common need.
295 Such interceding prayer belongs not
To the dead, withdrawn by God
From our company.
Though ever growing is their love toward us—
Bound as they are to us
300 In the one faith in Christ—
Still speak with them we cannot
Or hear their voice.

To declare otherwise—

What is this but in fevered frenzy
305 To bypass God's Word
And break in upon His judgments,
Trample on Scripture?
The prudence of our flesh
Is God's wisdom's enemy;
310 Vain, vain are our minds.
The Scripture warns:
Lay low your reason,
Look to God's will alone.

And so Scripture offers
315 To us Christ alone,
To us sends Him,
Establishing us in Him.
Through Christ our mouth
We speak to the Father;
320 Through Christ our eye
We see the Father;
Through Christ our right hand
We offer ourselves to the Father;
Converse with God we and all saints cannot
325 Unless Christ intercedes for us.
So spoke the blessed Ambrose.

What insolence to the saints
For us to choose from them a patron,
For us to hope from them
330 Some special commendation!
If we do this, we drag the saints
Away from that one will,
A will they hold to be
Set and unmoved in God,
335 The will that God's kingdom come.
If we do this, we forge for the saints
Some physical affection
That makes them favor
One worshiper above another.

340 To make a saint our mediator
Is to say Christ failed us,
Was too severe for us.
Will you dishonor Christ,
Strip the name of Mediator from Him,
345 A name uniquely given by His Father,
A name that cannot be transferred
To another?
Will you obscure the glory of His birth,
Make nul and void His cross?
350 Strip, defraud of rightful praise
All He has done or suffered for our salvation?
Christ is alone and must be believed to be
The Mediator.
Will you cast out God's kindness,
355 The kindness of a Father?
God is not our Father
If we do not deem Christ our brother.
Will you deny this brother's love,
This gentlest love of all?

360 But you may answer:
Do we not read in Scripture
Of saints' prayers answered?
Of course: they prayed, were heard.
The prophet speaks:
365 "In Thee they trusted,
Were saved;
To Thee they cried,
Were not confounded."
Like them, we too must pray;
370 Like them, we too will be heard.
But some men say to us:
"Only those once heard by God
Will be heard again."
To this James speaks:
375 "Elijah, a man like us,
Prayed fervently

That rain should cease.
Three and one-half years
No rain fell upon the earth.
380 Once again he prayed:
The heavens gave rain
And the earth fruit."
In this Elijah had no special track to God.
Here Scripture teaches rather
385 The power of prayer,
That we too may pray
With equal fervor.

Components of Prayer

Prayer has two parts:
Petition and thanksgiving.
390 Petitioning, we lay before God
The desire of our hearts,
Thus seeking from His goodness
What serves His glory,
And then what is useful to us.
395 In giving thanks, we own
His benefits to us,
With praise confess them,
To His goodness alone
Attribute all our blessings.
400 David, speaking for God, says:
"In day of need, call on Me;
I will deliver you,
And you shall glorify Me."
Poor indeed we are,
405 Pressed on all sides
By great anxiety;
So even the holiest
Must ever groan and sigh to God,
Beseech Him suppliantly.
410 Well-nigh overwhelmed

Are we by the outpouring
Of God's great blessings,
By the many, mighty miracles
Discerned where'er we look.
415 How then can we fail to turn
In praise and thankfulness
To God?

All our hope and wealth
So reside in God
420 That neither we nor what we have
Can prosper unless
His blessing is ours.
This fact we know.
Then commit ourselves we must
425 Constantly, with all we have,
To Him.
All we plan or speak or do,
Let us plan, speak, do
Under His hand and will,
430 Hoping for His help.
All men confident in themselves
Or in another's help,
Who hatch and carry out their plans,
Who undertake or try to start anything
435 Apart from God's will,
Apart from calling upon Him—
Such persons are declared
Accursed by God.
Author of all blessings
440 God truly is;
Receive then we must
All from His hand
With continual thanksgiving.
Make proper use we cannot
445 Of His benefits streaming down to us
Unless we continually praise Him
And give Him thanks.

97

Paul tells us these benefits
Are hallowed by the word and prayer;
450 Without the word and prayer
They go unhallowed.
(And *word* means "faith.")
"Pray without ceasing," says Paul,
Meaning that all men
455 Should lift to God their desires
At all times,
In all places,
And in all situations;
Meaning too that all men
460 Are to expect all things from Him,
Give praise for all things to Him,
For to us God gives
Unfailing reasons to praise and pray.

Public and Private Prayer

Such constancy in prayer
465 Applies to private devotion,
But not to the public prayers
We offer in the church.
Such are not constant
And are to be given only
470 By the common consent of all.
Paul's words "decently and in order"
Mean that certain convenient hours
Are humanly agreed upon, appointed,
Accommodated to the need of all—
475 But not divinely set.
"Temples" we call the public places
Appointed for such rites.
No secret temple-sanctity makes
Prayers more holy or causes
480 Them to be heard by God.
A temple is but to accommodate

The believing congregation
As it gathers to pray,
To hear the Word preached,
485 To take the sacraments.
"True temples of God," says Paul,
"Are we." Do you wish to pray
In God's temple? Pray in yourself.
Like Jews and pagans are those
490 Who think God's ear comes closer
In a temple, or fancy their prayer
More holy by the holiness of the place.
Such physical worship goes against
The words of John: "Worship God
495 In spirit and in truth"—
Think not of place.
And so, because the goal of prayer
Is to arouse and bear our hearts
To God (praising or beseeching),
500 The essence of prayer is set
In mind and heart; or better said:
Prayer is an emotion of the heart within,
Poured out, laid bare before God,
Searcher of hearts.

505 Christ told us the best way to pray:
"In your bedroom, with door closed,
Pray in secret to your Father,
That He who is in secret
May hear you."
510 No prayer of hypocrites,
Vainly, showily grasping
After men's favor, is this
Call to secret prayer.
And so Christ bids us
515 Descend into our hearts
With our whole thought,
Promises us God will be near us
In the affection of our hearts,

Entempled in our bodies.

520 Pray you may in other places too,
But prayer is something secret,
Lodged chiefly in the heart,
Requiring tranquillity
Far from all teeming cares.

525 Voice and song interposed in prayer
Must spring from one's deepest heart.
To pray with the lips alone or from the throat
Is to abuse God's holy name,
Deride His majesty, and
530 Bring down His wrath.
In the prophet's words He speaks:
"With their mouth the people draw near to Me,
With their lips honor Me,
But far from Me are their hearts;
535 And it is by the command and teaching of men
That they have feared Me.
A marvelous miracle will I do
Among this people:
The wisdom of their wise shall perish;
540 The prudence of their elders shall vanish."

And so speaking and singing
Must be tied to the heart's affection,
Must serve it.
Shifty, slippery, inattentive
545 Is the mind toward thinking of God
Unless exercised by prayerful
Speech and song.
The glory of God ought to shine
In the various parts of our bodies,
550 And especially in the tongue,
Created to sing, speak forth,
Tell, proclaim
The praise of God.

And the tongue's chief task is,
555 In the public prayers offered
In the assembly of believers,
With one common voice,
With a single mouth,
To glorify God together,
560 To worship him together
In one spirit, one faith.
Openly, mutually we receive
Our brother's confession
And are in turn by his example
565 To give our own.

Not in Greek among Latins,
Not in Latin among French or English,
But in the daily language,
Understood by the whole assembly,
570 Are public prayers to be voiced.
Edify thus the whole church:
A sound not understood
Cannot benefit.
Not moved to this by love?
575 Let Paul then tell you clearly:
"How can the unlearned say amen
To your blessing by the spirit
If he is ignorant
Of what you are saying?
580 Unedified is he
By your giving thanks."

Private or public—
Tongue-prayers without the mind
Are not heard by God.
585 In fact the force and ardor
Of the mind must outstrip
Whatever the tongue in speaking
Can express.
One final word:

590 In private prayer
No tongue is needed,
For inner feeling will suffice
To rouse us to the best,
The silent prayer,
595 As Moses and Hannah knew.

The Form of Prayer

Now to the very form of prayer itself we turn:
What our heavenly Father has
Through His beloved Son
Taught us, in which to own
600 His boundless, kindly goodness.
As children fly to the protection
Of their parents,
He bids us, urges us
To seek in Him our every need.
605 Ignorant, too, He saw us
In our dire poverty
Of what was fair and profitable
To request of Him.
From His own wealth
610 He provided for our ignorance,
Supplied our lack.
In a table, as it were,
He composed, set forth for us
What we may ask of Him,
615 What benefits us,
What we need ask of Him.
Great consolation to us this provides:
Nothing absurd, nothing strange,
Nothing unseemly or inacceptable to Him
620 We ask, because we use
Almost His very words.
Six petitions—not seven—
(We follow Luke here)

Are in the prayer,
625 All to God's glory.
And yet the three first
To God's glory particularly refer,
Not to our own advantage.
The final three concern
630 The care of ourselves,
What we should ask
For our own sake.

"Thy name be hallowed":
Set before our eyes we must,
635 Gaze with eyes intent we must
Upon His glory.

Hallow God—then hallowed we become.
But blind your eyes to such personal gain!
If all our private good were cut,
640 Yet should we not cease
Both to desire and to entreat
With prayers this hallowing
And all else that redounds
To God's glory.
645 Like Moses and Paul,
Turn eyes and mind away from self,
Long with fierce and burning zeal
To be ourselves destroyed
So that, despite that loss of self,
650 God's glory and God's kingdom
May advance.
Even when we ask our daily bread,
Let it be only to seek God's glory
And only when it redounds to His glory.

655 **Our Father Who Art in Heaven**

All prayer to God
Is offered, commended to Him
In one name only—Christ's.

100

The very name of "Father"
660 Puts forth Christ's name.
Adopted to Christ as children of grace—
Is this not our sole assurance
To address God as Father?
Who, otherwise, would be so rash
665 To claim the honor
Of a child of God?
To us God has given His true Son,
Our brother bringing to us by adoption
What is Christ's own by birth.
670 But we must with firm faith
Embrace this great blessing.
John's words: "To those believing
In the name of God's only begotten Son
Is given the power
675 Also to become God's sons."
So does He call Himself our Father
And wills we call Him so.
Freed from unfaith we are
By this sweetest name of all,
680 For in the Father alone can we find
This greatest love.
As He exceeds all men
In goodness and mercy,
So is His love more excellent
685 Than all parental love.
It is as if all fathers on this earth
Were stripped of piety,
Were to forsake their children—and yet,
He would not fail us,
690 For He cannot deny Himself.
We have His promise:
"Evil though you are, yet you know
How to give good to your children:
How much more does your Father
695 Who is in heaven?"
If a son entrusts himself

To a stranger's safekeeping,
He at the same time
Is complaining of cruelty or want
700 At his father's hand.
If we then are God's sons
And seek help in any other quarter,
We are reproaching Him
For poverty, want of means,
705 Cruelty, or excessive rigor.

Do our sins then make us timid
Before our Father, kind and gentle as He is,
Because they displease Him?
Among men a son can have
710 No better advocate
To plead his cause before his father,
No better intermediary
To win back his lost favor,
Than if the son himself,
715 Suppliant, humble,
Acknowledging his guilt,
Implores his father's mercy.
His father then cannot
Conceal his compassion,
720 Fail to be moved
By such entreaties.
How then responds
The Father of mercies,
God of all comfort?
725 Will He not heed
His children's tears and groans,
Entreating for themselves?
Since He invites, exhorts us so to do,
Will He not be moved
730 By their pleas
Rather than by those
Of other advocates to whose help
They have recourse,

Doubtful as they are
735 Of their Father's merciful compassion?

A parable of abundant fatherly compassion:
A son had estranged himself from his father,
Had dissolutely wasted his substance,
Had grievously offended against him.
740 Yet the father embraces him with open arms,
Does not wait for him to ask for pardon,
But anticipates him,
Afar off recognizes him returning,
Runs willingly to meet him,
745 Comforts him,
Receives him into favor.
Great though this human compassion is,
He teaches us a greater.
No mere father He, but the best
750 And kindest Father of all
He is to us—
Provided we cast ourselves,
Ungrateful, rebellious, froward children
Though we are,
755 Upon His mercy.

The "our" He put with "Father"
To strengthen, assure us Christians
He is such a Father to us.
We are addressing Him:
760 O Father, utterly devoted to Thy children,
Utterly ready to forgive,
We Thy children call upon Thee,
Make our prayer,
Assured, persuaded
765 Thou bearest toward us
Only the affection of a Father,
Unworthy though we are
Of such a Father.

Not "my" Father do I call my God,
770 But in common with all Christians
We call Him "our" Father.
Children together of such a Father,
We must have among us
The greatest feeling of brotherly love.
775 Since all we have comes from Him,
Let us not keep it divided among ourselves
But be prepared (as need demands)
With eager hearts to share it.

Extend our hands to one another,
780 Help one another we must,
And especially must we commend
Our brethren to the providential care
Of the best of Fathers.
For if He is kind and favorable,
785 Nothing else at all can be desired.
This very thing, indeed, we owe
To our Father.
Love the father of the family
And you will embrace
790 In your love and good will
His entire household.
To His people, His family,
And His inheritance
We must needs then show
795 The same zeal and affection
We have toward this heavenly Father.
For them He has honored
By calling them
The fullness of His only begotten Son.

800 And so the prayer of the Christian man
Should embrace all
His brothers in Christ,
Both those he sees and owns as brothers
And all men who dwell on earth.

805 What for them the Lord has determined
Is beyond our knowing;
Yet we ought to wish
And hope the best for them.
To those of the household of faith
810 We ought with special affection to be drawn,
Commended as they are to us in everything
By the apostle.

Let all our prayers then look
To that community
815 Established by the Lord
In His kingdom and His household.
Pray for ourselves and certain others
We can, but never letting our minds
Wander or turn aside
820 From the community of faith;
All things to it we must refer.
Though some prayers are individually framed,
Directed to this end, they cease not
To be common.
825 A comparison will make this clear:
God bids us relieve the need
Of all the poor,
But we can only succor those
We know or see are suffering,
830 While many pressed by equal need
We have to overlook,
Not knowing all
Or unable to provide for all.
And so we particularly commend
835 To God, in words distinctive
Yet of public concern
And of common affection,
All persons God has pleased
To make intimately known.
840 When we so pray,
We are not resisting God's will.

Still in general prayer we can reach
Beyond the narrow limits
Of giving only to those we know:
845 Multitudes far away, unknown to us,
We can reach in prayers
Embracing all God's children.

In heaven?
Not bound, shut up, circumscribed
850 In a barred enclosure,
For the heaven of heavens
Cannot contain Him;
Heaven is His seat,
The earth His footstool.
855 Our God is, then, everywhere diffused.
But to our crass minds
His glory is unspeakable.
Hence "heaven" says to us
Our God is infinitely great, lofty,
860 Incomprehensible in essence,
Boundlessly mighty,
Beyond our mortal ken.
When "heaven" falls upon our ears,
Higher, higher we must raise our thought,
865 Beyond all earthly, physical measure;
Not by our puny measure,
Not to our weak emotions
Are we to confine His will.

Hallowed Be Thy Name

870 God's name comprises all His excellences:
Might, righteousness, wisdom, mercy, truth.
Great and wonderful is He
For He is righteous,
For He is wise,
875 For He is merciful,
For He is mighty,

For He is true.
And so we petition that
In excellences like these
880 His majesty be hallowed.
Not in God Himself can
His majesty be hallowed,
For to His presence nothing can be added
And from it nothing can be removed.
885 Holy, holy it must be held by all,
Truly recognized and magnified.
Whatever God does,
Let all His works appear
Glorious as they are.
890 If He punishes,
Let Him be proclaimed righteous.
If He pardons,
Let Him be hailed as merciful.
If He does what He has promised,
895 Let Him be known as truthful.
Nothing, nothing there is to be
In which His deep-graved glory
Does not shine;
In all hearts,
900 On all tongues
Let praise of Him resound.
All ungodliness
Besmirching and profaning His holy name
(Obscuring, diminishing this hallowing)
905 Is to perish and be confounded:
And so God's majesty
Shines more and more.
In hallowing God's name,
We also thank and praise Him,
910 Source of all our blessings.

Thy Kingdom Come

What is God's kingdom?
By His Holy Spirit

To act and rule over His own people
915 That in all their works
The riches of His goodness and His mercy
May clearly stand out.
But His kingdom is also
To ruin and cast down the reprobate
920 Because they do not acknowledge
Their loyalty to God and to the Lord,
And refuse to come under His rule.
It is to destroy, lay low
Their sacrilegious arrogance,
925 Thus making clear
That no power is able to withstand
His power.
Yet daily before our very eyes
We see His holy Word:
930 Raised like a sceptre,
Even underneath the cross itself,
Even amid the world's contempt, disgrace
It grows, reigns, prospers, flowers.
Not of this world, yet in this world
935 This kingdom flourishes,
Spiritual, incorruptible, eternal.
We therefore pray:
"God's kingdom come."
We pray the Lord may, day by day,
940 Add new believers to His people,
That they may celebrate in every way
His glory;
That He may ever more widely
Pour out His rich grace,
945 Living and reigning day by day
More and more in them
Until their perfect union with Himself
Is at last fulfilled.
We pray the Lord will shine
950 More and more His light and truth,
Dispelling, snuffing out, destroying

The darkness and falsehoods
Of Satan and his kingdom.

"God's kingdom come":
955 May it at last be perfected, fulfilled
In revelation of His judgment.
In that day He alone
Will be exalted,
Will be all in all,
960 When His own folk
Are gathered and received into glory,
But Satan's kingdom
Is disrupted utterly,
Laid low.

965 **Thy Will Be Done,**
As in Heaven So on Earth

O God, we ask Thee
In heaven and on earth—everywhere—
To temper, compose all things
970 To Thy will;
To govern the outcome of all things,
To use according to Thy decision
All Thy creatures,
To subject to Thyself
975 The will of every being.
O God, we ask that all
Equally obey Thy will:
Some (Thine own) willingly;
Others (the devil's crew)
980 Unwillingly, reluctantly;
For they try to evade Thy rule,
Try to give Thine obedience the slip.

By this petition
We renounce all our desires,
985 Resign and turn over to the Lord
All affections within us,

Ask God to answer our prayer
Not as we wish
But as He has foreseen and decreed.
990 We ask God not merely to crush
Our affections warring against His will,
But, extinguishing our own,
To create in us
New minds, new hearts.
995 We ask no prompting of desire in us
Save one pure and agreeing with His will.
Not what we will of ourselves
But what His Spirit may will in us—
This is our prayer.
1000 Let the Spirit teach us within
To love what pleases God,
But to hate, abhor
What displeases Him.

In this first half of the prayer,
1005 We are to keep before our eyes
The glory of God alone;
We are not deliberately
To consider ourselves
Or seek our own advantage.
1010 Though in their due season
All these things will come to pass
Whether we petition or no,
Still we ought to make known
Our desires and requests.
1015 What profit is there for us
So to pray?
Thus praying, we testify, profess ourselves
Servants and children of God;
Thus we serve His honor
1020 As best we can.
No less than this we owe our Father.
Those men then who—devoid
Of desire and zeal to further God's glory—

105

Do not pray:
1025 "Hallowed be Thy name;
Thy kingdom come,
Thy will be done,"
Such men are not to be counted
God's children and servants.
1030 Since all will come to pass
Even against their consent,
Their end will be
Confusion and judgment.

Give Us This Day Our Daily Bread

1035 In the last three petitions
We turn to ask of God
To help us in our need.
By this petition
We ask in general
1040 That God will supply
Under the elements of this world
Whatever our bodies need:
Food and clothing, but also
Everything God sees as beneficial to us.
1045 We ask to eat our bread in peace.
By this we give ourselves
Over to His care,
Entrust ourselves to His providence,
That He may feed, nourish, preserve us.
1050 Our gracious Father does not disdain
To take even our bodies
Under His safekeeping,
Thus even in these small details
Exercising our faith.
1055 And so we await from Him
Everything—crumb of bread or drop of water.
In our wickedness
We are more concerned with body
Than with soul:
1060 Hence many minded to entrust the soul to God

Still trouble over flesh,
Still worry about what to eat,
What to wear;
Unless on hand they have
1065 Abundant wine, grain, oil,
Apprehensively they tremble.
So much more does the shadow
Of this fleeting life
Mean to us than
1070 Everlasting immortality!
But those who rely on God
Cast out once for all
Anxiety about the care of flesh
And await at once from Him
1075 Still greater things,
Even salvation and eternal life.
No light exercise of faith then
Is it for us to hope
From God for those things
1080 That otherwise cause us
Such great anxiety.
Put off then we must
This faithlessness that sinks its teeth
Into the very bones
1085 Of almost every man.

Hence we ask our bread
Of our Father.
But why "daily" and "this day"?
Thus we are taught not immoderately
1090 To long for fleeting things,
Afterwards flamboyantly plunging ourselves
Into sensual pleasure, show, or luxury.
Thus we are taught to ask
Only for enough to tide us over
1095 From day to day.
Assured we are that as today
Our heavenly Father nourishes us,

Tomorrow He will not fail us.

Though our storehouses are stuffed, our cellars full,
1100 Still we ought always to ask for our daily bread
And count all our possessions nothing,
Except our Lord pour out His blessing,
Prosper and bring it to fruit.
Yet only as God hour by hour
1105 Bestows it upon us
Is it really ours.
But those not content with daily bread,
Who pant unbridledly after countless things
Or wallow carefree in their piled-up riches
1110 And still pray this prayer to God,
Are mocking Him.

The greedy ask for what they do not wish,
In fact abominate—mere daily bread—
Seeking to cover up their greedy way
1115 Before God.
True prayer pours out to God
The whole mind itself
And all hidden within.
The lazy rich ask of God
1120 What they least long for—daily bread—
Thinking they already have within themselves
All they need.

"Our" bread?
To show God's generosity in making ours
1125 What is by no reckoning owed to us.
However it may come to us,
Even when obtained
By our own skill and diligence,
Even when supplied
1130 By our own hands—
It is a simple and free gift of God.

Forgive Us Our Debts
As We Forgive Our Debtors

By this petition
1135 We ask forgiveness of sins
Needed by all men, without exception.
Sins are "debts" because we owe
To God penalty or payment for them,
Payment we could not satisfy
1140 Unless released by His forgiveness.
This free pardon comes
From His mercy
By which He generously wipes out
These debts, exacts for them
1145 No payment from us.
Rather He makes satisfaction
To Himself by His own mercy
In Christ,
Who once for all gave Himself
1150 To the Father as a ransom.

This free gift is not shared by those
Who trust God is satisfied
With their own or others' merits,
Who think such satisfaction
1155 Pays for and buys forgiveness of sins.
Calling on God in this form
They do nothing but subscribe
To their own accusation
And seal by their own testimony
1160 Their condemnation.
Debtors they confess they are
Unless released by the forgiveness
Spurned by them,
Thrusting as they do upon God
1165 Their merits, satisfactions.
Thus they do not entreat His mercy;
They call down His justice.

We ask that forgiveness come to us
"As we forgive our debtors."
1170 We mean, as we spare and pardon those
Who in any way have injured us,
Treated us unjustly in deed
Or insulted us in word.
Not that it is for us
1175 To forgive the guilt
Of transgression or offense,
For this belongs to God alone!
Our forgiveness rather is:
Willingly to cast from the mind
1180 Wrath, hatred, desire for revenge;
Voluntarily to banish to oblivion
Remembrance of injustice.

Hence, unless we ourselves forgive
The offenses against us of all those
1185 Who do or have done us ill,
We ought not to seek from God
Forgiveness of sins.
If we hold hatred in our hearts,
If we plot revenge,
1190 Ponder occasion to cause harm,
(Even if we do not try to get back
In our enemies' good graces
Or deserve well of them,
Commend ourselves to them),
1195 In this prayer we are asking
God not to forgive our sins.
Do to us as Thou dost to others!
Do not do it to us unless we ourselves do it.
To unforgiving souls who pray this prayer
1200 Comes a heavier judgment.

The condition, "as we forgive our debtors,"
Is not intended to make us by our forgiveness
Deserving of God's forgiveness.

By it the Lord only intended
1205 To comfort the weakness of our faith.
By this sign the Lord has assured us
He has forgiven us,
As surely as we are aware
We have forgiven others—
1210 Provided our hearts
Have been emptied, purged
Of all hatred, envy, vengeance.
By this mark too the Lord excludes
From the number of His children
1215 Those eager to revenge and slow to forgive,
Who nurse enmity, against others
Foment the very enmity they pray
To be averted from themselves.
And these enemies of God thus dare not call
1220 Upon Him as Father.

**Lead Us Not into Temptation
but Free Us from the Evil One**

Many and varied indeed
Are the forms of temptation:
1225 Wicked conceptions of the mind,
Provoking us to transgress the law,
Suggested to us either by our own lust
Or devil-prompted;
Also things not evil by nature
1230 Become temptations through the devil's devices
When thrust before our eyes
To draw us away or turn us
Aside from God.
Some temptations come at us from the right,
1235 Some from the left.
Right-hand temptations include
Riches, power, honors,
By their glitter and seeming goodness
Dulling men's keen sight,
1240 Alluring men with their blandishment.

Such tricks so captivate,
Such sweetness so inebriates,
That men forget their God.
Left-hand temptations include
1245 Poverty, disgrace, contempt, afflictions.
Thwarted by their hardship, difficulty,
Men's minds grow despondent,
Cast away assurance and hope,
At last are completely estranged
1250 From God.

O God our Father, let us not yield
To such temptations
Born of our own lust
Or held out to us by devil's guile,
1255 For they war against us.
We pray Thee, sustain, encourage us
By Thy hand so, strengthened by Thy power,
We may stand firm against all assaults
Of our deadly foe,
1260 Whatever the thoughts
He smuggles into our minds.
We pray that we may turn to good
The prosperity that puffs us up
And the adversity that casts us down.

1265 We do not ask, though, that we feel
No temptations at all, for we must
Be pricked, aroused, urged by them
Lest with inactivity we grow sluggish.
David wished to be tempted,
1270 And the Lord daily tests His elect,
Chastising them by disgrace,
Poverty, tribulation, and other afflictions.
God tests us in one way,
Satan in another.
1275 Satan tempts us
To destroy, condemn, confound, cast down;

But God tempts us
To prove and exercise His own children;
To mortify, purify, cauterize their flesh.
1280 For unless so restrained,
Flesh would play the wanton,
Vaunt itself beyond measure.
Satan attacks the unarmed, the unprepared,
To crush them unawares.
1285 God, while tempting, provides escape,
That His own may patiently bear all
He lays upon them.

This then is our plea:
Not to be vanquished, overwhelmed
1290 By temptations,
But by the Lord's power to stand unmoved
Against all hostile powers attacking us.
This it is not to succumb to temptations.
Our plea: received into His care
1295 And safekeeping, secure in His protection,
Grant us victoriously to endure
Sin, death, the gates of hell,
The devil's whole kingdom.
So it is to be
1300 "Freed from the evil one."
Mark this clearly:
Not in our power is it for us
To engage in combat
That great warrior the devil
1305 Or bear alone the force of his onslaught.
Otherwise pointless it would be
To ask of God what already
We have in ourselves.
Those who, self-assured,
1310 Ready themselves for combat, know not
Their ferocious, well-equipped adversary.
As from the jaws of a mad and raging lion,
We seek now to be freed from his power.

If the Lord did not snatch us
1315 From the midst of death,
We would by his fangs and claws immediately
Be torn to pieces,
Swallowed down his throat.
Still we know
1320 If the Lord is with us,
If He fights for us while we keep still,
In His might we shall do mightily.
Let others trust in their free choice,
Their own capacities—
1325 For us enough it is
To stand, be strong
In God's power alone.

From these last three petitions
In which we especially commend to God
1330 Ourselves and our possessions,
We reiterate our previous conclusions:
The prayers of Christians ought to be public,
Ought to look to the church's upbuilding,
To the advancement of the believers' fellowship.
1335 Of God we do not ask any private benefit;
No, together we ask in common
For our bread,
For forgiveness of sins.
We ask in common
1340 Not to be led into temptation
And to be freed from the evil one.

Emboldened still more to ask are we
By what is added.

Thine Is the Kingdom, the Power,
1345 the Glory, Forever

Here is a firm, tranquil repose for our faith.
If by our own worth our prayers were to be
Commended to God,

Who would dare even mutter
1350 In God's presence?
Yet, however miserable we may be,
Even the unworthiest of all,
However devoid of anything to commend us,
Still will we never lack reason to pray,
1355 Never be shorn of assurance,
Since His kingdom, power, glory
Can never be snatched away
From our Father.

Amen

1360 With this concluding word
Expressed is the warm desire
To obtain of God what we have asked.
With this is our hope strengthened
That all these things have been brought to pass,
1365 Will surely be granted us,
For it is by God, who cannot deceive,
They have been promised.

In this form of prayer, this rule
Handed down by our best Master, Christ
1370 (Whom the Father appointed our teacher,
Whom alone He would have us heed and harken),
Is set forth for us
Everything we ought or at all are able
To seek of God.
1375 For Christ has always been
The eternal Wisdom of God;
And, made man, has been given to men,
The Angel of great counsel.

So perfect in all respects is this prayer
1380 That any extraneous, unrelated addition
Is impious and unworthy
To be conceded by God.
For here He has summed up

110

What is worthy of Him,
1385 Acceptable to Him,
Needful for us—
What willingly He would grant.

Consequently all daring to go beyond
And ask of God anything apart from this,
1390 Are first wishing to add
To God's wisdom from their own—
Insane blasphemy!
Are secondly not confining themselves
Within God's will;
1395 Rather, holding it in contempt,
Panting, they stray farther away;
And lastly will never obtain anything
For they are praying without faith.
All such prayers are prayed
1400 Apart from faith,
For absent from them is the Word of God,
On which faith (if it is to stand at all)
Must always rely.
Such persons not only lack God's Word;
1405 With all their strength
Contend against it.

Do not suppose we are so bound
By this form of prayer as not to permit
Some word or syllable to change.
1410 Here and there in Scripture one reads
Many prayers, in words far different from it,
Yet composed by the same Spirit.
And these prayers are very profitable
For us to use.
1415 This is what we teach:
We should ask for, expect, demand
Only what is summed up in this prayer;
The words may be different;
The sense should not vary.

1420 In this all Scriptural prayers
Are surely to be referred to it.
None there is that equals it
In perfection, let alone surpasses it.
Here nothing is left out
1425 Of which we should think
In praising God,
Nothing that should come into our minds
For our advantage.
Indeed, so precisely framed is it,
1430 Any hope of attempting better
Is taken away from all men.

To sum up: let us remember
This is the teaching of divine Wisdom,
Teaching what it willed
1435 And willing what was needful.

Perseverance in Prayer

Already we have stated that,
Lifting up our hearts,
We should ever aspire to God
And pray without ceasing.
1440 Still, such is our weakness
It must be supported by many helps,
Such our sluggishness
It needs to be goaded.
Consequently fitting it is
1445 That each one of us should set apart
Certain hours for this exercise,
Hours that should not pass without prayer,
Hours when all the heart's devotion
Should completely engage in prayer.
1450 When should we pray?
Upon arising in the morning,
Before we begin daily work,

111

When we sit down to a meal,
When by God's blessing we have eaten,
1455 When we are preparing to retire.

No superstitious observance of hours, this,
Whereby, as if paying our debt to God,
We fancy ourselves paid up
For the remaining hours.
1460 No, it must be a tutelage for our weakness,
Exercised and repeatedly stimulated.
Whenever we are pressed
Or see others pressed
By any adversity,
1465 Let us hasten back to God,
Not with swift feet
But with eager hearts;
On the other hand,
Let us not permit the prosperity
1470 Of ourselves or others to go unnoticed,
Failing to testify, by praise and thanksgiving,
That we discern God's hand therein.

Lastly, in every prayer let us observe
Our intention is not to bind
1475 God to particular circumstances,
Not to prescribe at what time,
In what place, in what way
He is to do anything.

We are accordingly taught in this prayer
1480 Not to make any law for Him,
Impose any condition upon Him,
But to leave to His decision
To do what He is to do,
In what way, at what time,
1485 In what place seems good to Him.

Before we pray for ourselves,
We pray His will be done,
Thus subjecting our will to His,
By this bridle restraining it
1490 From presuming to control God,
But making Him the arbiter, director
Of all its entreaties.
With minds composed to this obedience,
Letting ourselves be ruled by the laws
1495 Of divine providence, readily
We shall learn to persevere in prayer;
With desires suspended,
Patiently to wait for the Lord.
Assured then we shall be that
1500 Though He does not appear,
He is always present to us,
Will in His own time declare
He has never been deaf to the prayers
That (in men's eyes) He seems
1505 To have neglected.

An ever present consolation, this:
If God should not respond to our first requests,
We should not faint
Or fall into despair.
1510 Such is the way of those who,
Carried away by their own ardor,
So call upon God
That unless He jumps at their first act of prayer
And brings them help at once,
1515 They immediately fancy Him angry,
Hostile toward them,
And, abandoning all hope of being heard,
Cease to call upon Him.
Too, let us not tempt God,
1520 Wearying Him with our depravity,
Provoke Him against ourselves.
This is the usual thing with those

112

Who only under certain conditions
Covenant with God;
1525 As if He were the servant
Of their own appetites,
Bind Him to laws of their own dictation.
If He does not obey them at once,
They become indignant,
1530 Grumble, protest, murmur,
Rage at Him.
To such, therefore, often in wrath and fury
He grants what in mercy He denies
To others to whom He is favorable.
1535 Proof of this is in the children of Israel—
Better it would have been for them
Not to be heard by the Lord
Than to swallow His wrath
With their meat.

1540 If, finally, after long waiting
We cannot sense benefit received from prayer
Or perceive any fruit from it,
Still our faith will assure us
Of what sense cannot perceive:
1545 That we have obtained what was expedient.
So will our Father cause us in poverty
To possess abundance,
In affliction comfort.
Though all else fail us,
1550 God will never forsake us,
For He cannot disappoint
His expectant, patient people.
In place of all things, He alone
Will be for us, since all good things
1555 Are contained in Him; them will He reveal
To us on the day of judgment,
When plainly manifested
Will His kingdom be.
By this patience believers need to be sustained;

1560 Without reliance on it, they will not long stand.
By no light trials the Lord proves His people,
Not softly exercises them;
Often He drives them to extremity,
Allows them so driven for a long time
1565 To lie in the mire before He gives them
Any taste of His sweetness.
As Hannah says: "He kills
And brings to life;
He brings down to hell
1570 And brings back."
What but be discouraged,
What but plunged into despair,
If they were not—while afflicted,
Desolate, already half-dead—
1575 Revived by the thought that
God has regard for them
And will end their present misfortunes?

Notes

Note: Calvin's treatise "On Prayer" (chap. 3 of the 1536 edition of the *Institutes* and chap. 20 of book 3 of the 1559 edition), which includes a brief commentary on the Lord's Prayer, is here translated in strophic form from the edition of 1536. It was slightly modified and expanded in later editions of the *Institutes*, reaching its final form in the edition of 1559. For fuller notes on this chapter, see *Institution of the Christian Religion . . . 1536*, trans. and an. Ford Lewis Battles (Atlanta: John Knox, 1975); and *Institutes*, McNeill-Battles. The chief contemporary source for Calvin was Martin Bucer's discussion of Matthew 6:1–13 in *Enarrationes Perpetuae in Evangelia* (1530), which I have translated in *Institution*, pp. 441–61. A second source was Bucer's *"Disputatio de Precatione"* ("Dissertation on Prayer"), a portion of his *"Familiaris Explanatio in Psalmum Quintum"* in *Sacrorum Psalmorum Libri Quinque* (1529). For the latter I am indebted to R. Gerald Hobbs, whose dissertation, "An Introduction to the Psalms Commentary of Martin Bucer" (Thesis, Strasbourg, 1971), exhaustively examines Bucer's commentary on the Psalms.

5. Cf. chap. 2, lines 202ff. above.

22f. Ps. 36:9.

28f. Cf. Col. 1:19; John 1:16.

53–62. Dan. 9:18f.; cf. Vulgate.

64–74. Bar. 2:18f.; 3:2; cf. Vulgate.

91. Matt. 6:9; Luke 11:2.

100. Luke 17:7–10.

115. Cf. Luther's *Enchiridion* (in WA, 10:2:395) and *Treatise of Good Works* (in WA, 6:233f.).

118–22. Luke 11:9–13; John 16:23–29; Matt. 7:7; 11:28; Zech. 1:3; Ps. 50:15; Exod. 20:7.

145. Matt. 7:7.

146. Mark 11:24.

147. Isa. 65:24; Ps. 50:15; 91:3; Matt. 11:28.

148. Exod. 34:14f.

149. Isa. 45:17.

184–86. James 1:6; cf. Luther, *Enchiridion*, in WA, 10:2:396.

189f. Matt. 8:13; 9:29; Mark 11:24.

198. I John 2:1; I Tim. 2:5; cf. Heb. 8:6; 9:15.

211f. Heb. 4:16.

219–22. John 14:13; 16:24.

229–32. II Cor. 1:20.

233f. Cf. John 14:6.

241f. Cf. John 6:27; Matt. 2:6.

242. I Cor. 11:3; Eph. 1:22; 4:15; 5:23; Col. 1:18.

251. John 14:6.

257–59. Col. 1:20; Eph. 1:10.

288f. I Tim. 2:1–7; James 5:15–18.

301f. I Cor. 13.

308f. Rom. 8:6–7 (Vulgate).

312f. Deut. 12:32.

318–25. Ambrose, *On Isaac; or, The Soul* 8.75; in CSEL, 32:694; PL, 14:520.

360–62. Cf. Eck, *Enchiridion*, chaps. 15–16.

365–69. Ps. 22:4f.; cf. 21:5f. (Vulgate).

375–82. James 5:17f.

401. Ecclus. 6:10.

401–3. Ps. 50:15; Luke 18:1; 21:36; Eph. 5:20.

424–26. Cf. James 4:14f.

436. Cf. Isa. 30:1; 31:1.

449. I Tim. 4:5.

453. I Thess. 5:17f.; cf. I Tim. 2:1, 8.

471. I Cor. 14:40.

486f. I Cor. 3:16; 6:19; II Cor. 6:16.

494f. John 4:13.

502. Cf. Bucer, *Enarrationes Perpetuae in Evangelia*, fol. 63ᵣ.22f. ET in Calvin, *Institution*, trans. and an. Ford Lewis Battles, pp. 444f.

504. Cf. Rom. 8:27.

517–19. Cf. II Cor. 6:16.

525ff. On singing in worship, see chapter 6 below.

532–40. Isa. 29:14; cf. Vulgate.

541ff. On the relation of mind and heart in faith, see the *Institutes* 3.2.33.

550. Cf. chap. 3, lines 189ff. above.

566ff. Calvin wrote in the "Letter to the Reader" in his *The Form of Prayers and Songs of the Church* (1542) that the common language of the people is to be used for prayers: the people cannot say amen to a prayer in a foreign language (I Cor. 14:16). In OS, 2:13. On the Roman Catholic rejection of vernacular worship, see Eck, "On the Mass Not to Be Said in German," chap. 37 in *Enchiridion*.

576–81. I Cor. 14:16f.

595. Exod. 4; I Sam. 1:13.

598f. Matt. 6:9ff.; Luke 11:2ff.

623. Luke 11:2–4.

645ff. Exod. 32:32; Rom. 9:3.

655. Matt. 6:9.

660. Calvin would not look with favor on the loose use of the fatherhood of God. For him the address of God as Father is essentially a Christological act and affirmation.

673–75. John 1:12.

692–95. Matt. 7:11.

724. Cf. II Cor. 1:3.

736ff. Luke 15:11–32.

743f. Luke 15:20.

745f. Luke 15:22–24.

772ff. Matt. 23:9.

797–99. Eph. 1:23.

800ff. True and Christian prayer, Calvin asserted, is social, not merely individual, in character. Cf. lines 1332ff. below.

809–12. Gal. 6:10.

848. Matt. 6:9.

848ff. The word *heaven*, which seems to confine God to a particular place, is really God's way of accommodating His utter transcendence of all human understanding to our limited capacity. On the exegetical principle of accommodation, crucial for Calvin's understanding of Scripture, see Ford Lewis Battles, "God Was Accommodating Himself to Human Capacity," *Interpretation* 31 (1977): 19–38. Cf. *Institutes* 4.17.26.

851f. I Kings 8:27.

853f. Isa. 66:1; Acts 7:49; cf. 17:24.

869. Matt. 6:9.

870ff. On the "excellences" of God (*virtutes Dei*), compare chapter 2, lines 6ff. above.

911. Matt. 6:10a.

934f. I Cor. 1:21; John 17:14; 18:36; Rom. 14:17.

936. Luke 1:33; Dan. 7:14.

938. Matt. 6:10a.

939ff. The correspondence of these lines to Calvin's teaching on gradual spiritual growth in chapter 3, line 275 above (see note) is to be marked. In his eucharistic teaching too Calvin regarded union with God the goal to which the faith-experience of this life points.

957–64. I Cor. 15:28.

965f. Matt. 6:10b.

993f. Ezek. 36:26.

1000. Calvin frequently described the Holy Spirit as our "inner teacher": e.g., *Institutes* 1.9.1; 3.1.4; 3.2.34; 4.14.9; 4.17.36; etc.

1034. Matt. 6:11.

1035ff. See chap. 3, lines 281ff. (note) above.

1041. Gal. 4:3.

1082–85. Matt. 6:25–33.

1089ff. On frugality see chapter 3, lines 2008f. (note) and 2109ff. (note) above.

1106. In editions of the *Institutes* subsequent to the first, the gift of "daily bread" includes the gift of digestion: "Indeed, not even an abundance of bread would benefit us in the slightest unless it were divinely turned into nourishment." McNeill-Battles, 3.20.44.

1125. Cf. Deut. 8:18.

1132f. Matt. 6:12.

1151ff. These lines reject Roman Catholic teaching on free will, works-righteousness, the treasury of merits laid up by the saints, and all forms of prayer associated with these doctrines. In his *Enchiridion* Eck countered Protestant teaching: "Because Luther has taught that all things happen by absolute necessity, and he has denied free will, very many of his followers, against express statements of Scripture, deny that one ought to pray, because Christ sufficiently prayed for us" (from chap. 31, "Concerning Free Will"). ". . . fasting and alms are not so superfluous that by them prayer is not lifted, as by wings, to heaven" (from chap. 32, "Concerning Prayer and the Canonical Hours"). (My translation.)

1177. Cf. Isa. 43:25.

1197. Matt. 7:12.

1221f. Matt. 6:13a.

1223–33. James 1:2, 14; cf. Matt. 4:1; I Thess. 3:5.

1234f. Cf. Prov. 4:27; Luther, *Fourteen Consolations*, in WA, 6:104–34. Calvin afforded a fuller exposition than he gave here in a sermon on II Samuel 16:1–4 (in SC, 1:459, lines 23ff.).

1268. James 1:2.

1269. Cf. Ps. 26:2.

1270. Gen. 22:1; Deut. 8:2; 13:3 (Vulgate).

1285–87. I Cor. 10:13; II Peter 2:9.

1297. Matt. 16:28.

1311. I Peter 5:8.

1322. Ps. 60:12; cf. 107:14.

1332ff. Cf. lines 800ff. (note) above.

1344. Matt. 6:13b.

1359. Matt. 6:13b.

1366. Cf. Luther, *Enchiridion,* in WA, 30:1:308.

1368ff. Calvin took seriously in his liturgy the teaching here expressed, that the Lord's Prayer is the perfect model of our prayers: see his long paraphrase of it in his Geneva Service, chapter 5, lines 218–309 below.

1371. Matt. 17:5.

1375f. Isa. 11:2.

1378. Isa. 9:6, conflated with Isa. 28:29 and Jer. 32:19.

1379–82. Cf. Augustine, *Letters,* 130.12.22f. (in PL, 33:502f.).

1439. I Thess. 5:17.

1445ff. Calvin's suggestions as to hours for prayer here seem to be an evangelical replacement for the medieval canonical hours still defended by Roman Catholic controversialists such as Eck (see "Concerning Prayer and the Canonical Hours," chap. 32 of *Enchiridion*).

1479–85. Cf. Luther, *Enchiridion,* in WA 10:2:397. Here Calvin seems to be obliquely refuting the Roman Catholic practice of vows. Cf. *Institutes* 4.13. See Eck, "Concerning Vows," chap. 18 of *Enchiridion.*

1487. Matt. 6:10.

1523f. See lines 1479ff. (note) above.

1536–39. Num. 11:18, 33.

1567–70. I Sam. 2:6.

Chapter 5

Prayers of Calvin

Having examined Calvin's theology of prayer, "the chief exercise of faith," let us see how he exercised his own faith and bade the people under his spiritual care to do likewise. Calvin's prayers have come down to us through three main channels: (1) the Strasbourg and Geneva liturgies,[1] (2) the Sermons, (3) the *Praelectiones,* or Lectures, on the Old Testament prophets. Because they found a certain sameness in them, the editors of the *Corpus Reformatorum* for the most part suppressed the prayers in their edition of the Sermons and the *Praelectiones.* One must therefore go to earlier editions of Calvin's works to find the prayers of the second and third categories. Fortunately for English readers, the *Praelectiones* prayers were translated in the Calvin Translation Society edition of the Old Testament Commentaries. Charles E. Edwards's anthology of these has recently been republished.[2]

Calvin introduced his liturgy in the "Letter to the Reader" that heads *The Form of Prayers and Songs of the Church,* published in Geneva in 1542.[3] Of the three chief elements of worship—preaching, prayers, and sacraments—the "Letter" concentrates on prayers, justifying the use of the vernacular and the restriction of singing almost solely to metrical Psalms. Since for their edification and for divine praise the worshipers must understand what goes on in the service, it is imperative that worship be in the language of the people and that the sacramental rites be clearly explained to them by the ministers. While God alone deigns to illumine the ignorant, *The Form of Prayers and Songs of the Church* was being published, Calvin stated, to protect the people from blind guides.[4]

There are two kinds of prayer: spoken and sung. Especial care must be given to sung prayers. Calvin was sensitive to the vast power of music to enhance the words whose vehicle it is. Therefore all lascivious or frivolous singing should be strictly avoided by evangelical Christians, and the holy, heavenly Psalms of David, set to grave and majestic tunes worthy of their thought, should be embraced. Yet Calvin allowed, in addition to the Psalms, the singing of the Creed, the Lord's Prayer, and such New Testament canticles as the *Magnificat* and the *Nunc Dimittis.*

Besides the liturgical prayers of the Sunday service, Geneva afforded the somewhat freer prayers of the weekday services, and as well the prayers expressly associated with the sermons. All these were in French; Latin was of course retained for the prayers that close each of the *Praelectiones.*

Of the extant spoken prayers of Calvin, we offer a strophic translation first of the Geneva Sunday Liturgy and of the Wednesday Service of Penitence (1542);[5] second, of the prayers of absolution and illumination and the prayer at the conclusion of the sermon;[6] third, of the prayers that introduce and conclude the *Praelectiones.* The sung prayers will be dealt with in the following chapter.

To provide a better understanding of the setting for Calvin's spoken prayers, some notes on the orders of service follow.[7] First, the Sunday service:

Invocation: Scripture sentences (see lines 3–4 below)
Confession of sins (6–47)
Singing of metrical Psalm (48)
Prayer for illumination before the sermon (48–54; for example, see p. 128 below)
Text and sermon (55)
Collection of alms
Final detailed prayer with paraphrase of Lord's Prayer
  Intercessions (58–217)
  Paraphrase of Lord's Prayer (218–309)
Benediction: Aaronic blessing (312–17)

Second, the communion service:
Preparation of elements during singing of Apostles' Creed
Words of institution
Exhortation
Consecration prayer (320–73)
Fraction
Delivery
Communion, while Psalm or Scripture is read
Postcommunion prayer (376–99)
Benediction (402–7)

And third, the Wednesday service of penitence:
Invocation
Confession of sins (5–47)
Singing of metrical Psalm (48)
Prayer for illumination (49–54)
Text and sermon (55)
Final detailed prayer with paraphrase of Lord's Prayer (436–628, 237–309, 632–67, 95–179)
Benediction (310–17)

Sunday Prayer

*On Sundays, in the morning, the following form
is commonly used.*
Let our help be in God's name,
Who made heaven and earth.

5 **Confession**

Brethren, let each one of you
Present yourself before the Lord's face,
With confession of your faults and sins,
Following with your heart my words.

10 Lord God, eternal and almighty Father,
We confess and truly recognize,
Before Thine holy majesty,
That we are poor sinners,
Conceived and born in iniquity and corruption,
15 Inclined to do evil,
Unprofitable for all good;
And that from our vice
We endlessly and ceaselessly transgress
Thine holy commandments.
20 So doing, we incur,
By Thy just judgment,
Ruin and perdition upon ourselves.
Nevertheless, Lord,
We are displeased with ourselves
25 For having offended against Thee
And condemn ourselves
And our vices with true repentance,
Desiring that Thy grace
Support us in our calamity.
30 Have pity upon us, then,
God and Father, most blessed
And full of mercy,
In the name of Thy Son,
Jesus Christ our Lord.

35 And in wiping out our vices and spots,
Pour upon us and increase
From day to day
The gifts of Thine Holy Spirit,
In order that, recognizing
40 Our unrighteousness with all our heart,
We may be touched with displeasure,
Which engenders true repentance in us,
Which, mortifying us in all sins,
Produces in us fruits
45 Of righteousness and innocence
That may be agreeable to Thee,
By Jesus Christ our Lord. Amen.
> *This done, in the assembly some Psalm is sung;
> then the minister begins straightway to pray, to ask
> 50 of God the gift of His Holy Spirit, in order that His
> Word may be faithfully expounded to the honor of
> His name and to the edification of the church; and
> that it may be received in such humility and obedi-
> ence as is meet. The form is at the minister's discre-
> 55 tion. At the end of the sermon, the minister,
> having made exhortations to pray, begins thus:*

Intercession

Almighty God, heavenly Father,
Thou hast promised us
60 To grant all the requests we make
In the name of Thy Son, Jesus Christ,
Well-beloved, our Lord;
And also we are instructed,
By His teaching and that of His apostles,
65 To gather together in His name,
With promises that He will be
In the midst of us
And that He will be
Our intercessor toward Thee,
70 To implore and obtain all things
Of which we have need on earth.

119

First, we have Thy commandment
To pray for those
Whom Thou hast set over us
75 As superiors and governors;
Thereafter, for all the necessities
Of Thy people,
And the same of all men.
Wherefore, in trust
80 In Thy holy teaching
And Thy promises,
Being here gathered before Thy face,
And in the name of Thy Son,
We implore Thee affectionately,
85 Our good God and Father,
In the name of Thine only Son and Mediator,
Pray by Thine infinite kindness
Freely pardon our offenses
And so draw and lift
90 All our thoughts and desires unto Thyself
That with all our heart
We may seek and ask—
According to Thy good pleasure and will—
That alone which is reasonable.

95 We therefore pray Thee, heavenly Father,
For all princes and lords,
Thy servants to whom Thou hast committed
The rule of Thy justice,
And especially for the lords of this city,
100 That it may please Thee
To communicate Thy Spirit to them,
Daily to increase unto them
The only and truly chief good,
So that, recognizing in true faith
105 Jesus Christ Thy Son, our Lord,
To be King of kings
And Lord over all lords,
As Thou hast given Him

All power in heaven and on earth,
110 They may seek to serve Him
And exalt His kingdom in their rule,
Conducting and governing their subjects,
Who are the creatures of Thy hands
And the sheep of Thy pasture,
115 According to Thy good pleasure;
In order that here,
As well as throughout all the earth,
Being sustained in good peace and tranquillity,
We may serve Thee
120 In all holiness and honesty;
And being delivered and freed
From the fear of our enemies,
We may be able to give praise
To Thee throughout our life.
125 Amen.

Also we pray Thee,
True Father and Savior,
For all those whom Thou hast ordained
By Thy believers
130 And to whom Thou hast committed
The care of souls
And the dispensing of Thy sacred gospel,
That Thou mayest lead them
And conduct them
135 By Thy Holy Spirit,
In order that they may be found
Faithful and loyal ministers
Of Thy glory,
Having always this end,
140 That all the poor wandering and lost sheep,
Being gathered and led back
To the Lord Jesus Christ,
Chief pastor and prince of bishops;
In order that, from day to day,
145 They may profit and grow in Him

Unto all righteousness and holiness.

Moreover, pray deliver all churches
From the clutches of ravening wolves
And from all hirelings who seek
150 Their own ambition and profit,
And not the exaltation
Of Thy holy name alone
And the well-being of Thy flock.

Thereupon we pray Thee,
155 Most blessed God and merciful Father,
For all men generally,
That as Thou dost will to be recognized
As Savior of all men,
By the redemption made through Thy Son, Jesus Christ,
160 That those who are still estranged from knowing Him,
Being in shadows and captivity
Of error and ignorance,
By the illumination of Thy Holy Spirit
And the preaching of Thy gospel
165 May be led back to the straight road of salvation,
Which is to know Thee as the only true God
And Him whom Thou hast sent,
Jesus Christ.

May those whom Thou hast already visited
170 By Thy grace
And illumined by the knowledge
Of Thy Word,
Daily grow in good,
Being enriched with Thy spiritual blessings;
175 In order that all together
We may adore Thee
With one heart and one mouth
And may give honor and homage to Thy Christ,
Our Master, King, and Lawgiver.

180 In like manner,
O God of all consolation,
We commend to Thee
All those that Thou visitest
And chastisest with cross and tribulation,
185 Whether with poverty,
Or prison, or sickness,
Or exile, or other calamity of body,
Or affliction of spirit,
That Thou mayest make known to them
190 And incline Thy fatherly affection,
Which is to chastise them for their amendment;
In order that they may wholeheartedly
Turn unto Thee and, being converted,
May receive full consolation
195 And be delivered from all evil.

Finally, O God and Father,
Grant us also for our benefit,
Who are here gathered
In the name of Thy Son, Jesus,
200 For the sake of His Word,
That we may recognize,
Straightway, without hypocrisy,
In what perdition we are by nature;
And what condemnation we deserve
205 And heap up from day to day upon ourselves
By our unhappy and disordered lives.

This we ask in order that,
Seeing and understanding
That there is no good in us
210 And that our flesh and our blood
Are not capable of possessing
Thy kingdom as an inheritance;
With all our affection
And in firm trust,

215 We may give ourselves completely
To Thy dear Son, Jesus,
Our Lord, our only Savior and Redeemer.

This we ask also in order that He,
Dwelling in us,
220 May mortify our old Adam,
Renewing us unto a better life,
By which Thy name,
According as it is holy and worthy,
May be exalted and glorified
225 By all and in all places;
That we, with all creatures,
May render unto Thee
True and perfect obedience;
Even as Thine angels and heavenly messengers
230 Ask only to execute Thy commandments,
And even as Thy will may be done,
Without any contradiction;
And that all may endeavor
To serve and please Thee,
235 Renouncing their own will
And all the desires of their flesh.

In this manner mayest Thou have
Lordship and government over us all;
And daily more and more may we learn
240 To submit and subject ourselves
To Thy majesty.
In such manner mayest Thou be
King and Ruler everywhere,
Guiding Thy people
245 By the scepter of Thy Word
And by the power of Thy Spirit,
Confounding Thine enemies
By the strength
Of Thy truth and justice.

250 And so let all power and loftiness
That contravenes Thy glory
Be from day to day destroyed and wiped out,
To the point that the fulfillment of Thy kingdom
May be revealed,
255 When Thou shalt appear in judgment.

Let us, walking in love
And in the fear of Thy name,
Be nourished by Thy goodness,
And do Thou minister all things to us
260 Which are necessary and expedient for us
To eat our bread in peace.

This we ask in order that,
Seeing that Thou hast care over us,
We may better recognize Thee as our Father
265 And await all goods from Thy hand,
Removing and withdrawing our trust
From all creatures
To put it completely in Thee
And in Thy kindness.
270 And because during this mortal life
We are poor sinners,
So full of frailty that we repeatedly fail
And depart from the straight path,
May it please Thee to pardon us
275 All our faults
That make us liable to Thy judgment;
And by this remission do Thou deliver us
From the bondage to eternal death
Wherein we now are.

280 May it please Thee therefore
To avert Thine anger from us
And not to impute to us
The evil that is in us;
So also let us by Thy commandment

285 Forget the injustices done to us
And, in place of seeking revenge,
Procure the good of our enemies.
Finally, may it please Thee hereafter
To sustain us by Thy power
290 In order that we may not stumble
By the weakness of our flesh.
And inasmuch as we ourselves are so weak
That we cannot remain firm
For a minute of time;
295 Further, as we are surrounded
And assailed continually
By so many enemies;
As the devil, the world, sin, and our own flesh
Cease not to war against us—
300 Strengthen us, we pray Thee,
By Thy Holy Spirit,
And arm us with Thy grace,
In order that we may be able
Constantly to resist all temptations
305 And to persevere in this spiritual battle,
Until we obtain full victory,
To triumph sometime in Thy kingdom
With our Captain and Protector,
Our Lord Jesus Christ. Amen.
310 *The benediction is to be given at the departure of*
the people, as our Lord has ordained (Num. 6).
"The Lord bless you and keep you.
The Lord make His face to shine upon you
And be merciful to you;
315 The Lord turn His gaze upon you
And maintain you in good prosperity."
Amen.

On the day the Lord's Supper is to be celebrated,
the following is to be added to what went before.

320 And as our Lord Jesus
Not only offered for us
Once on the cross

His body and His blood
For the remission of our sins,
325 But also willed to share them with us
As nourishment in life eternal,
Give us such grace that,
With true sincerity of heart
And a burning zeal,
330 We may receive from Him
Such a great benefit and gift
That in sure faith we may receive
His body and His blood.
Likewise it is entirely His
335 As He, being true God and true man,
Is verily the holy, heavenly bread
To quicken us,
So that we may no longer
Live in ourselves and according to our own nature,
340 Which is entirely corrupt and vicious,
But that He may live in us
To lead us to the holy life,
Blessed and everlasting.
In this way may we be truly made
345 Participants in the new and eternal testament,
That is to say,
The covenant of grace,
Being certain and assured that
It is Thy will to be eternally
350 A propitious Father to us,
Not imputing to us our faults,
And as Thy children and beloved heirs
To provide us with all things necessary,
Both for the body
355 And for the soul,
In order that ceaselessly
We may render unto Thee
Glory and thanksgiving
And magnify Thy name
360 By works and by words.

123

Grant us therefore in this manner,
Heavenly Father,
To celebrate today
The happy memory and recollection
365 Of Thy dear Son
To exercise us
And to announce the blessing of His death,
So that, receiving a new increase
And strengthening of faith and of all good,
370 We may, with the greatest trust,
Call Thee once more
Our Father
And glory in Thee. Amen.
    After the supper is finished, this thanksgiving or a
375   *similar one is to be used.*
    Heavenly Father,
    We give Thee praise and everlasting thanks
    That Thou hast bestowed such good
    Upon us poor sinners
380 To draw us into the communion
    Of Thy Son, Jesus Christ, our Lord,
    Having freed us from death,
    And giving Him to us
    As the food and nourishment
385 Of eternal life.
      Now also grant us this boon
      Of never letting us become
      Forgetful of these things,
      But rather, having them impressed on our hearts,
390 We may grow and increase continually
    In the faith, which labors in all good works;
    And in so doing
    We may order and lead our whole lives
    To the exaltation of Thy glory
395 And the upbuilding of our neighbor
    By this Jesus Christ, Thy Son,
    Who in unity of the Holy Spirit
    Lives and reigns with Thee,

O God, eternally. Amen.
400   *The benediction is to be given at the departure of*
      the people, as our Lord has ordained (Num. 6).
    "The Lord bless you and keep you.
    The Lord make His face to shine upon you
    And be merciful to you;
405 The Lord turn His gaze upon you
    And maintain you in good prosperity."
    Amen.

Prayer for Wednesday
Service of Penitence

Inasmuch as Scripture teaches us that plagues,
wars, and other such adversities are visitations of
410 *God by which He punishes our sin, when we see*
them coming we must recognize that God is
angered against us, and then, if we are truly faith-
ful, we have to recognize our faults, become dis-
pleased with ourselves, turning to the Lord in
415 *repentance and amendment of life and in true*
humility, praying to Him in order to obtain
pardon.

For this reason, if we sometimes see that God is
threatening us, in order that we may not try His
420 *patience but rather may anticipate His judgment*
that we see readied against us, it is good to have
one day ordained each week for remonstrances, to
make prayers and supplications according to the
need of the times. There follows a form proper to
425 *that purpose.*

For the beginning of the sermon, there is the
general confession of Sunday set forth above.

At the end of the sermon, remonstrances having
been made as to how God now afflicts men on
430 *account of the things they commit through all the*

earth and abandons the world to all iniquity;
exhortations also having been made to the people
to return and amend their lives, as well as to pray
God to impart mercy, one uses a form of prayer as
435   *follows:*

Almighty God, heavenly Father,
We recognize in ourselves
And confess it as the truth
That we are not worthy
440   To lift our eyes to heaven
To present ourselves before Thy face
And that we must not presume
Our prayers have to be answered by Thee
If Thou regardest only what is in us.
445   For our consciences accuse us
And our sins testify against us,
And we know Thou art a just Judge
Who dost not justify
The sinners and wicked ones
450   But punishest the faults of those
Who have transgressed Thy commandments.
Thus, Lord, in considering our whole lives,
We are confused in our hearts
And can do nothing else
455   But cast ourselves down in despair,
As if we were already
In the abyss of death.
However, Lord,
Since it has pleased Thee
460   By Thine infinite mercy
To bid us call upon Thee,
Even from the depths of hell,
And—the more we fail in ourselves—
To know we have our shelter and refuge
465   In Thy sovran goodness;
Since also Thou hast promised us
To receive our requests and supplications,
Not considering what is our proper due,

But in the name and by the merit
470   Of our Lord Jesus Christ,
Whom Thou hast established
As Intercessor and Advocate,
Renouncing all human confidence—
We take our strength in Thy goodness alone,
475   To address ourselves before Thy majesty
And to invoke Thy holy name
To obtain grace and mercy.

First, O Lord,
Beyond the infinite benefits
480   Thou distributest indiscriminately
To all men on earth,
Thou hast given us
So many special gifts
That it is impossible for us
485   To enumerate them
Or even sufficiently to comprehend them.

Especially has it pleased Thee
To call us to the knowledge
Of Thy holy gospel,
490   Drawing us back
From the miserable bondage of the devil
Wherein we were,
Delivering us from cursed idolatry
And superstitions in which we were plunged,
495   To lead us into the light of Thy truth.
Do this, we pray Thee,
Even though, by ungratefulness and forgetfulness,
Having forgotten the goods we have received
From Thy hand,
500   We have declined,
Turning ourselves from Thee
According to our lusts,
Not having rendered honor or obedience
To Thy sacred Word as we ought.

505 We have not exalted and magnified Thee
As is meet,
And although Thou hast always faithfully
Admonished us by Thy Word,
We have not listened to Thy remonstrances.
510 We have therefore sinned;
O Lord,
We have offended Thee.

Accordingly confusion and disgrace are upon us;
We recognize that we are
515 Grievously blameable before Thy judgment;
And if Thou wouldst treat us
According to our worth,
We could expect only death and condemnation.
For when we would excuse ourselves,
520 Our consciences accuse us;
And our iniquity is before Thee,
To condemn us.
Actually, O Lord,
We see how by the chastisements
525 That have already come to us,
Thou hast rightly been angered against us.
For since Thou art just and equitable,
It is not without reason
That Thou afflictest Thine own.
530 Having therefore been beaten with Thy rods,
We recognize that Thou art irritated against us.
And now we see Thy hand again raised up
To punish us,
For the swords with which
535 Thou art accustomed to execute Thy vengeance
Are now deployed,
And the threats that Thou hast made
Against sinners and the wicked
Are all made ready.

540 But when Thou wouldst punish us

Much more harshly
Than Thou hast done until now,
And that for one wound
We should have to receive a hundred—
545 Even that the curses with which
Thou hast formerly corrected
The faults of Thy people Israel
Would fall upon us—
We confess this would be with good reason
550 And do not gainsay
That we have indeed deserved it.

Yet, O Lord, Thou art our Father,
And we are but earth and mire;
Thou art our Creator,
555 And we are the work of Thy hands;
Thou art our Shepherd,
We are Thy flock;
Thou art our Redeemer,
We are the people Thou hast bought back;
560 Thou art our God,
We are Thine inheritance.
Therefore, be not angry against us,
To correct us in Thy wrath.
Recall not our iniquity,
565 To punish it;
But chastise us gently
In Thy kindliness.
Because of our demerits,
Thine anger is enflamed.
570 But be mindful
That Thy name is called upon among us
And that we bear Thy mark and badge.
Undertake rather the work
Thou hast already begun in us
575 By Thy grace,
In order that the whole earth may recognize
That Thou art our God and our Savior.

Thou knowest that the dead
Who are in hell
580 And those whom Thou wilt undo and confound
Will not praise Thee;
But sad and desolate souls,
Hearts cast down,
Consciences oppressed with the feeling of their evil
585 And hungering with desire for Thy grace,
Will give Thee praise and honor.
Thy people Israel several times
Stirred Thee to wrath by their iniquity;
Thou afflictedst them
590 By Thy just judgment.
But when they returned to Thee,
Thou always didst receive them with pity.
And grievous as were their offenses,
For the love of Thy covenant
595 That Thou hadst made
With Thy servants Abraham, Isaac, and Jacob,
Thou didst turn aside
Thy rods and curses
That were prepared for them,
600 So that their prayers
Were never rejected by Thee.
We have, by Thy grace,
A covenant much better
That we can cite to Thee:
605 It is the one Thou hast made and established,
In the hand of Jesus Christ,
Our Savior,
A covenant Thou willedst to be
Written in His blood,
610 Ratified by His death and passion.
Therefore, O Lord,
Renouncing ourselves
And all human hope,
We appeal to that blessed covenant
615 By which our Lord Jesus,

Offering His body as sacrifice to Thee,
Has reconciled us to Thee.
Look then, O Lord, upon the face
Of Thy Christ, not upon us,
620 So that by Thine intercession
Thine anger may be placated
And Thy countenance may shine
Upon us in joy and in salvation;
And henceforth mayest thou
625 Receive us into Thy holy charge
And govern us by Thy Spirit,
Who regenerates us
Into a better life, etc.
Here is to be added the paraphrase set above, at the
630 *end of the Sunday prayers, after which the sermon*
is preached. Then one says the following:
And although we are not worthy
To open our mouths for ourselves
And to make request of Thee
635 In our need,
Nevertheless it has pleased Thee
To bid us pray for one another.
We pray Thee for all our poor brothers and members
Whom Thou visitest with Thy rods and chastisements,
640 Supplicating Thee to turn Thy wrath away from them;
Namely, for N–– and N––.
Be mindful, O Lord,
That they are Thy children
As are we;
645 And if they have offended Thee,
Fail not to pursue them
With Thy bounty and mercy,
Which Thou hast promised
Is to be perpetual unto all the faithful.
650 Please therefore look with pity
Upon all Thy churches
And all Thy peoples
Whom Thou hast now afflicted,

127

Either by plague,
655 Or by war,
Or by other rods;
And let not Christianity
Be entirely forsaken;
Let not the memory of Thy name
660 Be abolished in the earth;
Let not those
Upon whom Thou hast willed
Thy name to be invoked,
Entirely perish;
665 And let the Turks and pagans,
In blaspheming Thee,
Glorify Thee.

The rest is set out above, on the second page of the Sunday prayers, after the sermon.

Formula of Absolution and Prayer for Illumination

Here the minister speaks some word of Scripture to comfort the consciences and makes absolution in this manner:[8]

May each of you
Truly recognize yourself
A sinner groveling before God
And believe that the heavenly Father
In Jesus Christ wills
To look on you with favor.
Unto all those who in this manner
Repent and seek Jesus Christ
As their salvation,
I declare absolution
In the name of the Father,
Of the Son, and of the Holy Spirit.
Amen.

Here the church sings; then the minister says:
The Lord be with you.
Let us pray to the Lord.
Heavenly Father,
Full of goodness and grace,
As it pleases Thee to declare
Thy holy will to Thy poor servants
And to instruct them
In the righteousness of Thy law,
Mayest thou will it so
To be written and imprinted on our hearts
That in our whole lives
We seek only to serve and obey Thee,
Not imputing the transgressions
We have committed against it
In order that, feeling Thy grace
Multiplying upon us so abundantly,
We may have occasion
To praise and glorify Thee,
By Jesus Christ, Thy Son our Lord.

Here while the church sings, the minister goes into the pulpit and thereupon offers prayers of the following sort at the beginning of the sermon.

We shall call upon our heavenly Father,
Father of all goodness and mercy,
Begging Him to cast the eye of His kindness
On us His poor servants,
Not imputing to us
The many faults and offenses
Committed by us,
Whose great unworthiness
Can only arouse His wrath toward us,
But looking upon us in the face
Of His Son, Jesus Christ our Lord.
As He has appointed Him
Mediator between Himself and us,
We shall pray that He,
As all fullness of wisdom

And light is in Him,
May desire to direct us
By His Holy Spirit
To the true understanding
Of His holy doctrine,
To fructify it in us
In all the fruits of righteousness
To the glory
Of His name.
Recognizing we owe Him such obedience
As servants should render their master
And children their father,
We shall pray to Him
In the words of our good Master:
Our Father, etc.

Prayers After the Sermon on Working Days

It was customary on working days, instead of using the detailed paraphrase of the Lord's Prayer of the Sunday Service (lines 58–309 above), to follow the sermon with a freer form of prayer, in three parts. Part 1 is a brief opening formula, exhortatory in character, with slight internal variation from sermon to sermon; part 2 is a very short reflection upon the content of the sermon, generally containing two requests only; part 3 is a concluding statement taking one of two basic forms. Of the second part Rodolphe Peter said that it "often contains felicitous expressions stamped with real spirituality."[9]

The Beginning and the Middle

First, God was addressed in these or similar words: "Let us therefore bow before the majesty of our good God...." Then followed a brief reference to our sins, fashioned with variant forms, arranged in five "slots,"

and occasionally expanded at the end, as the following analysis shows:

1. Recognizing
2.   our
      all our
      the
      the infinite
      the great
      the great number of
      the innumerable
3.   faults
      offenses
      sins
      poverty
      misery
4.   and
      faults
      poverty
5.   of which we are guilty (before Him)
      which we have committed
      with which we have proked His wrath
      with which we are burdened
      which are in us

Thus you the reader can construct the introduction to your own prayer out of the same materials which Calvin himself used, varying the form according to your need.

Three examples follow of the beginning and middle portions of the prayer, in which the ideas of the sermon are rehearsed. All three come from Calvin's sermons on I Samuel 2 in *Homilies on I Samuel.*[10]

Let us therefore bow
Before the majesty
Of our good God,
Recognizing the great number of faults and offenses

With which we have provoked
His wrath against us.

Let us pray to Him
That He may etch the fear of His majesty
Upon our minds
And make us sharers in those things
That we have learned in this scripture,
That by His strength He may support
Our weakness and infirmity,
And may make us victors
By the power of His Spirit,
And provide sufficient strength
For us to withstand any temptations
To which we would otherwise be unequal,
And run the whole course of our lives
In obedience to Him,
Giving eternal thanks to Him
For His many and great benefits to us;
Finally, that all our senses
May be lifted up in worshiping Him
To His everlasting praise and glory,
And we may be led
In the pathway of salvation,
Not for our own private advantage,
But for the upbuilding of our neighbors.

———————

Let us therefore bow to God,
And, recognizing the innumerable sins
With which we daily provoke Him,
Let us pray to Him
That He may more and more affect us
By the power of His Spirit
And thus restore and reform us;
That, renouncing ourselves,
We may be wholly carried
Into obedience to His will;

That we may receive grace.
And since we are far removed
From this perfection,
Despoiled by our own infirmities,
Let Him clothe us with His righteousness
And, forgiving our offenses,
Embrace us with His bounty,
Until, fully cleansed of our vices,
We may reign with Him.

———————

Now let us kneel before God's majesty,
Making supplications for our many and great sins,
With which we daily stir up
His wrath against us.
Let us request Him
To open the eyes of our mind
That, touched with a deep repentance
And sense of our past sins,
We may compose ourselves hereafter
To His obedience,
In true faith and repentance:
Never doubting that we shall find Him
Ever ready to forgive our offenses,
Provided we do not hesitate
To take refuge with Him
Who by His Word seeks us;
And thus relying on His goodness,
Let us consecrate ourselves wholly,
That He may be glorified
In all our life;
And we may patiently and steadfastly await
His ever-ready help
Against all temptations.

The End

Two forms of the concluding portion of the closing prayer have been noted in Calvin's sermons, with some slight variation. The first and more common form generally begins, "May He bestow this grace not only upon us . . ." Sometimes, however, this first sentence is dropped and the concluding portion begins, "And for this reason may it please Him to arouse (or raise up) . . ." A second, less common form of the concluding portion of the closing prayer (not here translated in full) begins: "Thus we shall all say together, 'Almighty God, heavenly Father . . .' "

Here we give both a shorter variant of the more common form used by Calvin up to 1553 and also a longer variant used by him after that date.[11]

May He bestow this grace
Not only upon us
But upon all,
Inasmuch as we see that Christianity
Is so forsaken.
May we therefore be so moved to pray
In order that His kingdom
May be established in our midst;
To do this let Him raise up for us
True ministers
In order that His flock
May be maintained.
May it please Him to give
To princes and magistrates
Such zeal that they seek not
Their own honor;
May He bestow upon them the grace
To live to His glory,
Correcting all iniquity,
In order that all of us together
May render to Him the honor
That is His due.

May He bestow this grace

Not only upon us
But upon all peoples
And nations of the earth,
Calling back all poor,
Ignorant folk
From the blind captivity
Of error and ignorance
To the straight path of salvation.
And for this reason
May it please Him
To arouse the true and faithful ministers
Of His Word
Not to seek
Their own advantage and ambition,
But the exalting of His name
And also the welfare of His flock;
Conversely, that He may uproot
And destroy all sects,
Heresies, and errors,
Which are the seedbed
Of disturbances and divisions
In the church,
That we may all together
Live in brotherly concord.

May He by His Holy Spirit
Reign and govern over all kings,
Princes, and lords,
Who possess the administration
Of the sword,
That their rule
May not be exercised
In greed, cruelty, and tyranny,
But in all righteousness
And uprightness.
May we also, living under them,
Render the honor and obedience
Due them, that, enjoying

Peace and tranquillity,
We may serve God
In all holiness and honesty.
May it be His will
To comfort all poor, afflicted folk
Whom He visits with various kinds
Of crosses and tribulations,
People whom He chastises with plague,
War, famine, or His other punishments,
All men afflicted with poverty,
Prison, disease, exile,
Or other calamity of body
Or affliction of mind;
May He so support all
With firm patience
Until He shall utterly free His own
From all their misfortunes.

But chiefly may He strengthen
And confirm with true constancy
His faithful ones who have,
In Babylonian captivity,
Been scattered in various places
Under Antichrist's tyranny,
And who also suffer persecution
As a witness of heavenly truth;
May He comfort them
And not leave them to wicked
And rapacious wolves
To exercise their ferocity against them,
But let Him give them true constancy,
That His most holy name
May be glorified by them
Both in life and in death.
May it be His will
To confirm and protect
All His churches that today toil
And are besieged

As a witness
To His most holy name;
May He overturn and destroy
The counsels, plots, and undertakings
Of all His enemies
In order that His glory
May shine everywhere the more
And the kingdom of our Lord Jesus Christ
May be the more increased and furthered.
All these things therefore
We will seek from Him,
Even as our supreme Master and Lord
Jesus Christ has taught us
To pray to Him in these words:
Our Father, etc.

Prayers Before and After the Exegetical Lectures

It was Calvin's custom to open and close his lectures on the Old Testament prophets with short prayers. The opening formula is short and unvaried; the closing prayer follows a set form with variation of content to fit the particular lecture. These prayers, numbering 524, are omitted from the *Corpus Reformatorum* text. They are carried, however, in earlier editions of Calvin's works (e.g., that of Schipper) and are translated into English in the volumes of the Calvin Translation Society. Six examples are offered here following the initial prayer.[12]

Initial Prayer

May the Lord grant
That we may contemplate
The mysteries of His heavenly wisdom
With truly increasing devotion,
To His glory

And to our edification.
Amen.

Concluding Prayer

Almighty God,
We never cease to cut ourselves off
From Thee by our sins,
And yet Thou gently urgest us
To repentance
And promisest also
To hear our prayer with favor.
Grant we may not stubbornly keep in our sins
And be ungrateful to Thy great generosity,
But may return to Thee in such a way
As to witness by our lives
To the genuineness of our repentance
And may so rest in Thee alone
As to resist being buffeted
Hither and thither by the perverse lusts
Of our flesh.
Rather, grant we may stand firm and fast
In a right purpose
And so endeavor
To obey Thee throughout our lives,
At last receiving the fruit of our obedience
In Thy heavenly kingdom
Through Jesus Christ our Lord.
Amen.

—————————

Almighty God,
Thou settest before our eyes
The many evils and vices
By which we have provoked
Thine anger against us
And yet givest us the hope
Of pardon if we repent.
Grant us a teachable spirit

That with becoming meekness
We may pay attention
To Thy threatenings
And be so terrified by them
As not to despair
Of the mercy offered us,
But seek it through Thy Son.
As He has once for all
Made peace with Thee
By shedding His blood,
So cleanse Thou us also
By Thy Spirit
From all our pollutions,
Until at last we stand
Spotless before Thee
In that day
When Christ shall appear
For the salvation
Of all His people.
Amen.

—————————

Almighty God,
Thou hast in the gospel
Set clearly before us
With how many and how dreadful sins
We are crammed.
This Thou hast done
In order that we may learn
To be displeased with ourselves
And so lie down, confounded and despairing,
In our sins and in the guilt
Contracted from them;
Thus we may yet know the true glory
That has been offered us,
And we can be made
Partakers of it
If we embrace with true faith

133

Thine only begotten Son,
In whom perfect righteousness and salvation
Have been offered us.
Grant we may so cleave to Christ
And receive His benefits in faith
That we may be able,
Not only before the world
But also against Satan
And against death itself,
To glory in Thee.
For Thou alone art just and wise and strong:
May Thy strength, Thy justice, Thy wisdom
Shine upon us
In our iniquity and ignorance and weakness,
Until at last we may reach
That fullness of glory
Laid up for us in heaven
Through the same Christ our Lord.
Amen.

———————

Almighty God,
Thou didst frame heaven and earth
For our sake;
Thou didst witness to us
Through Thy servant Moses
That both sun and moon
(Foolishly held divine by the pagans)
Are under us,
And their resources we are so to use
As if they were our servants.
Grant then by Thy many blessings
We may be lifted up
And come to Thy true glory;
May worship Thee
In pure simplicity,
Wholly surrender ourselves to Thee;
Using the resources

Of all stars and even of earth itself,
May know ourselves
By that many benefits
Bound to Thee;
May more and more be kindled
To seek after righteousness
And strive to glorify
Thy name on earth,
At last coming to that blessed glory
Prepared for us in heaven
By Christ our Lord.
Amen.

———————

Almighty God,
Thou showest Thy glory
For us to see,
Not only in heaven and earth
But also in the law, the prophets, and the gospel;
And hast so intimately revealed Thyself
In Thine only begotten Son
That we cannot excuse ourselves
Out of ignorance.
Grant that we may advance in this teaching,
Wherewith Thou so kindly invitest us to Thyself,
And may thus steadfastly cleave to Thee
That no errors of the world
May lead us astray;
But may stand firmly fixed
In Thy Word,
Which cannot deceive us:
At last reaching heavenly blessedness,
Where we may enjoy
Thy glory face to face,
Conformed completely to Thee
In Christ Jesus our Lord.
Amen.

Almighty God,
Thou hast deigned to show Thyself
So intimately to us
And also daily deignest
To confirm us in Thy truth.
Grant we may turn aside
Neither to the right nor to the left,
But depend wholly on Thy Word
And so cleave to Thee
That no errors of the world
May lead us astray.
May we stand firm in that faith
Which we have learned from Thy law,
From the prophets and the gospel
(Wherein Thou hast more clearly
Shown Thyself through Christ),
That we may finally enjoy
Thy full and perfect glory,
Being transfigured into it,
At last attaining that inheritance
Acquired for us by the blood
Of Thine only begotten Son.
Amen.

Notes

1. The first Calvinian liturgy (that of 1539–1540, now lost) and all subsequent French Reformed liturgies of Strasbourg and Geneva rest upon Martin Bucer's *Psalter mit aller Kirchenübung* (Strasbourg, 1539). This in turn was the culmination, through nineteen stages, of what began with Diebold Schwarz (Th. Nigri) in the translation of the Latin Mass into German in 1525. Throughout this long succession of liturgies, the basic scheme was kept, but details were gradually changed with elimination of sacerdotal and sacrificial elements and the incorporation of corporate prayers, the emphasis upon preaching, etc. R. Will noted that even the titles of these successive liturgies indicate the reforming process: "German Mass," "German Church Office," "Order of the Lord's Supper," then "Church Practice." "La première liturgie de Calvin," *Revue d'histoire et de philosophie*

religieuses 18 (1938): 526f. See also William D. Maxwell, *John Knox's Service Book, 1556: The Liturgical Portions of the Genevan Service Book Used by John Knox . . . , 1556–1559* (Edinburgh: Oliver and Boyd, 1931), passim; and Hughes Oliphant Old, *The Patristic Roots of Reformed Worship* (Zurich: Theologischer Verlag, 1975), pp. 99f.

2. *Devotions and Prayers of John Calvin* (Grand Rapids: Baker, 1960).

3. In OC, 6:172–80; OS, 2:11–58.

4. OS, 2:15.

5. The text of the Sunday Liturgy is taken from OC, 6:172–80; cf. OS, 2:18–26. For the text of the Wednesday Service, see R. Peter, ed., *Sermons sur le livre de Jérémie et des Lamentations*, in SC, 6:xxxiii–xxxix; cf. OS, 2:26–30.

6. From *The Form of Prayers*, in OS, 2:19f.

7. See OS, 2:1ff.; SC, 6:xxxiii; William D. Maxwell, *An Outline of Christian Worship: Its Development and Forms* (London: Oxford University, 1936), pp. 114f.

8. To be inserted in accordance with rubric after line 47 above.

9. In SC, 6:xxxii.

10. Homilies no. 6 (Schipper, 2:25), 11 (ibid., 2:47), and 16 (ibid., 2:69), respectively. The middle begins, "Let us pray . . ."

11. The shorter variant is the concluding portion of the closing prayer found in the *Homilies on Jeremiah* (1549–1550), in SC, 6:6. The longer variant is the concluding portion of the closing prayer found in the *Sermons on Job* (1554–1555), in Schipper, tom. 2, fol. *2^V.

12. All six are from *Homilies on Jeremiah* (1549–1550). They conclude, respectively, lectures no. 14 (Schipper, 4:45), 37 (4:118), 38 (4:121), 39 (4:124), 40 (4:127), and 41 (4:131).

*   *   *   *

48–54. Cf. pp. 128f. below.

67. Matt. 28:20.

71. Matt. 18:19f.

75. I Tim. 2:2.

78. I Tim. 2:1.

107. I Tim. 6:15; Rev. 17:14.

109. Matt. 28:18.

114. Ps. 100:3.

120. I Tim. 2:2.

122. Luke 1:74.

143. I Peter 2:25; 5:4.

148. Matt. 7:15.

149. John 10:12.

167f. John 17:3.

180ff. Cf. pp. 59ff. above.

223. Matt. 6:9–13.

252. II Cor. 10:4f.

311. Num. 6:24–26.

318ff. For the French text of the Communion Service, see OC, 6:193–202; OS, 2:45–49.

581. Ps. 115:17.

Chapter 6

Metrical Psalms Translated by Calvin

The Genesis of French Psalmody

We have already alluded to Calvin's appreciation of the power of music, for good or ill.[1] While it was not until the spring of 1539 that his first collection of Psalms,[2] metrically paraphrased and set to appropriate tunes, was published, his modest effort had a rather complex origin and even more complex consequences for Reformed worship.

Profound forces were at this time working to transform the music inherited from the medieval church and that of the secular songs imbedded in popular culture. Both of these musical streams contributed, at once negatively and positively, to the psalmody that originated in the 1520s and 1530s.

Among the features of "papal" worship rejected by the Reformers in varying degrees and ways were mumbled Psalms, executed without understanding.[3] At the same time, men like Luther, Erasmus, Zwingli, and Calvin understood the dangerous effects, particularly on the young, of lascivious songs.[4] Like Plato, who excluded all but the Dorian mode from his Republic, these sixteenth-century writers sought to exclude such songs even from marriage festivities.[5] Perhaps a musician of such talent as Zwingli threw up his hands at the problem of domesticating music in the Reformed church of Zurich and so banished it altogether from divine service.[6] More realistically, Luther sought to adapt some medieval psalmody and hymnody to the new vernacular worship through the medium of simple poetic texts set to appealing tunes.

In his letter of 1523 to Spalatin, Luther sent out a call to German poets to translate the Psalms into hymns, simple, unadorned and direct, to make the Word of God through song to live among the people. Like Calvin later, Luther belittled his own poetic efforts, but unlike Calvin's, Luther's hymns and Psalms have endured.[7]

But it was not so much Luther who directly initiated Reformed psalmody. This task fell to Martin Bucer and to the Reformed church of Strasbourg, under the spiritual and theological direction of Bucer and his colleague Wolfgang Capito. In that city from 1524 onward Bucer undertook to provide Scriptural instruction in both Latin and German;[8] much of his exegetical labor was focused on the Psalms, eventuating in 1529 in the publication of his *Commentary on the Psalms*. It was from the Latin version of the Psalter contained in that commentary that George Joye made his important English translation.[9] Bucer's vision of a religion of the heart, going beyond mere words and shared by the whole people of God, was fed by the Davidic piety. The flowering of the German Psalter in Strasbourg began in 1524 and proceeded through the series of enlarged and improved editions to 1539, the year of Calvin's first effort.[10] Bucer's psalmody was abetted by the school renaissance instituted by Johannes Sturm, who came from Paris to organize an academy in Strasbourg in 1537. It was also helped by fine musicians like Mattheus Greiter and Wolfgang Dachstein, whose facility at providing suitable melodies insured the success of congregational singing.

How quickly psalmody took hold at Strasbourg is attested by Gérard Roussel, the early French Reformer, who during a six-month exile there wrote (in December 1525) the Bishop of Meaux (initially favorable to reform in France) of the intense piety of the Strasbourgers. His almost rhapsodic description of the frequent preaching and singing of Psalms in crowded churches makes one think that here, at last, was the laicization and vernacularization of the canonical hours of the older monasticism, but with a fervor worthy of the Apostolic Age.[11]

It was the singing of Psalms by German voices that Calvin heard on his visit to Strasbourg and that led him early in his exile there (1538–1541) to compile for French singers a comparable collection.[12] But doubtless long before Calvin took up his pastorate at Strasbourg and even before he was impressed by Farel into his Genevan career, he had had reports of the singing of Psalms in Strasbourg from countrymen like Roussel, who, as we have seen, had experienced the inception of psalmody. Farel's correspondence with Bucer dates from 1528, Calvin's from 1534.

Thus, some time before French psalmody formally began in 1539, there was a desire to inaugurate the singing of Psalms in the French Reformed service. This is seen in the petition of Farel and Calvin to the Council of Geneva in January 1537.[13] The decision of the city to embrace the gospel faith, made in May 1536,[14] did not at once bring the religious and moral transformation it at first seemed to promise.[15] In their request to the council, Calvin and Farel complained of the cold tone of worship and rightly sensed the power of song to lift hearts and bring fervor. While the council promptly approved this along with other requests, there is no evidence that singing was at once introduced into the services of Geneva.[16]

But when the two Reformers were banished on 23 April 1538 (for their refusal to accept the dictation of the council on disciplinary and liturgical matters and for their effort to safeguard the Lord's table against profanation), they did not forget the matter of singing Psalms. As they journeyed first to Bern (where psalmody was then being undertaken)[17] and to Zurich, where a synod was in session in early May, the two banished leaders incorporated both a proposal for psalmody[18] and a prohibition of lascivious songs[19] in their memorandum which, through the synod, they were forwarding to the Geneva council, setting forth the basis upon which they would return from exile to their old posts at Geneva. Their appeal in this latter regard, however, was rejected by the city fathers.

It was not therefore until Calvin took up his pastorate with the French émigré congregation in Strasbourg in September 1538 that the opportunity to attain his desire of having French psalmody presented itself. The congregation, which now had full worship with monthly communion from October on, wished to have Psalms to sing in French, for daily they heard their German fellow Christians singing. And just then Calvin came into possession (how, it is not clear) of some metrical paraphrases of the Psalms by the celebrated court poet Clément Marot, although not in the form in which they were subsequently published under Marot's name.[20] Further, the beauty of certain German tunes so struck Calvin's ear that he himself undertook composing first metrical paraphrases of Psalms 25 and 46[21] and then of several others, all but one rhymed,[22] to be sung to those tunes. In addition he put in meter the Ten Commandments (with the Kyrie Eleison as refrain), the Song of Simeon, and the Apostles' Creed.[23] Calvin's purpose was entirely utilitarian, but his work had greater poetic merit than later critics or even he himself would concede.[24] Although Calvin's texts continued to be used as late as the 1553 Strasbourg edition and, with the

exception of Psalm 113, were used in the Genevan *Form of Prayers and Songs of the Church* of 1542, all his texts were suppressed in favor of Marot's in the Genevan Psalter of 1551 and subsequent editions. There is a directness and strength to his poetry that one does not find in the more polished verses of Marot. It has been suggested that Calvin intended "the Song of Simeon, Psalm 113 and Psalm 138 . . . for the Communion and Post-communion Thanksgiving. Psalm 25 and the Ten Commandments were probably meant to be sung after the Prayer of Confession."[25]

It is of course idle speculation, but if Calvin had followed the leading of his work on Psalm 113 and produced other metrical but unrhymed versions of the Psalms to be sung to the vigorous German tunes, the whole history of psalmody both in French-speaking lands and elsewhere would probably have gone differently. To be sure the limits of the Psalter would eventually have to be breached (there was precedent already in the Canticles of the 1539 collection), but tasteless rhyming would not have so confined psalmody. But he left to others this task, concentrating his attention on the theological labor in all its vast ramifications.

The modest collection of 1539 was an immediate success. Even Geneva itself, shortly to urge his return, presumably received one hundred copies soon after publication.[26] Thus we see how the task of giving the people the Psalter in their own language and in tunes that spoke directly to their hearts, previously achieved by Bucer for the German evangelicals of Strasbourg, was now launched by Calvin not only in Strasbourg, but in Neuchâtel, Geneva, Lausanne, Montbéliard, and Metz, and in France itself. With the help first of Marot, then of Beza, he saw by 1562 the whole Psalter in French, and especially with the collaboration of Loys Bourgeois, he saw tunes worthy of the texts supplied for use not only in formal worship, but also wherever men and women were at work or leisure. And to make sure the rapid progress of psalmody, Calvin advocated the teaching of the Psalms to the children, who in turn by their singing would teach them to the adults.[27]

The Music of Calvin's Psalms

The purpose of presenting these musical settings of the Psalms is twofold. First, there is a desire to restore to the repertory of congregations and choirs for public worship Psalm melodies that recapture the early-sixteenth-century rhythms and meters, which are of much more interest and artistic import than those presently available. Second, there is an attempt to provide accompaniments and polyphonic settings that will maintain the unique metrical personality common to these melodies and texts. Only those Psalm texts attributed to Calvin are treated, but it is hoped that other musicians will seek out similar Psalms and enhance our repertory with additional settings for use as service music in the United States.

It will be immediately apparent that these Psalm texts are longer than the common meter versions to which we are accustomed. One of the goals of early Reformed liturgy was to present the entire Psalm in its musical setting.[28] In dividing the total Psalm into strophes at repetitions of the music, greater length of each musical repetition was necessary. And similarly, each line of the paraphrased Psalm text was longer than those in the usual body of our hymnody.

Another unique feature of these Psalms is that the music had previously been used for German texts and thus French texts had to be adapted to it. Yet there are surprisingly few changes in the melodies, a fact which attests to Calvin's literary ability as well as points up the difficulty of compromising one language in a musical setting intended for another.

With the interesting juxtaposition of lines of different length and metrical accent, the French texts and these musical settings share a gentle flow and remarkable symmetry of organization that makes them immediately singable and easy to memorize in spite of their length. In the English translations an effort has been made to retain these qualities as well as to restore some of the weight and accent associated with the original German texts.

Composers. Greiter (d. 1550) and Dachstein (d. 1561) were church musicians at Strasbourg who were also on the faculty at the school.[29] Their authorship of the respective Psalm melodies is not now contested.[30] Greiter's music for Psalm 119 in the 1539 Psalter was used by Bach in the German chorale "O Mensch, bewein' " in his celebrated organ chorale from *Orgelbüchlein* and in the closing of part 1 of *St. Matthew Passion.* Dachstein's Psalm 137, "An Wasserflüssen Babylon," not among the Psalms here under consideration, has been used in the music of Ducis, Hellingk, Wallister, and Tunder, as well as in Bach's alternate settings in the collection of *Eighteen Chorales* for organ.[31] Pierre Pidoux's suggestion that Luther wrote the melody of Psalm 130 (our Psalm 113), "Aus tiefer Not," may stem from a confusion of this melody with the more familiar Phrygian melody that appeared one year earlier and that was used in a Bach organ work quoted in *Clavierübung,* part 3.

Sources. A *unicum* of the Psalter of 1539 exists at the Royal Library of Munich, two facsimiles of which have been published.[32] However faithful the reproductions, it proved difficult to transcribe into modern notation portions of Psalms 91 and 113. In the first instance, the awkward leap from the penultimate to the final bar is a result of suppressing the penultimate bar of the original German melody. (The penultimate bar of the German melody was not needed in the French paraphrase; neither was the original repeat of the first four lines.) In Psalm 113 the final bar has a ligature intended to slur in long notes one syllable of the French text. Errors occur in both instances in Richard R. Terry's transcriptions, but our realizations are borne out in the original German as well as in the subsequent French Strasbourg Psalters.

Performance. Although the early Psalters contain only texts and melodic lines, there is no reason to hold that accompaniments were not employed.[33] Organs continued to be used in Strasbourg even after the instruments were silenced in Geneva in 1535.[34] The length of the Psalms suggests some sort of accompaniment for leading the congregation as well as keeping them on pitch.

In the versions that follow, the melodies maintain the modes and rhythms of the originals. But the longer Psalms provide opportunities for alternating the congregation with the choir for some strophes merely to avoid monotony. Occasionally polyphonic settings enhance the homophonic strophes, and while the modes and key centers will shift in other than *cantus firmus* voices for the sake of interest, the modes of the melodies remain true to the original in all cases but one.

These accompaniments encourage singing the Psalms quickly and sometimes quite lustily. The feeling that slow music is religious music just does not work here! The flow and breath-pauses will be easier if a good pace is established and maintained throughout. The accompaniments are basic and allow the melody to stand forward with clarity and without competition. Yet the accompaniments may receive discretionary alteration in succeeding strophes with good effect. In the same respect alternate polyphonic settings by Arcadelt, Bourgeois, Champion, Goudimel, Janequin, L'Estocart,[35] Le Jeune and Sweelinck may be used.

The early French congregations greeted these settings with enthusiasm, and it is hoped our congregations and choirs will as well. As in the sixteenth century,[36] children today can learn these Psalms quickly and accurately, and in singing them for their elders they will introduce a new song to present-day worship.[37]

Notes

1. See introduction to chap. 5 above.

2. *Alcuns pseaulmes et cantiques mys en chant* (Strasbourg, 1539); no publisher, editor, or compiler is listed. This is discussed further below.

3. The ministers of Geneva wrote the Council of Geneva (ca. 13 January 1537): "Besides, by this [the singing of the Psalms] we will be able to recognize of what good and what consolation the pope and his followers have deprived the Church, seeing that they have so used the Psalms, which must be true spiritual songs, to mumble them among themselves without any understanding." Herminjard, no. 602, 4:163.

4. Calvin and Farel wrote the Synod of Zurich in early May 1538: "[We] request that lascivious and obscene songs and accompanying dances be suppressed, following the Bernese precedent." Herminjard, no. 708, 5:6.

5. Herminjard has cited a council held in early August 1537 (at Gex?) that requested the Council of Bern to suppress the singing of lascivious *rondes* while dancing. No. 708 (note); cf. no. 650 (note 1). The following year Bern renewed the regulation, excepting only marriage days. *Manual*, 16 June and 5 July 1538.

6. For a comprehensive treatment of the subject, see Charles Garside, *Zwingli and the Arts* (New Haven: Yale University, 1966).

7. On Luther's hymns and Psalms see volume 53 of LW, *Liturgy and Hymns,* ed. Ulrich S. Leupold (1965). Luther provided, among his German hymns, paraphrases of Psalms 12, 14, 46 (*"Ein' feste Burg"*), 67, 124, 128, and 130 (*"Aus tiefer Not"*).

8. See R. Gerald Hobbs, "An Introduction to the Psalms Commentary of Martin Bucer" (Thesis, Strasbourg, 1971), pp. 48ff.

9. See G. E. Duffield, "Introduction," in Martin Bucer, *The Psalter of David* (Appleford, Eng.: Sutton Courtenay, 1971), pp. 7ff.

10. For a recently published list and discussion of this series, see Hughes Oliphant Old, *The Patristic Roots of Reformed Worship* (Zurich: Theologischer Verlag, 1975), pp. 97–100.

11. See Gérard Roussel's letter to the bishop of Meaux, written from Strasbourg in December 1525: "Here there are very many things that cannot but please you, namely that arouse and promote piety, because the ministers of the churches so keep the Word awake that, at almost no hour of the day is their own pure food lacking to the sheep. . . . From the fifth hour of the morning to the sixth, preaching is held in individual churches and common prayers offered. Then at the seventh hour the same is repeated; but at the eighth hour, or thereabouts, preaching takes place in the larger church, accompanied by songs translated from the Hebrew Psalter into the common language, where women wonderfully sing together with men, so that it is pleasing to hear. Also in the same church preaching is repeated at the fourth hour after lunch, not omitting likewise the songs that precede and follow the sermon, as it were, by the latter asking grace whereby they may be made fit to receive the Gospel seed, and may keep it, once received, with their thanks. And in order that more may be seen to frequent the services, it is of no little interest that a great crowd of people is eager for the divine Word. I long for nothing as much as that this desire be instilled into the breasts of our own people." Herminjard, no. 167, 1:406f.

12. See note 2 above.

13. The ministers of Geneva wrote the Council of Geneva (ca. 13 January 1537): "The second article concerns the Psalms, which we desire to be sung in the church, as we have the example of in the ancient church, and even the witness of St. Paul, who says it is good to sing in the congregation from the mouth and from the heart. We cannot conceive the advancement and edification that will proceed from this without having experienced it. Indeed as we do it, the prayers of the faithful are so cold that that must bring upon us great shame and confusion. The Psalms can arouse us to lift up our hearts to God and move us to an ardor both to call upon and to exalt by praises the glory of His name." Herminjard, no. 602, 4:162f.

14. On Sunday, 21 May 1536, the General Council of Geneva decided unanimously to abolish the Mass, images, idols, and other papal ceremonies and abuses, promising and swearing to live, with God's help, in the holy gospel law and the Word of God. Beza, *Vita Calvini,* in OC, 21:201f.

15. Among various evidences of this are the efforts of Farel and Calvin to get the citizens of Geneva to subscribe to and use the *Confession and Catechism of the Church of Geneva* of 1538. For details see the prefatory letter to that volume, ed. and trans. Ford Lewis Battles (Pittsburgh: Pittsburgh Theological Seminary, 1972), pp. i–xv. See also note 13 above.

16. The Council of Geneva approved on 16 January 1537 "the rest of the articles [including the one on Psalm singing] . . . as they were written." Herminjard, 4:165 (note 17). There is no further record on this, however, until Calvin's and Farel's request of the Council of Zurich in May 1538, mentioned above.

17. The *Manual* of Bern, 21 June 1538, said: "Write a letter to the judges of the consistory to acquaint them with the fact that the Lord desires that the youth learn to sing the Psalms, and that the principal of the school and his headmaster teach the music of the said Psalms." Herminjard, no. 708, 5:6 (note).

18. Calvin and Farel wrote to the Synod of Zurich in early May 1538: "Secondly, [we request] that at public prayers, the singing of Psalms take place." Herminjard, no. 708, 5:6.

19. See note 4 above.

20. See Pierre Pidoux, *Le Psautier huguenot du XVI*ᵉ *siècle* (Basel, 1962), 2:6f.; and Orentin Douen, *Clément Marot et le Psautier huguenot,* 2 vols. (Paris: Imprimerie nationale, 1878–1879).

21. Calvin wrote Farel on 29 December 1538: ". . . we both hope for and ponder another way of spreading Christ's Kingdom. Consequently we regret that the Psalms were sung among you [at Neuchâtel?] before they arrived at the place known to you [i.e., Metz]. For I have determined to publish them shortly. Because I find the German melodies rather pleasing, I have set myself to attempt what I can in verse. So two Psalms, 46 and 25, are my maiden attempts; I have afterwards added others." Herminjard, no. 762a, 5:447.

22. Psalms 36, 91 (listed by the Vulgate number, 90), and 138; Psalm 113 is unrhymed.

23. See Pidoux, *Le Psautier,* 2:3.

24. Douen, citing the earlier work of Felix Bovet, *Histoire du Psautier des églises réformées* (1872), did not find in Calvin's Psalms "the grace and suppleness of the style of Marot" and deemed Calvin less experienced in versification. *Clement Marot,*

1:307ff. But an experiment in singing the corresponding Calvin and Marot versions disclosed a directness and simple beauty and faithfulness to the Psalter in Calvin's text that is somewhat overlaid by the elegance of Marot.

25. Old, *Reformed Worship,* p. 89.

26. Calvin wrote to Farel on 27 October 1539: "I could not now write to Michael. Yet I should like you to urge him, by the first messenger, to write what is happening to the *Psalms.* I requested that one hundred copies be sent to Geneva." Herminjard, no. 832, 6:118.

27. The ministers of Geneva wrote the Council of Geneva (ca. 13 January 1537): "This way to proceed to this seemed good to us: if some children, to whom we have previously taught a simple church song, sing in a high, distinct voice, to which the people listen attentively, following with their hearts what is sung by mouth, until little by little they become accustomed to sing a song together. But in order to avoid all confusion, it would be needful that you not permit that anyone by his insolence, to hold the holy congregation in derision, set about to disturb the order that will be established for this." Herminjard, no. 602, 4:163f. Also see references in note 36 below.

28. Old, *Reformed Worship,* p. 40.

29. Comprehensive biographies are available in *Allgemeine deutsche Biographie* (1897); Robert Eitner, ed., *Biographisch-Bibliographisches Quellen-Lexikon,* 10 vols. (Leipzig, 1900–1904); Friedrich Blume, ed., *Die Musik in Geschichte und Gegenwart,* 15 vols. (Kassel and Basel, 1949–1968); *Neue deutsche Biographie* (Berlin, 1952–1974); and Clyde William Young, "School Music in Sixteenth-Century Strasbourg," *Journal of Research in Music Education* 10 (1962): 130–32.

30. The original German musical settings may be seen in facsimile in Pidoux, *Le Psautier,* 2:235ff., and are realized in modern notation in Johannes Zahn, *Die Melodien der deutschen evangelischen Kirchenlieder,* 6 vols. (Gütersloh, 1889–1893), numbers 7551 (Ps. 25), 8303 (Ps. 36), 4450 (Ps. 46), 8451 (Ps. 91), 4438a (Ps. 113), and 8466a (Ps. 138).

31. Young, "School Music," pp. 131f.

32. The more recent is Richard R. Terry, *Calvin's First Psalter* (London: 1932; reprint–Ann Arbor: University Microfilms, 1965). The earlier one is a limited edition published by Delétra in Geneva in 1919.

33. Robert Homer Leslie, Jr., "Music and the Arts in Calvin's Geneva" (Ph.D. dissertation, McGill University, 1969), p. 323. Also see *Institutes* 3.20.31–32.

34. Leslie, "Music and the Arts," pp. 124–27.

35. Ibid. Chapters 8 and 9 introduce a musical supplement comprising a transcription of L'Estocart's *Cent cinquante Pseaumes de David.* Also, references to editions of all these composers' Psalm settings by the American Institute of Musicology, Breitkopf and Härtel, Henry Expert, and others are available in Anna Harriet Heyer, *Historical Sets, Collected Editions, and Monuments of Music* (Chicago: American Library Association, 1969).

36. Students in Geneva were required by *"L'Ordre des escoles de Geneve"* to "return to the college in the winter and summer, after dinner at eleven o'clock, and are there to practice singing Psalms until noon." OS, 2:367. For comprehensive discussions of music education in Strasbourg and Geneva at this time, and of the city councils' interaction with school officials and churches, see Young, "School Music," and Leslie, "Music and the Arts."

37. For works on the music of Calvin's Psalms not already cited in the notes, see: Friedrich Blume et al., *Protestant Church Music: A History* (New York: Norton, 1974); Isabelle Cazeaux, *French Music in the Fifteenth and Sixteenth Centuries* (New York: Praeger, 1975); Charles Garside, "The Origins of Calvin's Theology of Music: 1536–1543," unpublished, 1977; Théodore Gérold, "Protestant Music on the Continent," in Gerald Abraham, ed., *The Age of Humanism: 1540–1630,* The New Oxford History of Music, vol. 4 (London: Oxford University, 1968); Waldo Selden Pratt, *The Music of the French Psalter of 1562: A Historical Survey and Analysis* (New York: Columbia University, 1939).

Psalm 25

John Calvin, 1539 *(A toy Seigneur)*
Translated by Ford Lewis Battles, 1969 (1976)

88 88 88 98

Melody by Mattheus Greiter, 1526*
Harmonization by Stanley E. Tagg, 1976

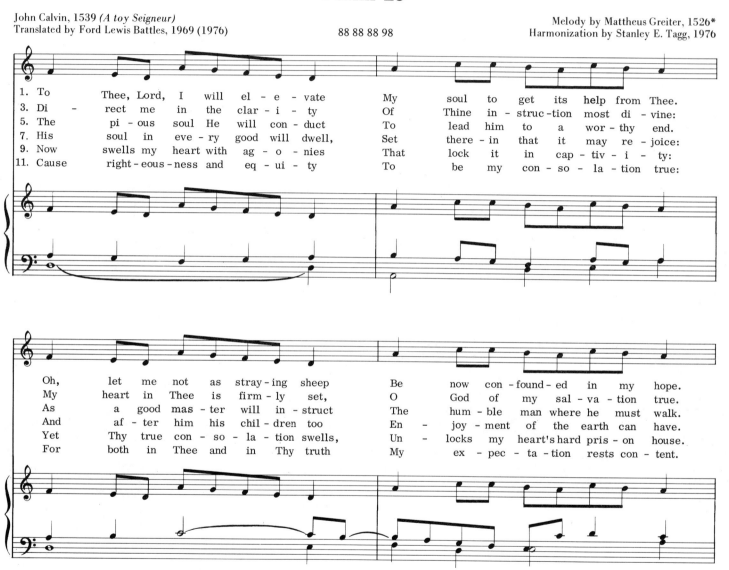

1. To Thee, Lord, I will el - e - vate My soul to get its help from Thee.
3. Di - rect me in the clar - i - ty Of Thine in - struc - tion most di - vine:
5. The pi - ous soul He will con - duct To lead him to a wor - thy end.
7. His soul in eve - ry good will dwell, Set there - in that it may re - joice:
9. Now swells my heart with ag - o - nies That lock it in cap - tiv - i - ty:
11. Cause right - eous - ness and eq - ui - ty To be my con - so - la - tion true:

Oh, let me not as stray - ing sheep Be now con - found - ed in my hope.
My heart in Thee is firm - ly set, O God of my sal - va - tion true.
As a good mas - ter will in - struct The hum - ble man where he must walk.
And af - ter him his chil - dren too En - joy - ment of the earth can have.
Yet Thy true con - so - la - tion swells, Un - locks my heart's hard pris - on house.
For both in Thee and in Thy truth My ex - pec - ta - tion rests con - tent.

*From *Psalmen Gebett und Kirchenuebung* (Strasbourg, 1526), fol. 40ᵛ, 41ʳ. (Pidoux, 1:34. 235; Zahn, 4:465. 7351.)
Harmonization copyright 1977, Stanley E. Tagg

1. Let not my foes, I pray Thee God, De - light in mak - ing sport of me,
3. Let me for - get not the long course Of all Thine an - cient ben - e - fits:
5. His stead - fast love, un - fail - ing truth, Whole and com - plete our Lord now keeps.
7. To His vast se - cret treas - ur - y God - fear - ing men are in - tro - duced,
9. The great dis - tress where - in I am, Please Thee, O Lord, to look up - on,
11. Oh, make Thy cho - sen peo - ple feel How sweet is Thy sal - va - tion, God:

Per - ceiv - ing me in ex - trem - i - ty From long op - pres - sion suf - fer - ing. *2 choir*
As Thou hast done ev - er to Thine own, Toward me ex - tend Thy pre - cious grace. *4 choir*
To all those men who in loy - al - ty Fol - low His law and tes - ta - ment. *6 choir*
And now by God's cov - e - nant are taught His sal - u - tar - y, blest de - crees. *8 choir*
Thus turn a - side Thy deep - pierc - ing gaze From my own sins that Thou pur - suest, *10 choir*
And at the end make them leave be - hind All mis - er - y and wear - i - ness.

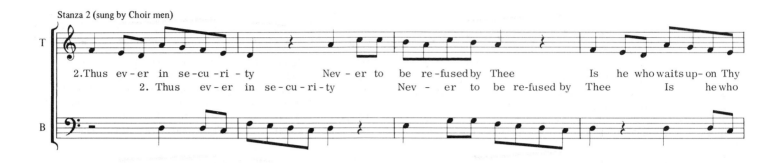

2.Thus ev - er in se - cu - ri - ty   Nev - er to be re -fused by Thee   Is   he who waits up- on Thy
2. Thus   ev - er in se - cu - ri -ty   Nev - er to be re-fused by Thee   Is   he who

truth,   Yet e - vil men he will con-found.   Cause me, O Lord, to keep my gaze   Up - on the
waits up -on Thy truth,   Yet   e - vil men he will con-found.   Cause   me, O Lord, to keep my gaze

road that I must hold,   The path that can   best lead to the goal   Of right-ly hon-or-ing Thy name.
Up - on the road that I must hold,   The path that can   best lead to the goal   Of right-ly hon-or-ing Thy name.

146

147

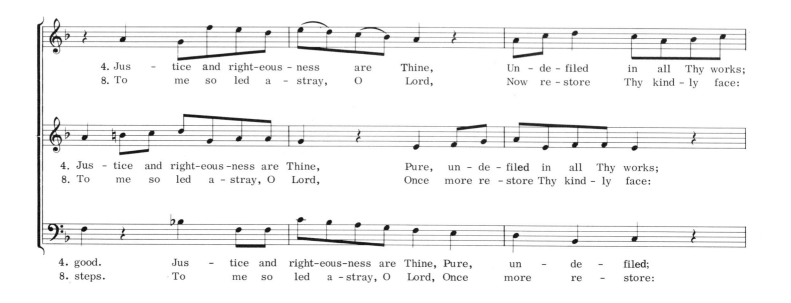

4. Jus - tice and right-eous - ness are Thine, Un - de - filed in all Thy works;
8. To me so led a - stray, O Lord, Now re - store Thy kind - ly face:

4. Jus - tice and right-eous-ness are Thine, Pure, un - de - filed in all Thy works;
8. To me so led a - stray, O Lord, Once more re - store Thy kind - ly face:

4. good. Jus - tice and right-eous-ness are Thine, Pure, un - de - filed;
8. steps. To me so led a - stray, O Lord, Once more re - store:

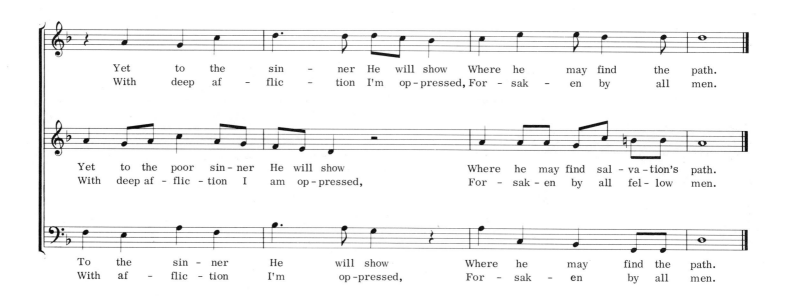

Yet to the sin - ner He will show Where he may find the path.
With deep af - flic - tion I'm op-pressed, For - sak - en by all men.

Yet to the poor sin - ner He will show Where he may find sal - va - tion's path.
With deep af - flic - tion I am op-pressed, For - sak - en by all fel - low men.

To the sin - ner He will show Where he may find the path.
With af - flic - tion I'm op-pressed, For - sak - en by all men.

Stanza 6 (sung by the Choir)

SA: 6. A - las, is my trans-gres-sion now Noth - ing but hor - ror, O Lord God:

T: 6. A - las, is my trans - gres - sion now Noth - ing but hor - ror, O God:

B: 6. A - las, is my trans-gres-sion now Noth - ing but hor - ror, O God:

Still, by the great-ness of Thy name, In me it yields to Thy strong love.

Still, by the great-ness of Thy name, In me it yields to Thy love.

Still, by the great - ness of Thy name, In me it yields to Thy love.

149

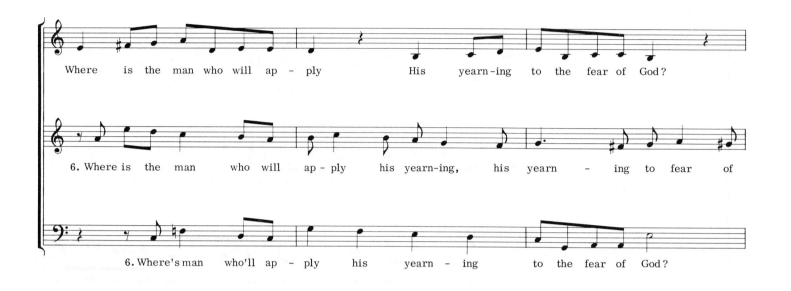

Where is the man who will ap-ply His yearn-ing to the fear of God?

6. Where is the man who will ap-ply his yearn-ing, his yearn - ing to fear of

6. Where's man who'll ap-ply his yearn - ing to the fear of God?

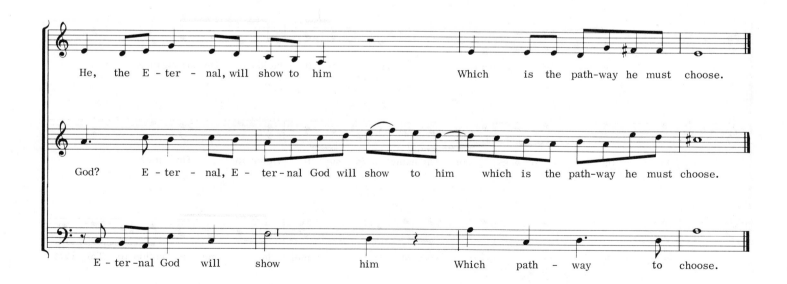

He, the E - ter - nal, will show to him Which is the path-way he must choose.

God? E - ter - nal, E - ter-nal God will show to him which is the path-way he must choose.

E - ter -nal God will show him Which path - way to choose.

Stanza 10 (sung by the Choir women)

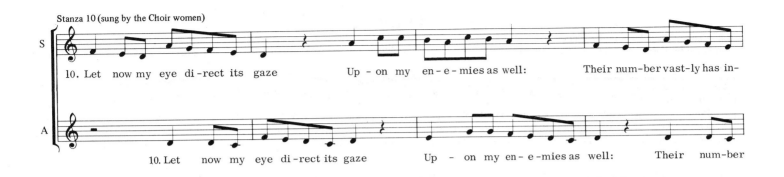

S: 10. Let now my eye di-rect its gaze Up - on my en - e - mies as well: Their num-ber vast-ly has in-

A: 10. Let now my eye di-rect its gaze Up - on my en - e - mies as well: Their num-ber

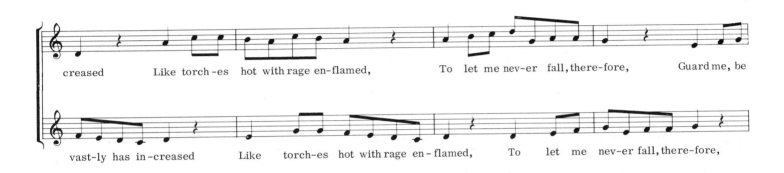

creased Like torch-es hot with rage en-flamed, To let me nev-er fall, there-fore, Guard me, be

vast-ly has in-creased Like torch-es hot with rage en-flamed, To let me nev-er fall, there-fore,

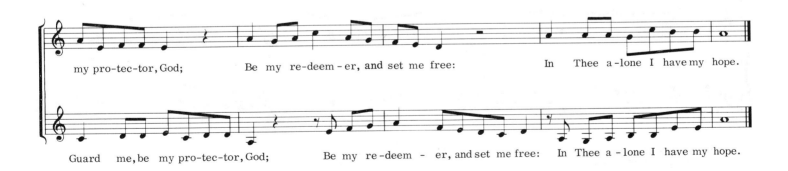

my pro-tec-tor, God; Be my re-deem - er, and set me free: In Thee a-lone I have my hope.

Guard me, be my pro-tec-tor, God; Be my re-deem - er, and set me free: In Thee a-lone I have my hope.

151

Psalm 36

John Calvin, 1539 *(En moy le secret)*
Translated by Ford Lewis Battles, 1969 (1976)

887 887 D

Melody by Mattheus Greiter, 1525*
Harmonization by Stanley E. Tagg, 1976

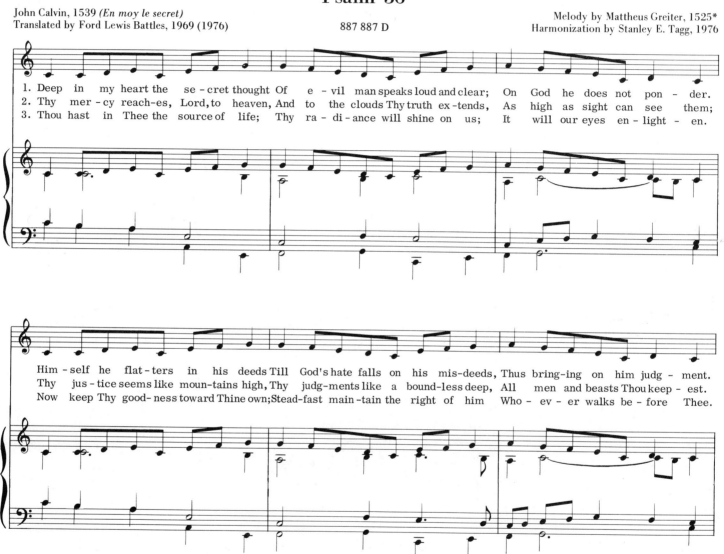

1. Deep in my heart the se-cret thought Of e-vil man speaks loud and clear; On God he does not pon - der.
2. Thy mer-cy reach-es, Lord, to heaven, And to the clouds Thy truth ex-tends, As high as sight can see them;
3. Thou hast in Thee the source of life; Thy ra-di-ance will shine on us; It will our eyes en-light-en.

Him-self he flat-ters in his deeds Till God's hate falls on his mis-deeds, Thus bring-ing on him judg - ment.
Thy jus-tice seems like moun-tains high, Thy judg-ments like a bound-less deep, All men and beasts Thou keep - est.
Now keep Thy good-ness toward Thine own; Stead-fast main-tain the right of him Who-ev-er walks be-fore Thee.

*From *Strassburger Kirchen ampt . . . das dritte Theil* (Strasbourg, 1525). (Pidoux, 1:44. 236; Zahn, 5:101. 8303.)
Harmonization copyright 1977, Stanley E. Tagg

152

1. His e - vil speak-ing spreads de - ceit; He does not seek to un - der - stand Or know, or do one good deed;
2. Thy lov - ing-kind-ness is well known; Un - der the shad-ow of Thy wings Men will re - pose se - cure - ly,
3. In or - der that in - hum - an man His foot up - on me may not set, His wick - ed hand af - flict me;

Ly - ing in bed he plots de - ceit; From the right way he goes a - stray. E - vil does not of - fend him.
By Thine own goods be sat - is - fied, And from the ri - ver they will drink Of Thine a - bun-dant pleas -ures.
The e - vil man is there cast down, Up - on the earth now pros -trate lies; Nev - er a -gain can he rise.

Psalm 46

John Calvin, 1539 *(Nostre Dieu)*
Translated by Ford Lewis Battles, 1969 (1976)

LMD

Melody by Wolfgang Dachstein, 1526[*]
Harmonization by Stanley E. Tagg, 1976

1. For us our God is firm sup - port, Strong - hold and for - tress, cer - tain help,
2. While seas are loud - ly thun - der - ing, As if with an - ger fierce they swell:
4. God of the ar - mies, lead - er, chief, The God of Ja - cob is for us:
6. Now be it known to eve - ry man That God it is who must be feared;

Where - in our plight we shall pos - sess A pres - ent ref - uge, hav - en safe.
And loft - y crags re - ver - ber - ate, Are bat - tered, top - pled by the waves.
And our pro - tec - tor He will be A - gainst our ad - ver - sar - ies all.
Be - cause of His tre - men - dous power, Through - out the world ex - alt - ed be.

Note: Choir sings Stanzas 3 and 5 polyphonically.

*From *Psalmen Gebett und Kirchenuebung* (Strasbourg, 1526), fol. 27ᵣ. (Pidoux, 1:55. 236; Zahn, 3:78. 4450.)
Harmonization copyright 1977, Stanley E. Tagg

1. Whence firm as - sur -ance we will have, E - ven when we will see the earth
2. The cho - sen cit - y of our God, House to which He has giv - en rain:
4. Come, raise your eyes then to be - hold, Each one of you now strain to see
6. God, rul - er o - ver heav - en's hosts, For us will ev - er guard-ian be,

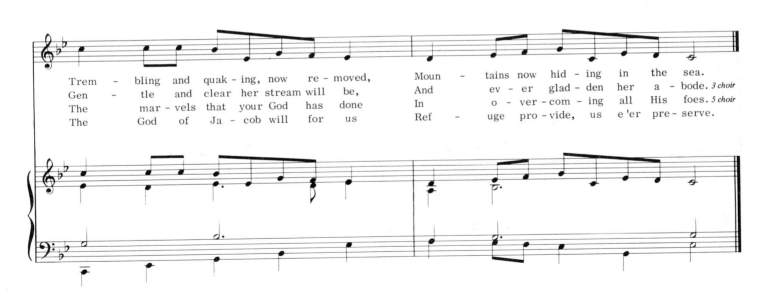

Trem - bling and quak - ing, now re - moved, Moun - tains now hid - ing in the sea.
Gen - tle and clear her stream will be, And ev - er glad - den her a - bode. *3 choir*
The mar - vels that your God has done In o - ver - com - ing all His foes. *5 choir*
The God of Ja - cob will for us Ref - uge pro - vide, us e'er pre - serve.

155

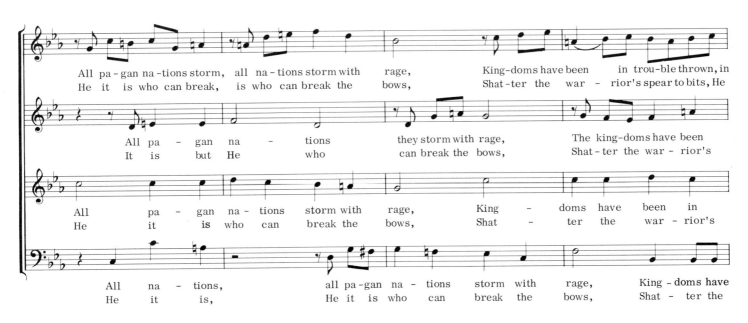

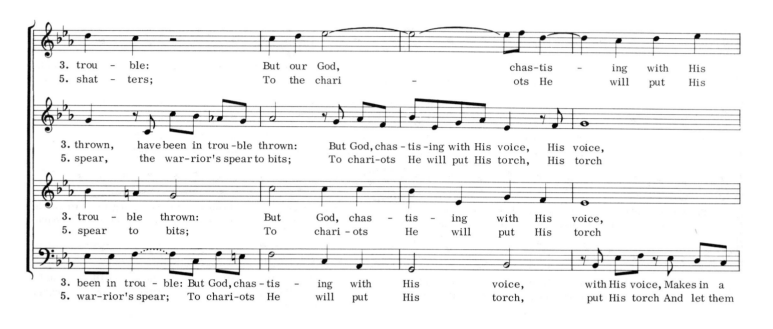

3. trou - ble: But our God, chas-tis - ing with His
5. shat - ters; To the chari - ots He will put His

3. thrown, have been in trou-ble thrown: But God, chas-tis-ing with His voice, His voice,
5. spear, the war-rior's spear to bits; To chari-ots He will put His torch, His torch

3. trou - ble thrown: But God, chas - tis - ing with His voice,
5. spear to bits; To chari - ots He will put His torch

3. been in trou - ble: But God, chas-tis - ing with His voice, with His voice, Makes in a
5. war-rior's spear; To chari-ots He will put His torch, put His torch And let them

voice, Makes in a mo - ment them all calm.
torch And let them fall con - sumed with fire.

Makes in a mo - ment, makes in a mo - ment, mo - ment them all calm.
And let them fall, let them fall con-sumed with fire, con - sumed with fire.

Makes in a mo - ment them all calm.
And let them fall con - sumed with fire.

mo - ment them, them all calm.
fall con - sumed, fall with fire.

158

Psalm 91

John Calvin, 1539 *(Qui en la garde)*
Translated by Ford Lewis Battles, 1969 (1976)

888 88 888

Melody by Mattheus Greiter, 1526*
Harmonization by Stanley E. Tagg, 1976

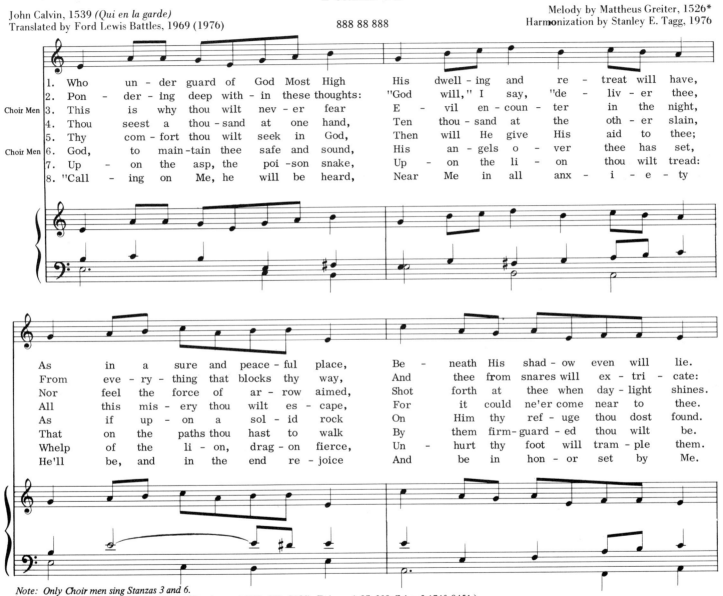

1. Who   un - der guard of God Most High   His dwell - ing and   re - treat will have,
2. Pon - der - ing deep with - in these thoughts: "God will," I say,   "de - liv - er thee,
Choir Men 3. This   is   why thou wilt nev - er fear   E - vil en - coun - ter   in the night,
4. Thou   seest a   thou - sand   at   one hand,   Ten thou - sand at the   oth - er slain,
5. Thy   com - fort thou wilt seek   in   God,   Then will He give   His aid to thee;
Choir Men 6. God,   to main - tain thee safe and sound,   His an - gels o - ver thee has set,
7. Up - on the asp, the   poi - son snake,   Up - on the li - on   thou wilt tread:
8. "Call - ing on Me, he will be heard,   Near Me in all   anx - i - e - ty

As   in   a   sure and peace - ful place,   Be - neath His shad - ow even will lie.
From   eve - ry - thing that blocks thy way,   And thee from snares will ex - tri - cate:
Nor   feel the force of   ar - row aimed,   Shot forth at thee when day - light shines.
All   this mis - ery thou wilt es - cape,   For   it could ne'er come near to thee.
As   if up - on a   sol - id rock   On Him thy ref - uge thou dost found.
That   on the paths thou hast to walk   By them firm - guard - ed thou wilt be.
Whelp   of the li - on, drag - on fierce,   Un - hurt thy foot will tram - ple them.
He'll   be, and in the end re - joice   And be in hon - or set by Me.

Note: Only Choir men sing Stanzas 3 and 6.
*From *Psalmen Gebett und Kirchenuebung* (Strasbourg, 1526), 561. 54 r-v. (Pidoux, 1:87. 238; Zahn, 5:174f. 8451.)
Harmonization copyright 1977, Stanley E. Tagg

1. Bold - ly will I say to my God: "Thou art my fort - ress and my hope;
2. Un - der His wings thou art at peace, Be - neath His pin - ions safe - ty hast,
3. Whe - ther in light or in the dark Ru - in may stalk with harm - ful force:
4. Clear - ly in - deed thine eye will see That on the wick - ed man will fall
5. Thee no mis - for - tune will come near. No wound to cause thee in - jur - y,
6. They in their hands will car - ry thee, And un - to thee such suc - cour give
7. God says to thee: "Him will I aid, Since in es - teem he holds Me fast,
8. My grace will on his life be - stow A hap - py, long, and bless - ed course;

In Thee my con - fi - dence will lodge, Most sure - ly will I rest in Thee."
Thou al - ways wilt have God's own truth As shield and buck - ler strong and stout." *3 choir*
Wreak - ing de - struc - tion here and there, Thou wilt be in tran - quil - li - ty.
Dead - ly af - flic - tion to con - found: This is the price that he must pay.
Or to op - press thy fam - i - ly Ev - er will come up - on thy tent. *6 choir*
That thy feet may never trip up - on Mis - chance or hin - drance in thy path.
Since He has rec - og - nized My name Him will I lift to eve - ry good.
And through My power, him will I help; To safe - ty lead him by the hand."

160

Psalm 113

John Calvin, 1539 *(Sus louez Dieu serviteurs)*
Translated by Ford Lewis Battles, 1969 (1976)

87 87 888

Melody by unknown composer, 1524-1525 (?)*
Harmonization by Stanley E. Tagg, 1976

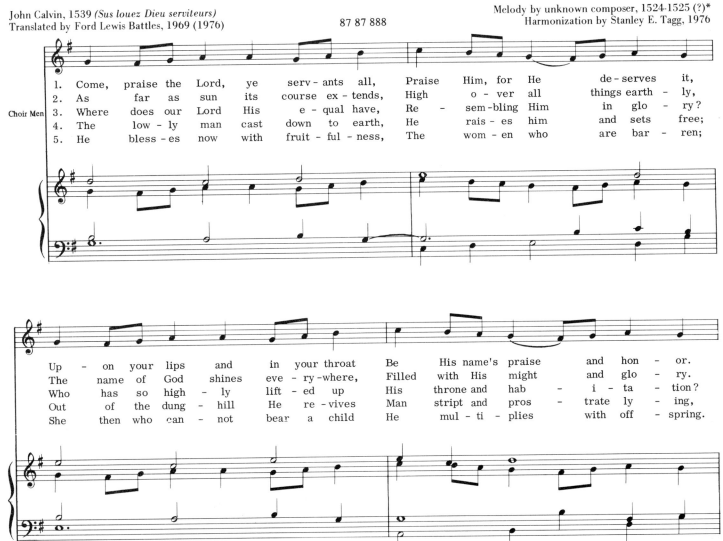

Choir Men

1. Come, praise the Lord, ye serv-ants all, Praise Him, for He de-serves it,
2. As far as sun its course ex-tends, High o-ver all things earth-ly,
3. Where does our Lord His e-qual have, Re-sem-bling Him in glo-ry?
4. The low-ly man cast down to earth, He rais-es him and sets free;
5. He bless-es now with fruit-ful-ness, The wom-en who are bar-ren;

Up - on your lips and in your throat Be His name's praise and hon - or.
The name of God shines eve - ry-where, Filled with His might and glo - ry.
Who has so high - ly lift - ed up His throne and hab - i - ta - tion?
Out of the dung - hill He re-vives Man stript and pros - trate ly - ing,
She then who can - not bear a child He mul - ti - plies with off - spring.

Note: Only Choir men sing Stanza 3. Play right hand an octave lower, omit tenor, and play bass where written.
*From *Teutsch Kirchen ampt* (Strasbourg, **1524-1525**[?]), fol. C 1 ʳ. (Pidoux, 1:102. 238; Zahn, 3:74. 4438a.)
Harmonization copyright 1977, Stanley E. Tagg

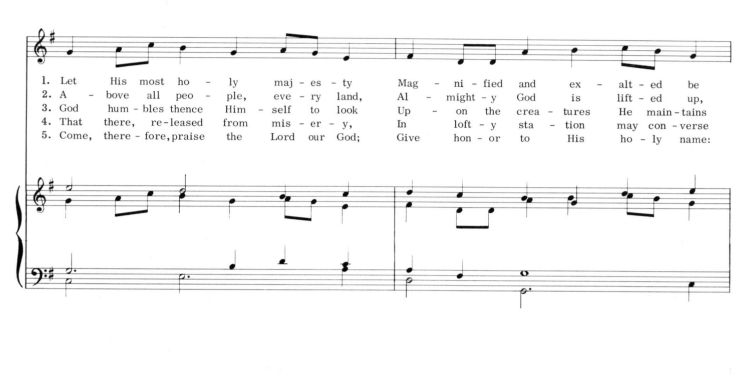

1. Let His most ho - ly maj - es - ty   Mag - ni - fied and ex - alt - ed be
2. A - bove all peo - ple, eve - ry land,   Al - might - y God is lift - ed up,
3. God hum - bles thence Him - self to look   Up - on the crea - tures He main - tains
4. That there, re - leased from mis - er - y,   In loft - y sta - tion may con - verse
5. Come, there - fore, praise the Lord our God;   Give hon - or to His ho - ly name:

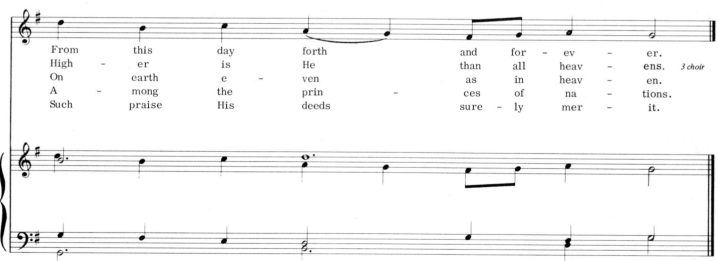

From this day forth and for - ev - er.
High - er is He than all heav - ens. *3 choir*
On earth e - ven as in heav - en.
A - mong the prin - ces of na - tions.
Such praise His deeds sure - ly mer - it.

Psalm 138

John Calvin, 1539 *(Louang' et grace)*
Translated by Ford Lewis Battles, 1969 (1976)

998 998 888 888

Melody by Mattheus Greiter, 1527*
Harmonization by Stanley E. Tagg, 1976

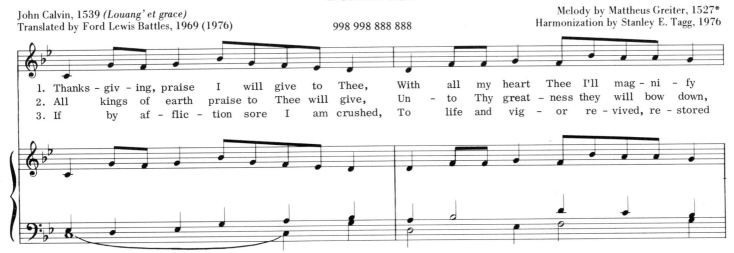

1. Thanks - giv - ing, praise I will give to Thee, With all my heart Thee I'll mag - ni - fy
2. All kings of earth praise to Thee will give, Un - to Thy great - ness they will bow down,
3. If by af - flic - tion sore I am crushed, To life and vig - or re - vived, re - stored

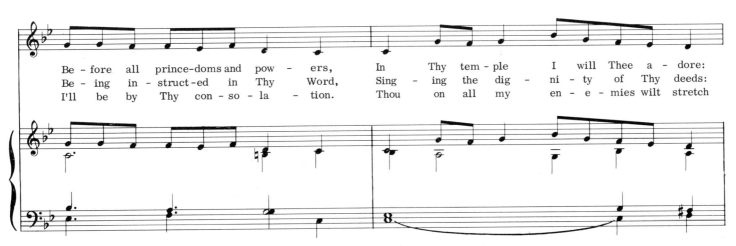

Be - fore all prince-doms and pow - ers, In Thy tem - ple I will Thee a - dore:
Be - ing in - struct -ed in Thy Word, Sing - ing the dig - ni - ty of Thy deeds:
I'll be by Thy con - so - la - tion. Thou on all my en - e - mies wilt stretch

*From *Die zween Psalmen Gebett und Kirchenuebung* (Strasbourg, 1527), fol. 70. (Pidoux, 1:122f. 239; Zahn, 5:185. 8466a.)
Harmonization copyright 1977, Stanley E. Tagg

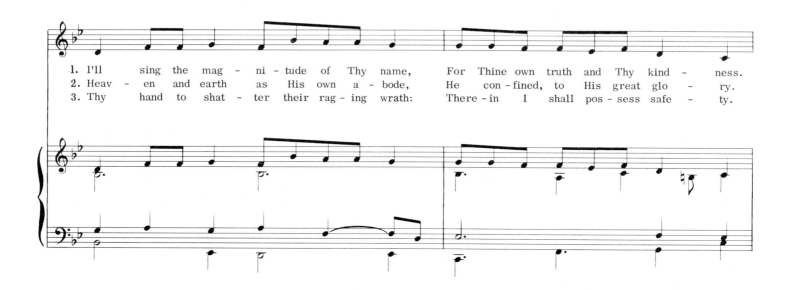

1. I'll sing the mag - ni - tude of Thy name, For Thine own truth and Thy kind - ness.
2. Heav - en and earth as His own a - bode, He con - fined, to His great glo - ry.
3. Thy hand to shat - ter their rag - ing wrath: There - in I shall pos - sess safe - ty.

God, Thou hast ex - alt - ed o'er all, By Thine own Word, Thy maj - es - ty. When with my voice I called on Thee,
High, lift - ed up our Lord in heaven Is seat - ed, to rule and com - mand. Yet none-the - less bends down His eyes,
For - ev - er in me will the Lord His won - der - ful kind-ness dis - play. Thy mer - cy, O God, will per - sist,

164

1. Straight-way Thou gavest an-swer to me, Sus - tain - ing me by Thy vast might, My soul main-tain-ing in Thy strength.
2. To gaze on the hum-ble and poor: In judg-ment He views from a - far Proud men and haugh-ty with con - tempt.
3. Sur - pass-ing the bounds of the earth. Thou ne'er wilt for - sake or for-get All works Thy hand has ta - ken up.

Hal - le - lu - ia, Hal - le - lu - ia.

165

Chapter 7

Prose-Poems Adapted from Calvin

Some of the finest poetry of the Christian faith is imbedded in the prose works of its greatest expositors. Even a theologian whose style is normally dry and halting—Of Calvin this cannot be said!—occasionally takes wing when the theme he is addressing lifts his exposition to a higher level of discourse. Scattered through the writings of John Calvin, in French as well as in Latin, are hymnic fragments that, if "lined out" and given strophic form, afford yet another source for discerning his spirituality.[1] Considering that Calvin was schooled in classical rhetoric but that he utterly subordinated the artificialities of literary heightening to his spiritual task, it is not surprising to find such rhapsodic passages in his works. Sometimes these are given in a single burst; at other times they run like a thread through longer, more diffuse expository passages. The technique of adapting these fragments must then vary with their setting. The short pieces here included illustrate, therefore, varied ways of bringing forward these "hymns" into separate literary existence. No two editors would necessarily choose the same passage in the same way. There is opportunity for experimentation; what follows here is not the final word.

What marks a "hymnic fragment"? There is usually a repeated phrase running through the passage like a refrain. There is also a series of short, parallel phrases over against which a subsequent antithetic series is set. There is cumulative movement from a first statement to a final summation, symmetrical with the first. These traits, expressed in varied ways, unmistakably mark the lyrics of the theologian.

To illustrate Calvin's "found poetry," we have chosen six passages, some from the French, some from the Latin, that cover the years 1534–1559.

A Hymn to the Gospel

Calvin's first strictly theological writing was his preface to Pierre Robert's French translation of the New Testament, the printing of which was finished at Neuchâtel on 4 June 1535. Since Robert's dedication is dated 12 February of the same year, it is quite possible that Calvin actually composed his preface as early as the end of 1534. At any rate it would seem to be the first fruits of his conversion. Our hymnic passage is taken from a portion near the middle of the preface that celebrates the call of the gospel.[2]

Without the gospel
All of us are useless and empty;
Without the gospel
We are not Christians;
Without the gospel
All wealth is poverty,
Wisdom is foolishness before God,
Strength is weakness,
All human justice is condemned of God.

But by the knowledge of the gospel,
We are made children of God,
Brothers of Jesus Christ,
Fellow citizens of the saints,
Citizens of the kingdom of heaven,
Heirs of God with Jesus Christ,
By whom the poor become rich,
    the weak powerful,
    the fools wise,
    the sinners justified,
    the desolate comforted,
    the doubting certain,
    the slaves set free.
It is the power of God
For the salvation of all believers
And the key to the knowledge of God
Which opens the door of the kingdom of heaven
To unbelievers lying in their sins.

Happy are all those
Who hear and keep it.
For by that they show
That they are children of God.
Miserable are those
Who wish neither to hear nor follow it:
For they are children of the devil.

A Hymn to God

The second theological tract of Calvin, directed against the French Anabaptists, was written around 1535 but not published until 1542. Here is Calvin's ringing defense of the soul's everlasting life against those who taught that it either dies or goes to sleep at earthly death and is restored only at the general resurrection.[3]

You are the life of my soul,
O God.
When You take Your presence away from me,
My soul is dead:
O Son of God, revive.

You are the light of my soul,
O God.
Outside You no light to light our night;
My soul is blind:
O Righteous Sun, shine forth.

You are my soul's salvation,
O God.
When it can't confess its faith in You,
My soul is mute:
O Word Incarnate, speak.

You are my soul's right hand,
O God.
Without You it stumbles, cannot stand;
My soul is lame:
O hand of God, heal me.

The two series, *life/light/salvation/right-hand,* and
dead/blind/mute/lame, suggest the strophic structure.
The added line of each strophe is inferred from them.

The remaining selections are drawn from various parts
of Calvin's *Institutes.*[4]

A Hymn to Creation

God Reveals Himself to Man

Great is the Artificer
Who station'd and arrang'd and fitted together
The starry host of heaven.

Wonderful is their order;
Beyond all imagining their beauty.

Great is the Artificer
Who set and fix'd some in their stations
Motionless; granted to others
A freer course, yet not to wander
Outside their appointed path.

Great is the Artificer
Who adjusted the motion of all, measur'd
Off days, nights; years and seasons
Of the year; who proportion'd the days
Unequal, daily visible to us.

Great is the Artificer
In His power sustaining
This great mass,
Governing the swiftly
Wheeling system of heaven.

Great is the Artificer
Who shows His pow'r in miracles,
His goodness and wisdom in all
The things of His creation,
Whether great or small.

Man Responds to God

God has set all things for our good
And our salvation; in our very
Selves we feel His pow'r and grace,
His great, unnumber'd benefits,
Freely conferr'd upon us.

What else can we then do but stir
Ourselves to trust, invoke, to praise and love Him?
For all God's handiwork is made for man.

169

Ev'n in the six days He shows a Father's care
For His child as yet unborn.

Away, ingratitude, forgetfulness
Of Him! Away with craven fear He may
Fail us in our need! For He
Has seen to it that nothing will be
Lacking to our own welfare.

Whene'er we call on God, Creator
Of heav'n and earth, we must be mindful
That all He gives us is in His hand
To give; our ev'ry trust and hope
We hang on Him alone.

Whatever we desire, we are
To ask of Him and thankfully receive
Each benefit that falls to us.
Let us then strive to love and serve
Him with all our hearts.

A Hymn of Faith

Not from afar do we now contemplate
Our Savior, Jesus the Christ.
No—Christ dwells within us,
Feeds our faith, and draws us onward
Through thick darkness of trials and fears
To our eternal home.

Not in our own hearts do we set our faith,
For in them we are nothing;
No—in the heart of God
We really are, in Him alone
We firmly ground our every hope
Beyond mortality.

Despair of self we must, for by ourselves
Unaided, weak fools we are;
No—in Christ God offers
To us, adopted children,
Increase in wisdom, day by day,
Until our eyes can see.

An Ordination Hymn

This text is a much freer adaptation of Calvin's thought. The starting point is the contrast of the inward-outward call of 4.3.11, but the content is drawn from the larger context. The refrain is generally inferred.

Who calls this man?
In the secret place of prayer, O God,
You spoke, he heard and gave assent
In trembling to Your call.
Blessed be Christ our head;
Blessed Your Spirit who sustains;
Blessed be You, O Father of us all.

Who calls this man?
In this public place of praise, O God,
We prayed, You heard and counseled us
In fear to call him ours.
Blessed be Christ our head, etc.

Who calls this man?
Unless You first called him inwardly,
Before our hands were raised, O God,
Our call was given in vain.
Blessed be Christ our head, etc.

Seal then this call:
Give us firmness of faith, O God,

Assurance and hearts attentive
To Your Word from his lips.
Blessed be Christ our head, etc.

A Communion Hymn

There are many passages of high poetry in the chapter on the Lord's Supper (4.17); it is in fact difficult to cull out a short hymn from such a rich store without doing grave injustice to the original. Here the effort has therefore been not so much to be guided by the immediate rhythms of the text as to follow the grander themes expressed in a more extended passage.

All speech far transcending
And beyond all thought,
Wonderful exchanging—
Poverty for wealth:
To our hopeless weakness,
Give Your mighty power;
Through this body's eating,
Grant our souls new health.

Son of God now with us,
Make us sons of God:
Coming from the Father,
Raise us now to Him.
Dying with us human,
Give us Godlike life;
Knit our members to You,
Fasten limb to limb.

Word of God now calling
Us to purity,
Of this supper make us
Worthy to partake;

Flood us with thanksgiving
For Your sacrifice,
Once for all time offered
Humbly for our sake.

Author of all justice,
Turn our unjust ways;
Healer of all sickness,
Cure our dread disease.
In this meal declaring
Your death till You come,
Make all men our brothers,
Living in Your peace.

Amen.

Notes

1. Passages of hymnic quality previously quoted include chapter 3, lines 310–26, 1240–54; chapter 5, lines 552–61.

2. OC, 9:807.

3. For an English translation of the *Psychopannychia*, see John Calvin, *Tracts and Treatises in Defense of the Reformed Faith*, ed. Henry Beveridge, 3 vols. (Grand Rapids: Eerdmans, 1958), 3:414–90.

4. "A Hymn to Creation" is from the *Institutes* (1543) 1.14.21–22; "A Hymn of Faith," from the *Institutes* (1559) 3.2.17ff.; "An Ordination Hymn," from the *Institutes* (1559) 4.3.11; "A Communion Hymn," from the *Institutes* (1559) 4.17.2, 31, 37, 39, 42. "A Communion Hymn" has been set by Joseph Willcox Jenkins. For this, see Ford Lewis Battles, N. Mikita, and M. Ioset, *Adjutorium ad Cultum Divinum* (Pittsburgh: Pittsburgh Theological Seminary, 1977), no. 359.

Epilogue

Calvin on Christ and the Church

The Church as Pilgrim

Let us remember:
However low the church's outward state,
It shines in inward beauty;
Though shaken upon earth,
In heaven it is firmly seated;
Though in the world's sight it lies maimed and fallen,
Before God and His angels it stands whole and flour-
     ishes;
Though wretched after the flesh,
In the spirit it abounds in spiritual blessedness.

Even so, when Christ lay lowly in the manger,
In the clouds the angels sang His loftiness;
In heaven the star witnessed to His glory;
The wise men from a far-off land felt His power.

When He fasted in the wilderness,
Struggled against the mockeries of Satan,
Sweated unto death,
Still were angels ministering to Him.

When He was about to be imprisoned,
By His voice alone He drove back His enemies.

While He hung upon the cross,
The sun by its darkness proclaimed Him King of all,
The opened graves confessed Him Lord of death and
     life.

Now if we see Christ
In His body troubled by the proud insults of the
     wicked,
Oppressed by their savage tyranny,
Exposed to their abuse,
Driven to and fro by their violence:
However insolent, none of these things can frighten us.
Rather let us ponder
That the church is ordained,
So long as it is pilgrim in the world,
To fight under a continual cross.

A Meditation upon Christ

The whole of our salvation is in Christ.
Where is our salvation?
The very name of Jesus teaches us
It is in Him.

The whole of our salvation is in Christ.
Whence came the Holy Spirit's other gifts?
These we find
In His anointing.

The whole of our salvation is in Christ.
Where is our strength?
It we will obtain
In His dominion.

The whole of our salvation is in Christ.
Where is our purity?
Find this we will
In His conception.

The whole of our salvation is in Christ.
Where is tenderness for us?
This He offers us
In His nativity:
     For like us He was made
     In all things, to learn
     With us to suffer.

The whole of our salvation is in Christ.
Where is our redemption?
He gives us this
In His passion.

The whole of our salvation is in Christ.
Where is our absolution?
This we receive
In His condemnation.

The whole of our salvation is in Christ.
Where is our curse lifted?
This He takes away
By His sacrifice.

The whole of our salvation is in Christ.
Whence are we cleansed?
Our purgation comes
From His shed blood.

The whole of our salvation is in Christ.
Whence are we reconciled to God?
He draws us to the Father
In His descent to hell.

The whole of our salvation is in Christ.
Whence is our flesh mortified?
Our old man must needs lie
In His sepulchre.

The whole of our salvation is in Christ.
Where lies our newness of life?
Our life is renewed
In His resurrection.

The whole of our salvation is in Christ.
On what rests our immortality?
Deathless we become
In that same resurrection.

The whole of our salvation is in Christ.
How may we inherit the heavenly kingdom?
He makes us its heirs
By His entrance into heaven.

The whole of our salvation is in Christ.
Where defense, safety, store of all blessings?
All these we find
In His blest kingdom.

The whole of our salvation is in Christ.
If we would steadfastly await the judgment,
We must rest in the power
Given Christ as Judge.

The whole of our salvation is in Christ.

Notes

"The Church as Pilgrim" is from *On Scandals* (OS, 2:180.13–31); "A Meditation upon Christ" is from the *Institutes* (1559) 2.16.19.

Index of Scripture

When page numbers are followed by, for example, *n 3*, this means either "note number 3" or "note on (or concerning) line number 3."

178